The Price of Experience:
The Rewards of Life

(Poetic Short Stories)

Janet – that you may enjoy your journey into the "golden years" as much as I —

By

Rodney Francis Foster

PUBLISH AMERICA

PublishAmerica
Baltimore

First printing

PublishAmerica has allowed this work to remain exactly as the author intended, verbatim, without editorial input.

ISBN: 1-60441-835-4
PUBLISHED BY PUBLISHAMERICA, LLLP
www.publishamerica.com
Baltimore

Printed in the United States of America

Dedication

To Patsy for her passion, enduring love and support

Acknowledgments

My older brother, Duane, a little brother's mentor and role model,
Aunt Lu, for her lifetime of encouragement,
Rosemary, for her enthusiastic appreciation of my writing!

Table of Contents

INTRODUCTION

FREEDOM 15
REFLECTIONS 18
A WALK 20
PRODIGAL SON—MOTHER'S IMMACULATE PERCEPTION 22
LOUISE 26
GOD WITHIN 27
THOUGHTS AT TWILIGHT 30
ABOUT GOLF AND LIFE 31

THE PRICE OF EXPERIENCE

ROLE MODELS 35
BOUNCING BACK 39
LITTLE LEAGUE BASEBALL 44
BAGGAGE FROM YESTERDAY 46
A FATHER'S COUNSEL—FAILURE OR SUCCESS 50
BELIEF AND FAITH 52
CREATING CONFIDENCE—AVOIDING ARROGANCE 56
THE VALUE OF FEAR 61
A DECISION TO BE HAPPY 65
FACE TO FACE WITH GUILT 69
ENDURING PAIN 72
SATAN'S SALE—THE PRICE OF DOUBT 74
FROM HOPE TO ACHIEVEMENT 77
NOT RIGHT OR WRONG—JUST FEELINGS 80

IMAGINATION'S POWER 83
PROBLEMS, CHALLENGES OR OPPORTUNITIES 86
I HAVE TO GIVE A SPEECH! 90
WHO DECIDES? 93
AM I AN AMATEUR OR A PROFESSIONAL? 96
ACCIDENTS LARGE AND SMALL 100
PREPARED FOR AN EMERGENCY? 103
JUST WALK 107
LIFESTYLE CHOICES—LIFE OR DEATH 110
RUN AWAY—RUN TOWARD 114
WHAT IS "OLD AGE"? 117
LAST DAY 120
WHO'S THE BOSS? 123
I'M SORRY 127
RETIREMENT—PURGATORY OR PARADISE 129
SURVIVAL 138
LONG-TERM CARE—NO MONEY, NO SALE 143
NO TIME FOR CHRISTMAS (A Parody) 145
SURGERY—YOU'RE GOING TO DO "WHAT" 146
TAXES—GOING IT ALONE 151

REWARDS—PERSONAL, POLITICAL AND RELIGIOUS

OUR JUSTICE SYSTEM—FOR ALL? 161
SEARCH FOR GOD 164
PUBERTY'S GOD 172
SIN IS SIN 175
WITHOUT HONOR—A KOREAN VETERAN 179
MEMORIES OF YOUTH 182
LETHAL FIGHTER 188
DENIAL—ACCEPTANCE—HOPE 191
AT DEATH DO I PART 193

REWARDS—A LOVE AFFAIR

SYMPTOMS OF A LOVE AFFAIR 199
WE'RE GETTING MARRIED TODAY 200
CELEBRATING A BIRTHDAY AND ANNIVERSARY ON OUR
    WEDDING DAY 201
WE'RE NOW LEGALLY ONE 202
THE DAY WE MET—A DAY TO REMEMBER 203
THE HOLIDAYS—A LIFE FILLED WITH LOVE 204
CHRISTMAS WITH MY SOUL MATE 205
A VALENTINE'S DAY (NIGHT) DREAM 206
LITTLE THINGS ON MOTHER'S DAY 208
TOGETHER AS ONE 209
DESIRE UNLEASHED 211
I FEEL YOUR PAIN, MY DARLING 213
JUST THINKING OF YOU 214
ANOTHER DAY IN PARADISE 216
MY VALENTINE—FOREVER 218
REFLECTIONS FROM YOUR GOLFING LOVER 220
SPECIAL MOTHER 222
WE 224
LOVE'S SYNERGY 226

REWARDS—OUR FAMILY BIRTHRIGHT

MOTHERHOOD 229
MOTHER—THE CONSERVATIVE 230
MOTHER—FINAL CONFUSION—FINAL PRAYER 232
MY FATHER... 233
FATHER AND EXTENDED FAMILY—ANGER TO RAGE 238
TOO YOUNG—TOO LATE 244
GOD'S GIFT—FOUR CHILDREN 245
FIRST-BORN DAUGHTER 249
A LITTLE BIRTHDAY TRIBUTE 251
DAUGHTER'S FIRST HALF CENTURY 253
DAUGHTER ON MOTHER'S DAY 254

A FATHER'S REMORSE—AN UNINTENDED HURT 255
BREAKING SILENCE 257
SECOND BORN 258
HAPPY BIRTHDAY 262
THIRD BORN 263
"OLD MAN" TO SON 264
MY NEW STEPSON 265
PERNICIOUS PERSONALITY 268
TOUGH LOVE 271
TO MY GRANDCHILDREN 274
FROM SURROGATE TO REALITY 276
A BEAUTIFUL PERSON 278
DWY—DRIVING WHILE YOUNG 280
SOUL MATE RELATIONSHIPS (CHOICES—Getting PRIORITIES
    Right) 283
RENEWING RELATIONSHIPS—MY BROTHERS AND SISTER 286
OLDER BROTHER—A ROLE MODEL 290
HAVE STRENGTH, MY OLDER BROTHER 292
YOUNGER BROTHER 293
GRANDMA'S CREAM CANDY 297
A VERY SPECIAL AUNT 299
GLEN—VISIT FROM A TOUGH AND LOVING COUSIN 300
FAMILY AT CHRISTMAS 301
SEVENTY-FIFTH BIRTHDAY 303
SHOPPING—A PARODY 304

REWARDS—LASTING FRIENDSHIPS

A CHRISTMAS GIFT 311
LIFETIME FRIENDS 312
FRIENDSHIP 315
A HOME SHARED WITH FRIENDS 317
LOST FRIEND—LONELINESS—FRIENDSHIP FOUND 320
THE STROKE 323
CLIMBING BACK 324
BIG ED—BIG "C" 326
ROSEMARY 329

MARY 331
MARY LOU 336
BOB & JOAN 339
ANITA 342
DOCTOR "ED" 344
THE BULLY 345
BEAUTIFULLY UGLY 348
COPS 351
OTHER COMPANIONS 353
MY FRIEND—HUGO, THE DOG 356
SEASON'S GREETINGS TO FRIENDS: DECEMBER 2004 359
MUCH LOVE—BEST WISHES—HAPPY HOLIDAYS: DECEMBER
    2005 361
DECEMBER 2006 363
CHRISTMAS TRADITIONS 365

REWARDS—LOCATION AND LIFESTYLE

MY COLORADO—EVENING IN GOD'S COUNTRY 369
FORMATIVE YEARS IN THE VALLEY 370
THE VALLEY—REVISITED 376
ARVADA, COLORADO 380
SPRINGTIME IN THE ROCKIES 382
MY NEIGHBORHOOD 383
A TRIP TO ESTES PARK 386
SEARCH FOR BAGELS 388
COLORADO WEATHER REPORT—FAIR AND BREEZY 391
FIRST CAR—MY MODEL "A" 393

REWARDS—A SENIOR GOLFER

AVID GOLFER'S LOVE LETTER—A PARODY 399
DESPERATE FICKLE LOVE 400
COLORADO WINTER GOLF—FIRST VISIT TO A GOLF
    COURSE 404

HOME GOLF COURSE 407
NATURAL BEAUTY 411
FIRST WINTER GOLF—FIRST FREEZE 414
A MATCH—A LITTLE BET 416
MATCH PLAY BETS WITH A DUFFER 418
SPRING GOLF IN THE ROCKIES 420
"OLD GEEZER" TOURNAMENTS 422
LADY GOLFERS 424
THE "EASY" 7TH HOLE 425
10TH HOLE—"NEW BEGINNINGS" ON THE BACK NINE 427
SENIOR GOLFER TOURNAMENTS 430
MEMORABLE GOLF SCENES 432
A TASTE OF HUMILITY 434
RUB OF THE GREEN 435
FOURSOME 437
ANOTHER LOUSY ROUND 439
IT'S THE EQUIPMENT 441
COLORADO WEATHER REPORT—LET'S GO GOLFING!! 443
DON'T MESS WITH THE "GOLF GODS" 445
FROM WINTER TO SPRING—THE SEASON BEGINS 447
TIPS FROM GOLF MAGAZINE 448
I QUIT THIS &%#@ GAME 450
IT'S LADIES' DAY 452
TAKE IT TO THE COURSE 454
OLD GEEZERS 456
THE "GORILLA" 457
MID-SEASON FORM 459
A "YOUTHFUL" MIND VERSUS AN "OLD MAN'S" BODY 460
GOLF PARTNERS 462
COURSE UNDER REPAIR—WHO CARES? 464
OUR "NEW" HOME COURSE 466

INTRODUCTION

Over three quarters of a century has passed since I was shockingly introduced, early one Sunday morning, to planet Earth. I didn't realize until much later the blessings that had been bestowed on me by my birthright. Surrounded by strict, but caring parents, three siblings, a massive extended family, social, school and business friends and all of the opportunities that are present in this great country for those who care to pursue them, my life, now in its fourth quartile, has been rich and fulfilling. I've been so broke I couldn't afford the dime for bus transportation to my work and I have been wealthy beyond my dreams. In my personal life and work I have been impotent and omnipotent. I have experienced the romance of adventuring into uncharted territory during the genesis of business computer technology. I have enjoyed the unstinting support of corporate executives at all levels and from all business cultures throughout the world; and I have felt the ruthlessness of corporate competition at the top. I have fallen, and risen. I have felt the warmth of acceptance and the bitterness of rejection.

Finally, near the end of my seventh decade I found requited, romantic love from a soul mate that, fifty years earlier, had been my high school sweetheart. With her love I have finally become the man, the person that I have always strived to become.

In this Introduction I share some of the principles guiding my philosophy of life; the lessons of life that are treated in greater detail in the poetic short stories that follow.

FREEDOM

It's great to be an American, where everyone is free.
And equal opportunity prevails for you and me.
Where men and women from abroad are welcomed to this land!
And all who labor honestly receive a helping hand.

The founders of this land showed everyone how much they care.
For freedom's price proved greater than the bravest were aware.
Courageously they fought the wars, in which they all believed.
Some lost their lives in battles leaving families who then grieved.
Forefathers fought and died so their posterity could live.
Their sacrifice was great, for they gave all that they could give.
These patriots had volunteered to fight until the death.
And fight they did until they didn't have another breath.

Our freedom's not a given; it's a privilege we must earn,
for history tells the story, and it's one that all should learn.
We need to fully understand that freedom is not free.
It doesn't matter what you think; you don't have to agree.

Each young adult should understand that freedom has a price.
To keep the freedom others earned requires some sacrifice.
For many gave their lives so that their families could enjoy
a country that is free, that some aggressors would destroy.
Aggressors wait, each looking for a chink in our defense.
"Prepared for battle" helps assure our freedom's permanence.
The price of freedom could take everything you have to give.
And you ascend to Heaven where the bravest heroes live.

If you come from another land, perhaps your skin's not white.
Your origin just doesn't count; you have a basic right.
The freedom each of us enjoys is not reserved for some.
It's yours and mine, for no one cares from where we might have come.

Our Constitution sets the legal system we employ.
Our Bill of Rights assures the many freedoms we enjoy.
And we can vote for candidates to represent our needs.
How long they represent us is determined by their deeds.
You're free to speak of anything, to praise or to condemn.
You're free to worship as you wish; attend a requiem.
Or you can be an atheist, without a God at all.
The choice is yours and only yours, for that is freedom's call.

We call our flag "Old Glory", for it's rich in history.
And it personifies how we have fought for liberty.
It's battle scarred and bloody, but it's beautiful to me.
For it's the flying symbol of a people who are free.

Yes, I am proud to live in this great land of liberty.
And I'm prepared for combat to assure that we stay free.
As my forefathers fought so that this country might exist,
I'll carry on that battle against any terrorist.

To give one's life is just about the greatest sacrifice.
Yet, there's a larger calling; just to die does not suffice.
For we're a land that's governed by the people we elect.
And every vote determines whom the citizens select.
You need an education; it is free for those who choose.
You'll learn about the freedoms that you never want to lose.
You'll study history learning about patriots of note.
Then you will be imbued to always exercise your vote.

New immigrants come to this land until the borders strain.
And those who live within the laws are welcome to remain.
You may have come from somewhere else; you may have been born here.
The laws of this great land assure a life that's free of fear.
There's equal opportunity for you, for me, for all.
You start a business, work for others; you can play baseball.

For you and only you select the work you want to do.
But your success is not assured; it's really up to you.

Yes, you will love this country just a little more each day.
To leave would be verboten; you will always want to stay.
And you must be prepared to fight, to fight until the death,
so all of your posterity enjoys sweet freedom's breath.
Pledge your allegiance to the flag; give freedom its full due.
For more than you can ever give will be returned to you.
Hold freedom in your heart; sing freedom's song with all your might.
Help keep this country strong so we will never have to fight.

I thank God every day for all the freedoms we enjoy,
while knowing we're the mark that some aggressors would destroy.
Our country is a role model for people everywhere.
And, we give them a helping hand to show them that we care.

Rejoice with me, but pull your weight; there are no guarantees.
Appreciate all that you have; give thanks on bended knees.
And welcome others into this free land of liberty.
Then separate, yet together, we'll all live here happily

REFLECTIONS

The sunbeams rise across the eastern plains; white clouds above.
Its rays cut through the gentle breeze; its warmth reflects God's love.
A love so great it fills our lives with happiness and joy,
for she's a pretty teenage girl and I'm a teenage boy.

The evening sky is crimson, now the setting sun departs.
Like angels sent from Heaven as the summer evening starts.
My soul mate sits beside me; her soft hand is clasped in mine.
Each evening she's more beautiful as loving hearts entwine.
That we are now together is a miracle, for sure.
Our lives have been fulfilling; yet with her there's so much more.

The moon now brightens the night sky; enhanced by chirping birds.
This moment complemented by the soft sound of our words.
As everything we've done, each action, thought and loving glance
is shared by lovers, both of us, as we live this romance.

How beautiful this world became as love consumed our hearts.
Yes, every day is perfect, yet each new day our life starts.

We lock the doors and pull the shades and then adjust the heat.
Then hand in hand we climb the stairs; the day's almost complete.
And though each day's ideal, spoken words do not suffice.
For as we end each day we know we'll enter Paradise.
She's beautiful beyond compare as she lies close to me.
We're one as we embrace with love that's given, totally.

Yes, I'm in Heaven here on earth each morning, evening, night.
My world's a wondrous place; it's crystal clear and oh, so bright.
I see her standing there; I feel her touch; I hear her voice.
I close my eyes; she's etched into my mind; I have no choice.

She fills my every waking moment, perfect as it seems,
there's more, she's omnipresent as she fills my sleep with dreams.

We've each found peace with our soul mate, and everything's okay.
We'll live each day in harmony till God takes us away.

A WALK

The Maple stands majestically, its boughs raised to the sky.
The Weeping Willow hangs its limbs as though it's going to cry.
A Pine grows through the trees and brush; it reaches for the sun.
Each tree gives shade to cool my soul until my walk is done.

With pride a Columbine opens its buds to say, "Hello".
Bright colors like the rainbow; it's the star of nature's show.
Though small, its flowers whisper, "I am strong, I have no fear".
Perennial, the Columbine survives beyond the year.
The whisper of the mighty Oak, as wind blows through its leaves.
Sounds like a parent whose child has died, a parent who sadly grieves.
The Cottonwood has blossoms that flow gently in the breeze.
They come to rest on grassy slopes and the surrounding trees.

Beside the path a creek flows over roots, between large rocks.
The birds in branches of the trees sing tunes, like cuckoo clocks.
The clouds up in the heavens add their color to the sky.
They flutter in the gentle breeze like doves as they fly by.
I see the gardens in the backyards of the homes I pass.
The flowers bloom; they border lawns of neatly trimmed green grass.
Each yard is like a little park; small children play nearby.
The children laugh with glee as they pursue a butterfly.

Clear water in the lake reflects the trees along the shore.
The beavers felled a bush and now return to fell some more.
The Honkers blow their horns as they descend upon the lake.
Their feet hang low like landing gear, creating a white wake.
The Mallards duck their heads in search of food that they can eat.
Then dive and surface with a trout; a special breakfast treat!
Like paddles on the stern of the old Mississippi Queen,
their feet create small ripples; quiet water in between.

The breeze upon my brow is like the touch of God's cool hand.
Soft music filters through the air; it's from the high school band.
I walk in blissful peace, yet there's excitement everywhere.
The flight of tiny insects on my path makes me aware,
how precious is this life that we accept without a thought.
How wonderful our world and all the things that God has wrought!

Then crystal beams break through the clouds, a stairway to the sun.
I'll climb those stairs to Heaven someday, when my life is done.

PRODIGAL SON—MOTHER'S IMMACULATE PERCEPTION

She's been there all my life to help with every need I've had.
It didn't matter how I'd acted, whether good or bad.
Her love was unconditional; her words displayed her care.
And every night at bedtime she engaged her God in prayer.
A volunteer, her husband served his country, long ago.
The dangers that he faced were more than anyone could know.
The tragedy played out when she received a telegram,
for he had lost his life while fighting Cong in Vietnam.

My mother had to struggle just to earn our livelihood.
Some things were hard to comprehend, but most I understood.
She faced each day with hope inside a body, taught and gaunt,
while stretching every penny so that I would never want.
She read to me from childhood; books about geography.
We couldn't travel much, so through her words the world I'd see.
And it was her belief in me that opened every door.
The needle in her fingers made the only clothes I wore.
When I got stuck in school she always lent a helping hand.
Her words offered encouragement; there was no reprimand.
To her the world was beautiful; she shared it all with me,
from hummingbirds at feeders to the splendor of the sea.

Her home was filled with nature's best, bright flowers, everywhere.
All life to her was special, like a pristine love affair.
She shed a tear of happiness when I became a man.
Although I left the home we'd shared, and where my life began.
I went to visit lands that through her eyes I'd seen so well.
Her final words encouraged me, "My son you shall excel".
I had a great foundation upon which to build my life.
I started my career and then I took a lovely wife.

For twenty years I labored in a business of my own.
I made a lot of money, yet my work was a millstone.
Instead of taking time to call my mother, just to talk,
or visit her on weekends so that we could take a walk,
I literally forgot that Mom had given me my start.
The thoughtlessness that I displayed would almost break her heart.

And then one day I got a call from one of Mom's close friends.
And just like that I realized I had to make amends.
For Mom was failing fast, she'd lost the health she always had.
I visualized her loneliness; the visions made me sad.
I called her on the phone to see if I could help, some way.
She simply asked if I could come and visit her one-day.
There wasn't any choice; I quickly put my work on hold,
so I could give some back to Mom, whose heart is filled with gold.

When I arrived she greeted me; a kiss, a loving touch.
A visit once in twenty years, that isn't very much.
She asked if I was happy with my work, with my career.
She spoke of all the beauty she'd enjoyed, year after year.
Mom's home was filled with flowers; there was color everywhere.
With nature she had always had a wondrous love affair.
The flowers and the plants bespoke the care she gave each day.
A sanctuary where small birds and butterflies could play!
Mom had just one request for she'd grown old and didn't drive.
To see the Great Divide once more, while she was still alive!
To cross the Great Divide had been her dream for many years.
That she might not see it again was one of her last fears.

So from her home in Boulder we departed in my car.
Through Lyons, then to Estes Park, it wasn't very far.
The winter snow was melting; signs of spring were all around.
The sun bounced prisms from the lake, like diamonds to be found.
We walked down to the valley floor; we sat upon the ground.
Words flowed like water from a well; there was no other sound.

Mom asked a hundred questions as we breathed the mountain air.
The splendor was so humbling all that I could do was stare.
The mountains stood before us piercing through a hanging cloud.
An elk stood in the shadows, like a stranger in a crowd.
The Columbines were blooming; purple sprays against the green.
We sat in awe while drinking in this captivating scene.
Tears came to Mother's eyes as we discussed the scenes above.
Her voice broke with emotion; I was sure she felt God's love.
She asked me to describe exactly what I sensed and saw.
This tested my vernacular, for I was filled with awe.

Back in the car I drove into the Rocky Mountain Park.
The sun behind the towering trees, the day turned almost dark.
Then over Milner Pass; almost eleven thousand feet,
I stopped so Mom could rest; our special day was not complete.
We looked out over distant slopes with green and bluish hues.
The patterns formed by Junipers, like colorful tattoos.
Enormous Ponderosa pines, majestically reached out.
Their shadows testified their size; there wasn't any doubt.
Long moments passed while Mom and I absorbed this stunning scene,
cliffs overhanging canyons; rugged boulders in between.
I searched for words to let her know the thrill I felt inside.
Her touch communicated, we had nothing left to hide.

The sun approached the mountaintops as we drove back toward home.
The world around us shifted to a stunning polychrome.
Reflections from the flowers rebounded from the setting sun.
A perfect day was ending for a mother and her son.

We hadn't traveled far, two hundred miles, more or less.
We'd crossed the great divide, its beauty and its ruggedness.
Now sitting in Mom's home, a glass of sherry in my hand,
I listened to her words and tried my best to understand.
I closed my eyes so I could visualize what Mom was saying.
The pictures formed as music, like a song she could be playing.

With eloquence she painted every scene we'd shared today.
So vivid I was certain not a word could be hearsay.

We sat there in her darkened room; there wasn't any light.
Yet everything was clear to Mom; she had a special sight.
Through Mother's words the "Great Divide" formed clearly in my mind,
for that's how she had seen it, too, for Mother is now blind.

LOUISE

When I awoke this morning, Pat beside me in our bed.
The usual thoughts of love, like dancing angels, filled my head.
While we are truly blessed with loving friends and family,
I couldn't help but think of what you mean to Pat and me.
You've been Pat's friend for many years; the years go by so fast.
Yet, friendships based on love don't falter, they forever last

We've thought of you a lot this year; the challenges you've had,
and how you've met them, every one, no matter, good or bad.
We've thought of how your family gives support and love to you.
Of all their thoughts and prayers, the many kindly things they do.
We've thought of all your friends who say a silent prayer each day.
And give you their support; each in their own and special way.

But we don't wonder why; you've earned the love of every one.
In every life you've touched, you've brought some joy, a little fun.
Yes, thoughtful little deeds for you are natural as can be.
You add some happiness to every person that you see.

Your friendship truly adds more love to every life you touch.
To Pat and me your friendship means a lot; so very much.
You add a little meaning to our lives each time we meet.
You're always so darned positive; so thoughtful and so sweet.
You know you're in our thoughts and prayers, a friend forever more.
Our love to you, our special friend; a friend that we adore!

Best wishes and much love from us!

GOD WITHIN

I've never heard him say a word; I've never seen his face.
Yet somehow I am certain every day when I say grace,
the words I speak create an aura blending soul with sound.
And somewhere deep inside me is the God that I have found.

When seeking faith I went to church to see if it was there.
I asked a lot of people; some would smile and some would stare.
In Sunday school I learned that I'm a child in Jesus' flock.
The minister's belief in God was solid as a rock.
I read the Bible every day; I read each word and phrase.
I learned of love and worship; of the God that I should praise.
The Elders said that God loves all, each person, everyone.
It doesn't matter if you're bright or you're a simpleton.
God loves each boy and girl, yes, every woman, every man.
And every person on the earth is part of God's great plan.

I looked around and saw that everyone in church was white.
Now why can't blacks be members too? I thought this wasn't right.
I asked the Elders why the blacks were not in church with me.
The Elders told me blacks are not God's children, equally.
The blacks were all good friends of mine; we went to school each day.
The church refused to change, so with that church I couldn't stay.
A church that teaches bigotry is not the faith I seek.
The membership may be aggressive or they may be meek.
Yet I believe that in God's view we're equal as can be,
for God's inside the soul of every person, you and me.

My father urged my study and to "witness" just like him.
I studied for a year, then two, but found his teachings grim.
There wasn't any love, just fear of sin and dying, too.
This fear of God applied to all, it wasn't for a few.

I want to feel the love of God within my soul each day.
I want to feel God's warmth each time I have a need to pray.
I know what's right and what is wrong; God's path for me is clear.
I do not need my head and heart maligned and filled with fear.

I studied Yoga with a friend; we'd meditate each day.
While silent and relaxed I'd often find the words to pray.
My body and my mind became a single entity.
I sensed God's love within my soul, in total unity.
Then like each other group I've known, my friend recited rules.
The stuff he wanted me to do was fodder, made for fools.
The more I learned the less I knew; a group omniscient.
Inside my heart I felt God's love; God's love was sufficient.

A Course in Miracles was next; a friend proclaimed its truth.
He preached it as God's word to all adults and to the youth.
His sermons lasted from the break of dawn to dusk each day.
For he was so sincere that all he did was teach and pray.
I listened to my friend and then I bought the books to read.
I had to see if these were God's own teachings I must heed.
And then I met the wife of a good friend that studied this.
In just one evening it was clear that something was amiss.
Where love and her respect should be, my friend received advice.
She criticized each word he spoke; her needs were avarice.
It only took a little while and I knew what was wrong.
The Course creates a vacuum where realities belong.

And then I met a minister with followers galore.
And every week his following grew larger; there were more.
Together with his wife he lived the way God wants us to.
A role model himself, he didn't tell me what to do.
He simply shared the beauty of belief in God within.
To love one's self as others is a blessing, not a sin.
My spirit or my soul is something I can't see or hear.
But I can feel its presence, for it's what makes life so dear.

The Reverend said to keep in touch with my own feelings, too,
and how God's presence in my soul will tell me what to do.
His teachings didn't hurt me and they didn't leave a scar.
God's love is there for each of us, no matter who we are.

It doesn't take a leap of faith to feel God from within.
For God is in your soul no matter where you might begin.
He's with you every day and night; with every breath you take;
and his forgiveness is your own, so give yourself a break.

Remember you are human and the God within you knows,
you'll do some right; you'll do some wrong; some feelings you'll expose.
Relax and let your God within, guide you to all your goals.
Your head will guide your body while your heart will guide your soul.

THOUGHTS AT TWILIGHT

The twilight portends darkness; it is quiet, calm; serene.
A western sky with setting sun, the air's so crisp and clean.
White clouds permute to scarlet as they give the sun a shove.
The shadows grow and fade as thunderheads form high above.

Too soon this day comes to an end, as twilight cloaks the earth.
Reflection! Deeds both good and bad! What has my life been worth?

The twilight, harbinger of darkness, death not far behind!
My search for friends was fruitless; not a one is left to find.
Each passed the twilight of this life, like shadows in the night.
Did twilight bring their stairs to Heaven clearly into sight?
Or, did the blackness of the night, another story tell?
A black hole, fire and brimstone, Lucifer, a burning Hell!

As twilight fades to darkness and the stars begin to glow.
I look around, I realize, so little do I know,
a miniscule of comprehension of God's master plan.
Is there a destiny for everything, including man?
Or, am I just a victim of the life I chose to live?
Take from the cup of life each day, no time to care or give.

I meditate in shades of gray, with twilight all around.
Dark images mock every thought; lost hope with every sound.
There's never been tomorrow in the presence of today.
Today bids fond farewell; it's gone, as daylight fades away.
Each yesterday's a hollow memory, gone forever more.
The years have come and gone till I can't count them, anymore.
How do I say goodbye when there is no one left but me?
I search my soul, an empty shell; there's nothing left to see.

I'll die or I'll forever live with God, if that's the plan.
Until the twilight takes me, I will be the best I can.

ABOUT GOLF AND LIFE

All golfers know the game's a metaphor of life, and more.
In both, with every action that you take, you know the score.
In golf and life your acts decide the outcome you'll achieve.
And when you win you celebrate; you lose and sadly grieve.
But there's a constant; it's the same; no person can deny,
what's fair; what's right and wrong; without regard to how you try.

In golf you tweak a shot, you nudge a lie; don't count a stroke.
It may win you the match, but your integrity is broke.
In life you tell a "small white" lie; you cheat a little bit.
It soon becomes a habit and you don't know how to quit.
The expectations others have of you become too great.
Like golf it started small, you're trapped, a victim of your fate.

You're world's become a fantasy; a wishful dream at best.
No matter how you try, you're going to fail life's every test.
When you do something that you know is wrong, you'll surely pay.
What goes around then comes around; it gets to you one day.

In golf you can resolve to let the rules control your game.
In life it's not that difficult to change, to do the same.
You're in the rough, your ball's so deep you barely see the top.
Just "nudge the thing" a little bit; and then you quickly stop.
You may not hit it very far, but you can dig it out.
You'll feel and be a better man; that's what life is about.

If you are fair and honest in your life, you'll feel the same.
Integrity guides all you do; there's no one else to blame.
With head held high you face each day, each person that you meet.
A lesson from your game of golf; that life can be so sweet.

Just treat your game of golf as life, "to thine own self be true".
And that reflection from your mirror, will smile right back at you.

THE PRICE OF EXPERIENCE

From our first "experience" of a swat on the butt to help us breathe life into our bodies to our last, gasping breath, we are "students" of the world in which we live, some formal, some informal, some planned, some accidental. In addition to the training and educational partnerships we form with our parents, other nuclear family members and then teachers and professors during our formal schooling, much of what we learn comes from personal experiences as we solve problems presented to us in our everyday lives. Occasionally we learn by observing the actions and experiences of others. Frequently we don't learn from either our own experiences or the "advice" of others, resulting in the "opportunity" to live the experiences again, particularly those that are downright unpleasant.

These poetic short stories discuss some of life's experiences along the paths that we traverse and the mountains that we climb. In some cases these "experiences" are pleasant and fulfilling; some are downright enervating. Many share philosophical hints for dealing with the unexpected challenges we meet in our daily lives.

ROLE MODELS

Is anyone responsible for children as they grow?
If asked, "Where are your kids right now", would many parents know?
For who's in charge when they're in school? Do teachers really care?
And who is shaping their young lives? Is anyone aware?

There are not many laws to guide new parents from the start.
Give shelter, food and clothing; some advice they may impart.
Don't physically abuse your kids, for that will break the law.
Their mental health is something else; is that a legal flaw?
Most parents love their children; well, at least their mothers do.
And when there's time away from work, most fathers love them, too.
But how much time do we devote to listening to them?
If something doesn't sound just right, do we quickly condemn?

We may try to remember just exactly how it felt,
when we were young, as they are now, the problems our life dealt.
Does life swing children round and round worse than a carousel?
Do parents serve as role models, and do they do it well?

If youngsters follow in your steps and do just as you do,
as an adult and parent would this make you happy, too?
They watch you when you drive your car for groceries that you need.
Do you comply with traffic laws and do you never speed?
You only travel thirty in a zone marked twenty-five.
It's no big deal like life or death; it's just the way you drive.

Are you sending a message to the children, one and all?
The laws apply selectively, for they're equivocal.

The phone rings and you answer it; your aunt is on the line.
When she gets going you are trapped, entangled in a vine.

You tell her you have got to run; it's just a little lie.
Your children hear; do they now feel that truth does not apply?

You have a party at your home, a few good friends of yours.
You're happy and excited for you don't invite the boors.
There's alcohol to drink and then a little pot to smoke.
It's nothing big like heroin; it's more a party joke.
Is this the message that you want your children to receive?
If doing drugs is right for you, then what will they believe?
Or will you make excuses with some "bill of goods" you sell?
Tell them a little lie so they'll think you're their role model.

You buy a pack of cigarettes; you buy one every day.
To hell with all that scary stuff! Your habits here to stay!
You find that in your son's backpack, he has some cigarettes.
Your son is smoking now; does that give you a few regrets?
You like to root and cheer for athletes who are superstars.
They dress up nice and pretty and they drive their fancy cars.
You hope your kids will understand and practice really hard.
They'll be so rich and famous that they'll need a bodyguard.
The super star makes headlines; he's accused of rape and more.
Convicted he must do his time and see a counselor.
What kind of message has he sent to young folks everywhere?
The money's not the thing; the guy could be a billionaire.

Are money and the things we own true measure of success?
Are "things we own" the basis for a life of happiness?
Is life simply a race to see how much we can acquire?
Are things we purchase from fine stores, for others to admire?

We sometimes get so busy that we may not take the time,
to help our children understand the mountains that we climb.
The conflicts that face each of us; how we prioritize.
How truthfulness is paramount, but why we tell "white lies".
Is raising kids so tough that we're unable to succeed?

Is it too much for us to try to fill their every need?
Are there too many ways for them to find a trouble spot?
Is everything okay as long as they do not get caught?

Perhaps there are some ways, some little things that we can learn.
Some "rules to live by" may assist us on our life's sojourn.
While words won't do it all, sometimes they help to pave the way.
Remember actions speak so loud, they won't hear what we say.

The things that we acquire will mean a whole lot more to us,
if they're acquired by honest means, without a lot of fuss!
Then as we walk through life and help a derelict or bum.
We find the greater good in knowing who we have become.
If we behave so we earn admiration from our peers.
Our self-esteem and confidence will mitigate our fears.
We make a wish; we hope, and then we pray a little, too.
We even might just ask ourselves, "Now, what would our God do?"
The people in our lives help, whether they are wrong or right.
For either way we learn if we just keep them in our sight.
To locate someone perfect we discover is quite rare.
But we'll be a lot closer if we say a family prayer.
Then once each day with family; with the parent in the lead,
we share thoughts inspirational, for all of us to heed.
For family is the place we learn what's wrong and what is right.
Morality exalts us like the honor of a knight.

Now, wouldn't you be honored and feel proud as you can be,
to learn that you're the role model for all the kids to see?
Each parent and each child wants you to tell what you have done
to earn respect and be the trusted friend of everyone.

Some things we learn so young that we're not certain what we know.
I had not entered school and I was just starting to grow.
My mother asked a question; it came right out of the blue.
She answered it herself; "Pretend the Lord is watching you".

I live my life just like a child, for there's a watchful eye,
that oversees my life, and it will be there till I die.

Make every action, thought or word, and every deed you do,
your best as a "Role Model" for "The Lord is watching you".

BOUNCING BACK

I fall; it hurts; I feel the pain; I sit for just a while.
I'm walking home; it isn't far; it's just about a mile.
I think I'll wait here on the ground; I'll lie here on my side.
Someone should be here pretty soon, and they'll give me a ride.
The pain persists; I rub my leg; there's not a car in sight.
Just standing makes me wince a bit, like I've just lost a fight.
Breathe in and out, do it again, then take a step or two.
I'll bounce back; I'll ignore the pain, and then I'll feel like new.

Today I learned a lesson and I wasn't very old.
To wait for help just wastes my time; it's better to be bold.
I take a step and take one more; it isn't very far.
The injury that I incurred won't even leave a scar.

We all have setbacks in our life, no matter how we plan.
Like scouts, just "be prepared", yes, every woman, every man.
Instead of giving up, you might just give yourself some slack.
Some energy, vivaciousness, and you'll come bouncing back.

When I was fourteen years of age, my parents split for good.
If they'd have asked I'd told them that I didn't think they should.
It happened fast, more quickly than a storm out of the blue.
I left my home and friends to be with mother, siblings, too.
From farm to city life I went; I gave it my best try.
I hated every minute, though it didn't help to cry.
The pain was mental but it hurt; I ached from head to toe.
Like torture I survived six months and then I had to go.

In this case bouncing back meant I'd return to my dad's farm.
Although I'd leave my mom behind, there wasn't any harm.
I'd miss her and my brothers and my little sister, too.
To see them I just drove an hour; that's all I had to do.

In '49 and '50 with a friend that I admired,
we started a small business on some land that we'd acquired.
We worked both day and night; we gave it everything we had.
We built a strong foundation, like a rocket launching pad.
The business was diversified and grew by leaps and bounds.
We sold the lumber by board feet; it wasn't sold by pounds.
We worked so hard we barely found the time to count our wealth.
Both young and strong; we didn't think it might affect our health.

For me it was the Army; Uncle Sam called me away.
I joined for just a little while; I didn't want to stay.
Before I'd finished training I received the awful news.
I had to get back right away or everything we'd lose.
My partner fell to polio; it had him on his back.
Our wealth was being stolen by a crooked lumberjack!
I had to stop him right away or nothing would be left.
We'd lose our business, everything, the victims of a theft.

The Army wouldn't let me go; we had a war to fight.
In disagreements such as this, the Army's always right.
Then two years later I returned; our business wasn't there.
And no one seemed to care that what had happened wasn't fair.

But I was glad I'd made it home, my mind and body whole.
To start again with nothing left took all my self-control.
As bullets ricochet when they hit something that's too hard,
I'd hit the bottom; I'd rebound, though I'd been badly scarred.

When I returned I found my wife in bed with a schoolmate.
She said that she'd been lonely, so I told her I would wait.
In just about a month she came to live with me, once more.
We left the past behind until she said she'd been a whore.
She wanted me to stay and share the pleasures she could give.
Each day she'd work the streets; for that's the way she liked to live.
At night we'd be together just like any man and wife.

She might as well have stabbed me in the heart with a sharp knife.
We talked and then we talked some more; it took a lot of grit.
Our talks were like a trial; I hoped the jury would soon acquit.
Could I accept the work she did and how she spent her days?
I made the choice; we parted and we went our separate ways.

I went to work and back to school; I had a life to live.
For work I found that finance was a great alternative.
And I attended school at night; learned what I had to know.
I worked some fifteen hours each day. That made my juices flow.
I had a great career; I worked for over thirty years.
I did it well and I advanced; I even earned some cheers.
No bouncing back for me, for I'm a big executive.
This time I've done it right and there is nothing to forgive.

If you don't learn from history, then you'll live it all again!
It's like I said my prayers each night but didn't say, "Amen".
The power structure changed; I must have blinked or turned my back.
"You're out"; I'd been derailed just like a train that missed the track.

This time I landed softer, for I'd earned retirement.
To bounce back at this age I'd need to be self-confident.
For just a while I wasn't sure how hard I'd like to drive.
For after thirty years and more, I'd just turned fifty-five.

No problem; I just started a new business of my own.
I built a network large enough I should have had a throne.
A network marketing approach, it fit me like a glove.
I talked to people everywhere; I'd just found my new love.
Then Sixty-Minutes aired a show that questioned what I did.
They didn't pull a punch; in fact they took off every lid.
The pot was black; the kettle burned; my network fell apart.
It wasn't true but no one cared; it nearly broke my heart.

How many times can I bounce back? I'm sixty years of age.
I'm healthy and I feel so good; I won't live in a cage.
I take a nice position with a friend I've known for years.
We're going into a marketplace that every banker fears.
With borrowed funds from other folks, our friends and family,
we knew we were the best, and we made money rapidly.
We financed cars for people who had never paid their bills.
And like a roller coaster ride, we got some real thrills.
We financed half a billion to these folks who had a need.
But over half were people who were mostly filled with greed.
They didn't make their payments so we repossessed their cars.
It didn't matter whether they were Fords or new Jaguars.
A guy from Texas bought our loans; we had a strong contract.
He breached it with a shrug; though it was wrong, it was a fact.
He simply laughed and said, "Up yours; there's nothing you can do".
It turned out that the guy was right; we couldn't even sue.
It happened pretty fast; we'd lost the millions we had made.
We faced investors, every one, not one did we evade.
Their money's gone; yes every cent, there wasn't any left.
While most accepted what we said, some thought there'd been a theft.
I lost my home and savings. Yes, I lost all of my wealth.
There wasn't any money left; it almost broke my health.
Once threatened with a pistol, I was sued by angry friends.
Ten million big ones down the tubes; I couldn't make amends.
The IRS laid claim to me for taxes that were due.
The state climbed on and said to me that they want their pound, too.

I'm broke and homeless living on a small retirement.
From stronger than Goliath, I am now an impotent.

It takes some courage, when you are down; it takes a little gall,
to raise your head with broken heart; to stand there strong and tall.
To face your friends and family who are ready to attack,
and promise them you've got the grit; that you'll again bounce back.

Well, here I am a writer and I'm sure that you'll admit,
so many stories that I can tell, I'll never need to quit.
I'm writing poems and novels. There is nothing I won't try.
I'll bounce back and pay every one their due before I die.

LITTLE LEAGUE BASEBALL

When I was young I loved the game; I played it every day.
At grade school on the hill, baseball's the only game we'd play.
Each grade had its own baseball field, on asphalt or on dirt.
In seventh and in eighth grades we each wore a special shirt.
I later played in high school, baseball season every spring.
We won a few and lost some, too, but baseball was my thing.
Although I loved the game, I didn't play exclusively.
Yet out of high school for a while, I played professionally.

To go to work I quit the game; baseball and I did part.
My father loved the game so much it nearly broke his heart.
I didn't know the time would come when once again I'd be,
on baseball fields most every day, these times my son with me.
There wasn't any little league where I played as a youth.
We organized ourselves to play, and that is God's own truth.
So when my son took up the game, it filled me with desire.
In uniform all black and blue, I worked as an umpire.

I knew the game but went to school to "relearn" all the rules.
I purchased all the gear I'd need; I wanted all the tools.
When I was on the field I always looked about the same
as those tough guys in black and blue, at any big league game.

I didn't know when I began, how much "appearance" means.
Things sometimes get emotional between opposing teams.
The kids are great for they just play; for them the game is fun.
When it's all over they just want to know which team has won.
But parents are another thing; an umpire's nemesis.
From bleachers they all scream and yell; some parents even hiss.
It didn't take me long to learn, I had to take control.
To let the game be for the kids, now that became my goal.

The very first league game I called, a parent charged at me.
His hand, a pumping fist, reached out for everyone to see!
I stood my ground and when he stopped, I spoke in a soft tone.
"Get off the field and leave the park; to me you're a millstone."
Another time a coach got mad; he grabbed me by the shirt.
He spat and then he shouted and he kicked up lots of dirt.
I backed away a step or two, with eyes of steel gray.
"You're out" I said; he sputtered some and then he walked away.

It wasn't always easy to be calm when others screamed.
It took a lot more self-control than I had ever dreamed.
I knew I had to keep my cool, no matter what the cost,
for otherwise I hurt the kids, and much more would be lost.

I've had my share of parents who attacked me on the field.
Some times I even wished the league had issued me a shield.
With firmness, no emotion, just as strong as I could be,
I counseled them or threw them out; the choice was up to me.
Most parents understood the game was for the youths that played.
They'd root for sons or daughters from the bleachers where they stayed.
For they knew we, the volunteers, who umpire every game,
have our own kids on other teams, for us it's just the same.

In little league, like all youth sports, the kids compete to win!
And hopefully they also learn to lose is not a sin.
The coaches mean a lot, much more than teaching kids the game.
Good sportsmanship means more most times than all the other fame.
In every competition you're allowed to use the tools.
You play with all your might, but you must not abuse the rules.
It may not make you happy when you're on the losing end.
But you'll have your integrity; for no rule did you bend.

I'm happy I could allocate the time to volunteer.
Most times I felt the benefits; sometimes it wasn't clear.
But in the end the boys that played were better than before.
For they had won in every game, no matter what the score.

BAGGAGE FROM YESTERDAY

The bag is here inside my head; it's filled with yesterday.
Each time I move forward with life, I throw the bag away.
But then when things go wrong it's here, and looks me in the eye.
It comes to life again; oh, how I wish that bag would die.

My yesterdays are part of me, no matter what I do.
I want to have good thoughts; get rid of all the bad ones, too.
Somehow I need to find a way to let the bad ones go.
So there's some space for all of my good memories to grow.
I've got this baggage in my mind; it weighs my very soul.
It stops me in my tracks each time I pursue a new goal.
I can't make a decision, for I think I might be wrong.
So here I sit, inactive, just like that's where I belong.

This baggage is the bane to everything that I pursue.
For years I did new things, and with each one I knew I grew.
But now I have experience; there's doubt in every move.
I cannot seem to get it right, to get into the groove.

The baggage started when I was a little boy in school.
I thought I had it right, for I had memorized each rule.
But then I got a problem about which I had to think.
I hadn't learned to reason, so my grades began to sink.
I had to find a whole new way to reason problems through.
Yet baggage filled my mind, so it was hard for me to do.
Then with some help from others, I learned how to analyze.
And found one isn't always right, no matter how one tries.

As I became a teenager I learned what's right and wrong.
My church taught "fire and brimstone" and each lesson was quite strong.
I learned each lesson thoroughly; I learned them very well.
I knew that if I sinned that I would go straight down to Hell.

I started dating girls; it was fun to neck and pet.
I didn't want to do much more; I wasn't ready, yet.
Sometimes it got a little warm, for girls enjoyed it, too.
Yet I refrained from all the things I knew I must not do.
Then without warning late one night, the rules seemed to subside.
My lady friend and I, I thought, would soon be groom and bride.
The petting got quite heavy, and it went a bit too far.
It wasn't what you think, but it still left an awful scar.
We didn't date again and we both went our separate ways.
I'd sinned against my God; it would be with me all my days.
I'd sinned against a lady whom I loved more than she knew.
With broken heart I left, for there was naught else I could do.

I can't "unspeak" a word I've said; it simply can't be done.
I can't "unrun" a race, in which I've run and have not won.
I can't undo a sin when I knew better all the time.
It's baggage in my mind, and to my God it is a crime.

My "Uncle" called and off I went and trained to fight a war.
When "drums and bugles" play, I'm patriotic to the core.
My father said, "To kill's a sin", conviction in his voice.
Yet this one time I felt I really didn't have a choice.
With rifle on my shoulder, I was in the infantry.
Yet in my heart I knew I could not kill the enemy.
Assigned a desk, the war and I were quickly far apart.
For once I felt God's love; or was I just a coward at heart?
Each time one of my buddies who had gone into combat
got wounded, maybe killed, as at my "warrior's" desk I sat.
I died a little, knowing they were there instead of me.
They risked and gave their lives so that our country would stay free.
On dates when veterans mourn their friends and buddies, who are dead,
I hide my face, embarrassed, and I weep inside, instead.
The war created baggage that I've carried since that day!
No matter how I try, these thoughts are in my mind to stay.

The war added more baggage that I've tried, but cannot shed.
It's there no matter what I do; it's deep inside my head.
Much like the gift of "guilt", it keeps on giving all my life.
It cuts small pieces from my soul, like it's a sharpened knife.

I made a lot of money then I lost it in a crash.
Some people say I may have acted, "just a little rash".
I lost it all; I'm broke and now I need to start again.
Yet carrying this bag is tough, it's one unholy pain.
No matter what I try, I think of those old friends of mine.
Who trusted what I told them when I said, "It will be fine"!
They loaned me lots of money, their life savings, sometimes more.
And when they lost it all, they quickly let me know the score.
Some threatened with their guns while others organized a Class,
to file with the DA and have him hang my sorry ass.
I somehow made it out; but I'd lost everything but hope.
Now looking back, I realize, I'd been a stupid dope.

In golf you're in the "zone" when you score par on every hole.
You're in the "zone" in football when you win the Super Bowl.
I've not been in the "zone" since I lost everything I had.
There's got to be a "zone" for me; or am I really bad?

I prayed unto my God to give me strength and guidance, too.
I seemed to hear a voice, "What are you qualified to do"?
That didn't help a lot for I had lost most everything.
My past's all baggage in my mind; what will the future bring?
I scribble a few notes and then I doodle for a while.
The jury's in; I'm guilty; it's the end of my life's trial.
Then as I read the words that I have written on the pad,
A tear forms in my eye; the words I've written are so sad.
Then like a bolt of lightning striking from the cloudy skies,
I know exactly what to do; hot tears now fill my eyes.
For every piece of baggage that I've carried all this time,
is fodder for a novel, though it may be one tough climb.

Make lemonade from lemons, stumbling block to stepping stone.
I'll be the "King of Tragedy"; I'll sit upon my throne.
And tell all of my stories, so that others learn from me.
Where I have failed, they will win; and that will make them free.
From writer on to author, I'll write books from dawn to dark.
A best seller or two and I will really make my mark.
I'll help poor souls who otherwise would never have a chance.
They'll never carry baggage just because of ignorance.
And then when Hollywood picks up my book for a movie,
the story will top the charts, be great, and critics will agree.
I've told the greatest story anyone has ever told.
With ticket sales beyond what any movie ever sold.

These stories are the bequest that I'll leave posterity.
No greater value could I leave; I know they'll all agree.
Each life's a story waiting for a writer to record.
And it's worth more than all the money anyone can hoard.

Your baggage need not hold you back. Just keep it in your mind.
There's value in experience of every single kind.
So keep a journal every day, record the things you do.
And value quite beyond your dreams will be returned to you.

A FATHER'S COUNSEL—FAILURE OR SUCCESS

Son

"Oh Father, if I miss a goal, does that mean I have failed?
I break a law, a small mistake and then find I am jailed.
Or, maybe something looks so tough I barely even try.
I walk away before it's done. Is this a self-told lie?
If I associate with 'losers' does that mean I'm wrong?
If they rough up a kid or two and I just tag along?
Does my association with these 'losers' define me?
Are my actions as wrong as theirs, if I do not agree?
Is my association with these 'losers' a mistake?
How will I ever know for sure good choices I forsake?
Can I be sure what's right or wrong in what I do each day?
Why can't all things be black or white and not just shades of gray?
Can't several 'rights' correct my 'wrongs' so they're gone from my past?
Can anything I do correct mistakes, if they are vast?
Am I a failure now before I've grown to be adult?
If failure's all I've known, am I part of a 'failure cult'?
My bank account is empty and I've got a lot of debt.
Instead of money all my work just creates beads of sweat.
And every time I think it's going to go right for a while,
Some dumb thing happens and I feel that I've been placed on trial.

Have I been singled out to be a failure all my life?
Has God made me the target of some everlasting strife?
Why must I suffer every day while others do quite well?
Sometimes I feel I'd like to quit, and end it all in Hell."

Father

"Your failure is a given Son, if that's what you decide.
The only thing that matters is who you become, inside.
A failure keeps on saying, 'Well, oh hell, what is the use?'
To be a failure all your life, you just need one excuse.
Success, Son is an attitude; it's not about your goals.
Success is found in everyone; sometimes deep in their souls.
The PROCESS is success; it's not the goals that you achieve.
You'll have success throughout your life, if that's how you believe.
It's always just as easy to be on a winning team.
One small success and just like that, it builds your self-esteem.
Success begets success and there you are, right on the top.
And winning will continue all your life, if you don't stop.
Enjoy the PROCESS every day; enjoy the work you do.
Then happiness beyond your dreams will be in store for you.
And you'll achieve your goals because your life is so much fun.
You'll feel fulfillment every hour, until each day is done.

Be honest with yourself; add to your knowledge every day,
Thank God that you are healthy every time you kneel and pray.
Reach out and give to those who are less fortunate than you.
Success will be your partner, Son, in everything you do."

BELIEF AND FAITH

Sometimes it doesn't matter whether you believe or not.
The morning sun arrives and then the day gets surly hot.
The evening breezes play with leaves; the sun sets in the west.
And quietly the night arrives when you are at your best.

Claude Bristol wrote a book about the "The Magic of Belief".
If I write his ideas here, you'll think that I'm a thief.
Yet much of what he has to say is fundamental truth.
The power of belief's been with me since I was a youth.
Now, what I have to say is from experience I've had.
So you may find some good advice; you may think some is bad.

They say you have to have a dream to make a dream come true.
But if you have a dream and don't believe, will it work, too?
And is the dream a thing that happens when you are asleep?
Or is the dream inside your head and there for you to keep?

Believe in something or you'll fall for anything, I'm told.
It happens to the poor and to the rich, who own the gold.
Belief defines the boundaries of the life you're going to live.
It helps you know what you'll accept, and what you have to give.
Beliefs may change their forms as years pass by and you mature.
The ones that dominate in youth may gradually obscure.
To be replaced by others that become your guiding light.
They help you differentiate what's wrong, and what is right.

Religions are all system of beliefs; some false, some true.
The challenge is to find the system that is right for you.
If from the pulpit every word you hear is how you feel.
You're lucky for most folks find some "beliefs" a bit surreal.
Belief is quite important to a pastor and a priest.

Their congregations may be from the west or from the east.
Their system of beliefs is what defines the groups they lead.
They have to "brainwash" followers, if they wish to succeed.
And to be brainwashed isn't bad; it's who has brainwashed you.
In fact if you think back you'll find you've brainwashed yourself, too.
It's just a way of changing your beliefs and how you feel.
Like you have had a wound and now you've helped the wound to heal.

A 'goal' is what you want that's just outside your 'comfort zone'.
You want it now for it's something you don't wish to postpone.
Yet, there's a little apprehension in the plan you've made.
You know that you'd achieve it now, if you were not afraid.

So write an affirmation, make it positive and strong.
Then charge it with emotion; read it like a battle song.
And read it every day so it will strengthen your belief.
Then fear will vanish and you'll feel the comfort of relief.
Your "comfort zone" gets larger, for the goal now fits inside.
To execute your plan is something you now take in stride.
And suddenly your goal is a reality of life.
For with belief, your goal's achieved; you've overcome the strife.

When I was young my mother said that I could have a bike.
A tricycle was what I'd had, for I was just a tyke.
My brother bought a new bike so I got the 'hand me down'.
I got excited for I now could ride all over town.
Without a second thought I jumped right on the seat to ride.
A bike with just two wheels is something I had never tried.
I hit the curb and then the ground; the bike was on my head.
I left the bike right there and rode my tricycle instead.

My mom had watched what I had done; she did not say a word.
She knew the way I acted that I had not been injured.
She picked the bike up off the ground and stood it by the fence,
then said, "Let's try again so you can get experience".

I didn't want to ride that thing; I did not have belief.
One try had been enough for me; I did not need more grief.
We talked a little while as Mom explained the way it's done.
She told me all the different ways that riding would be fun.
As we were talking I forgot the crackup I just had.
A little bump and scratch now didn't seem so very bad.
My mother had a dream and she instilled that dream in me.
I learned what fun I'd have with just two wheels, instead of three.
I tried again for I believed that I could ride it now.
There wasn't any question; I'd achieve success, somehow.
My mother held it steady as I jumped up on the seat.
With new belief I rode away, no thought that I'd retreat.

That day I learned a lesson and it didn't cost me much.
My mom explained that most times one's excuses are a crutch.
Replace excuses with your dreams, and visualize them, too.
They build belief, and with belief there's little you can't do.

Years later I discovered what a challenge it can be,
to overcome a latent fear that's in control of me.
No matter how or what I tried I couldn't do it right.
Each time I tried I knew that I again would lose the fight.
I learned all the mechanics from a lady therapist.
I knew each move and gesture; there was nothing that I'd missed.
I went to school at night to learn exactly what to do.
It worked for other students. Could it solve my problem, too?
No matter what I did I faced the fear each time I tried.
I tried to bow out graciously; sometimes I even lied.
But duty forced me to the podium to make each speech.
Immobilized, I knew this was a skill no one could teach.

For years I'd overlooked the most important lesson, yet.
It takes belief to overcome a fear that's really set.
Belief grows from your dream; a dream you really must achieve.
I hadn't formed a dream, so I had nothing to believe.

Yet, courage was inside my heart; it filled me with desire.
I learned to love each audience that I wished to inspire.
Within my heart were words I knew that everyone should hear.
With this belief I loved to speak; I'd overcome my fear.

I fully comprehend the awesome power of belief.
Yet it sometimes escapes me, I'm a victim of a thief.
The thief is doubt, or maybe fear, that creeps into my mind.
When overcome by doubt and fear, belief is hard to find.
The lesson should be clear for everyone that wants to know.
It doesn't take a lifetime, though for me it seemed that slow.
You visualize your dreams and you affirm them every day.
Belief enters your conscious mind, and there belief will stay.

When you believe you can, you'll get it done, sans fear or doubt.
Belief is what accomplishment of goals is all about.
And to believe, you simply have to visualize your dream.
Accomplishing your goals will then enhance your self-esteem.

Beyond Belief
If you believe in something that you cannot see or feel,
and you cannot be certain that what you believe is real.
Don't worry or have fear, for it's as natural as can be.
It's just an act of faith and faith does not need secrecy.
For faith is just a little leap beyond belief, you see.
Faith lets you trust completely; it's as easy as can be.
When you have faith in anything, even some crazy scheme,
then you'll achieve fulfillment quite beyond your wildest dream.

CREATING CONFIDENCE—
AVOIDING ARROGANCE

It's not there when you're born, yet you don't miss it then at all.
Two fears at birth; loud noise and as a baby you might fall.
And every other fear you get to learn as life goes by.
You cannot learn them all no matter how hard you may try.

Your confidence is like a "kissing cousin" to your fears.
It's neither there nor missing till you pass your early years.
You'll never miss it till you try a task that's new to you.
A task that doesn't work the way you really want it to.

You learn the "ABC's" and then you try to read a book.
The letters all look strange to you, no matter how you look.
They're strung in rows with lots of little spaces in between.
It doesn't make much sense, and it's the strangest thing you've seen.
The more you try, the less you understand about these things.
The teacher tries to help by making sounds; she even sings.
You try and try again, and finally close the book and cry.
For not a soul here understands how hard you've had to try.
You never want to see those words or read a book again.
Your confidence is shattered like a broken windowpane.
It takes too darned much effort; you're embarrassed to admit,
if it had just been easier, then you would not have quit.

You're ready to give up on reading; it's too hard to do.
Your mother says that's okay; I'll just read a book to you.
The book is small with little words you almost understand.
The pictures match the words; it's like your mother had this planned.
And pretty soon you mouth the words, as Mother reads each page.
This reading thing is easy if you don't get in a rage.
You take the book up to your room and read it through and through.

You're confident you now can read, and any book will do.
It takes a little while but you now know what reading takes.
You sound out every word and just accept there'll be mistakes.
You read books from the library and buy books from the store.
And then you let your mother know you'll read these books, and more.

Now you've developed confidence in one important way.
You've learned that if you try enough and work at it each day,
that you can overcome the lack of confidence you had.
And, making some mistakes along the way is not that bad.

The boy next door is playing tennis with a friend of yours.
You walk across the street to watch since you've finished your chores.
They ask you if you'd like to play for just a little while.
The game does not look hard and they give you a friendly smile.
Your friend loans you his racquet and you step out on the court.
You've been an academic and you've not played any sport.
He hits a ball to you and you swing at the ball, quite hard.
You miss the ball completely; you now feel like a retard.

Discouraged, you decide to leave before this thing gets worse.
To play a game of tennis there are things you must rehearse.
You feel like you're a fool for having tried to play at all.
So you return the racquet and retrieve the tennis ball.

But something deep inside you shouts a message loud and clear.
The words come through quite clearly, and the message you can hear.
It says that it's okay to do it badly when you start.
Although this time you may have put the horse before the cart.
The voice from down in side your head continues its dispatch.
You have to learn the basics long before you play a match.
So you go out and find yourself a racquet and a ball.
Then practice fundamentals; hit the ball against a wall.
You read about the game and then you practice every day.
The serve and hitting backhand; a strong forehand stroke you play.

You hit against the wall like your opponent's hitting back
And soon your tennis strokes are strong; there's nothing that you lack.

With confidence, you now approach the tennis courts to play.
Your friend is there again, for he plays tennis every day.
He asks you once again to play; he knows your worse than sin.
You walk onto the court and shout, "Now let the games begin".

You rally for a while and you return his every shot.
He serves and hits some lob shots just to see what you have got.
And then you play a game just like the pros do on TV.
You win with four straight points. It makes you almost shout with glee.
Your confidence increases every time you win a game.
You win some and you lose some, but the message is the same.
With practice and hard work you gain the confidence you need.
You're like a blooming flower that grew up strong from a small seed.

With all this confidence you've gained, you now know you are good.
And everyone should know this; or at least you think they should.
You strut around among your friends; you boast what you can do.
If they were tough and smart like you, then they could do it to.

And pretty soon you find when you arrive, the others leave.
They do not seem to care about the things you can achieve.
You find yourself alone with time to ponder who you are.
This isn't right; you've tried so hard; this whole thing seems bizarre.

Your mother comes into your room and sits with you a while.
She listens to your story and then she urges you to smile.
She tells you of some people in her life when she was young.
They organized a little group; a group she was among.
She speaks of this group's leader who had confidence galore.
With followers, his confidence kept growing, even more.
And soon the man was arrogant, conceited; pompous, too.
Into a haughty egotist is how this leader grew.

Then one by one his followers found someone else they liked.
And this continued day by day till all of them had hiked.
You cannot be a leader unless someone follows you.
If you are overbearing, that is not what folks will do.

A nuance is a little thing; it barely shows at all.
Like confidence and arrogance; the difference is so small.
You learn about respecting what the other people do.
And then to earn respect, you must respect the others, too.
You do not have to tell your friends how good or strong you are.
Performance speaks out for itself, and for life's course, that's par.
In fact when you have confidence it's easy as can be,
to compliment your friends, and then their happiness you'll see.

Just when you think you've got this down, a little golf you play.
You've practiced every shot; you know golf etiquette, okay.
With confidence you join a group of guys you've known for years.
Good friends, you've socialized, had parties; even drunk some beers.
At the first hole you're ready, ball with tee and driver, too.
Although you're last to play, you know exactly what to do.
The other three have driven balls straight down the fairway, green.
With bunkers on each side, you want your ball hit in between.
You take a mighty practice swing; the others are impressed.
And then you visualize your shot, so you will not feel stressed.
You want your tempo to be right, not slow or not to swift.
You're ready and you take your swing. My God, the shot was whiffed.

And just like that where confidence had been inside your head,
you feel like you're a zombie, body atrophied, brain dead.
The chuckles from your friends don't help the way you feel at all.
You set up; take another swing and pray you'll hit the ball.
It dribbles to the right, not even to the ladies' tee.
Now this is just about as bad as golf can ever be.
Your friends now make some choice remarks to help your confidence.
At times like this they demonstrate their verbal eloquence.

By now a group of golfers has assembled at the tee.
It's like you are a sideshow, and the price to watch is free.
There's nothing you can do to mitigate the way you feel.
Sans confidence about your game, the feeling is surreal.
Without another word you amble over to your ball.
The thing is almost hidden, for the grass is very tall.
You cannot use a wood so you select your pitching wedge.
Then you address your ball, between the cart path and a hedge.
And like a pro your stroke is just as smooth as it can be.
The ball jumps out and sails like you had hit it from the tee.
The crowd behaves politely as your group applauds a bit.
Your prayer to God paid off; the little ball is so well hit.

It took a swing or two for you to lose your confidence.
That it returned with just one swing was not coincidence.
You played the round as though you'd learned golf from a teaching pro.
With each success you realized your confidence would grow.

If you want confidence in every thing you try to do.
If it is your desire to vastly increase your purview
of life's activities that you can do with confidence,
without ambivalence that finds you sitting on a fence,
the principle is easy; it's as simple as can be.
Internalize this single rule; and soon you will agree.
Don't let a doubt invade your mind, for doubt destroys your will.
And every time you fail you'll feel that you're an imbecile.
It's okay to do something poorly, when at first you try.
It's okay to do badly when you start; you needn't lie.
Just draw on your persistence, and be sure you try again.
Don't let the early failures grow till they become your bane.

Just visualize success; make it a vision you can see.
Internalize the picture till it's clear as it can be.
With each attempt you'll find that your performance will improve.
And soon you'll find that your whole life is really in the groove.

THE VALUE OF FEAR

Psychologists will tell you that you have two basic fears.
If those who love you do not know, you won't find out for years.
They're basic, and they're buried inside your personality.
They have some tags but generally they're called security.
It's not security you have with money in the bank,
or fear when you find suddenly your minds a total blank!
They're much more basic; they are fears you have right from your birth.
For poor or rich you've got them, and they don't care what you're worth.

You have a fear of falling; it's as natural as can be.
The clothes you wear secure you starting as a small baby.
Your mother holds you in her arms; you have no fear at all.
For held so close you feel secure; you know you cannot fall.
Your other natural fear relates to sounds that you may hear.
A sudden unexpected noise depicts your second fear.
It's quiet inside your mother's womb, no noise to bother you.
Then you are born; you're in this world and hear the sounds we do.

The basic fear of sudden noise and fear of falling, too,
relate to your security, in everything you do.
You have to learn all other fears; they're not there from the start.
They work their way into your mind and creep into your heart.

I've learned some fears since I was young. With most I haven't tried.
With every fear I've learned a silent voice within me cried,
"What happened? What is going on?" or, "What is wrong with you?"
I rarely heed the warning; I just do what I must do.

I crawled through a small hole to do some work under my house.
I saw a rat; he jumped away, and then I saw a mouse.
I felt the claustrophobia surround, me like a wreath.

I stopped for just a moment; it was very hard to breathe.
I barely fit; I wriggled on; the space was really tight.
I stopped in the damp darkness; I could feel increasing fright.
A little apprehension; that is all I felt at first.
It quickly turned to terror, and I thought my lungs would burst.
I couldn't turn; I inched back some, back to where I began.
What am I doing in this small space? I didn't have a plan.
I squeeze and push; I'm finally back; there's something in my hair.
A spider, God, I'm out at last; that was an awful scare.

That lesson was okay because the fear I learned that day.
Helps me avoid these dark tight spots; I simply stay away.
If there's a job under the house or in between some stalls,
I don't think twice, I grab the phone and call professionals.

I climbed a ladder to the top; then shinnied up a wall.
I'm young and strong and agile so I never thought I'd fall.
The ladder slid away; a gust of wind attacked my chest.
I lost my balance, grabbed at space; I did my very best.
I slipped and I began to fall; I caught a windowsill.
I hung on by my fingertips; it took all of my will.
Some friends came by; they raised the ladder; held it to the wall.
I climbed right down, but now I felt about two inches tall.

I learned the fear of heights that day; it took me just one try.
I'm staying close to mother earth until I learn to fly.
I'm just like Dad, who said he'd fly the whole darned earth around.
But only if during the flight, one foot was on the ground.

I drove my car too fast when I was young, a "teen-a-cide".
And then one day in heavy rain, I took Mom for a ride.
Now I was proud of how I drove; my speed hit ninety-five.
I hit the brakes; we skidded, there was no way we'd survive.
The car careened; we slid and then we're backing down the road.
It skidded more; I spun the wheel; I felt a heavy load.

My mother screamed and grabbed my arms; I had to tear them loose.
In just that instant I was sure the Lord had cooked our goose.

Then when we pulled out of the skid, the car came to a halt.
A stupid episode; I knew the whole thing was my fault.
I hate to think what would have been if any car were near.
But luck was mine; the price was right for learning this new fear.

When I was in the second grade, I hadn't learned to swim.
My brother swam just like a fish, and how I envied him.
Our family traveled to Clear Lake to picnic and to fish.
The others swam around the lake; all I could do was wish.
We rowed across the lake, my dad, my mom and uncle, too.
If we had sunk I'd not have had a clue what I would do.
We made it clear across the lake and I was having fun.
We paddled back; it took a while; the picnic had begun.
The boat was moving slowly as we came up to the dock.
And nothing I had learned could have prepared me for the shock.
My dad threw me into the lake; he yelled, "It's time to swim".
I sank and then I sank again; the whole damned thing was grim.

My uncle jumped in after me; he pulled me from the deep.
I shivered; I was filled with fear; I then began to weep.
I've never cared for swimming, for that fear has stayed with me.
With choice, I joined the Army and I passed on the Navy.

Yes, learning fear is not that hard, we do it all the time.
Each lesson adds to judgment that will help us out, sometime.
We all have fear; some more, some less, it's there at work and play.
It builds a little safety net that's with us every day.
Your fear is healthy if you learn the dangers you may face.
You learn to plan, where not to go, so you avoid the place.
If you have some misgivings, some distress you feel, inside.
It's okay to just walk away. Let fear become your guide.

Fear isn't bad when it is real; sometimes it protects you.
So learn each lesson, learn it well and you'll know what to do,
when panic strikes or terror hits, you feel you want to hide.
Then don't be fearless; heed that voice and comfort will abide.

Just don't confuse anxiety with fears you know are real.
Some apprehension's good for you; it's not that big a deal.
Meet challenges with vigor, though it takes some discipline.
Respect your fears, yet face each challenge; you will always win.

A DECISION TO BE HAPPY

The memory is selective; it remembers what it wants.
It catalogues the pleasant and eliminates the taunts.
Unless I think it through quite well and focus very hard,
I recollect my greatest times; all else I disregard.

I always liked to go to school, to learn about new trends.
I'd answer questions in my class and play with all my friends.
The happiness I felt each day was greater than before.
I loved my schoolmates, but I may have loved my teachers, more.
In school the things I studied were as easy as can be.
I did the work assigned each day and nothing bothered me.
I played a lot of sports for competition seemed like fun.
I fished a lot and hunted ducks and geese with my shotgun.

At home it was another thing. My smile would disappear.
For more than apprehension, here I lived in mortal fear.
My father never seemed to think that what I did was right.
I often got the belt, and every stroke filled me with fright.
By bedtime every night I'd always try to just forget.
I'd say my prayers to God and then I wouldn't be upset.
My father worked most weekends so I didn't worry then.
I did my best each day and just ignored his regimen.

My happiness in youth related to the things I did.
It's pretty much the same, I guess, for almost every kid.
We had so much to do there really wasn't any time
to break the law in any way or be involved in crime.
I didn't own a lot of things; you might say I was poor.
My family didn't have a lot until the World War.
And then I got a paper route and made a buck each day.
It only took an hour of work; I still had time to play.

My happiness expanded now beyond just friends and school.
The beatings once a week or so, seemed kind of miniscule.
The joy of having money that was there for me to spend,
not only gave me pleasure, but it let me treat my friend.

To give without a thought of ever getting in return,
eventually meant more than other lessons I would learn.
The more I gave to others, then the better I would feel.
It's like an incongruity, a thing that seemed surreal.
The more I gave the more I got; it added to my wealth.
And I was blessed with happiness, enjoying perfect health.
A young adult, I understood how happy I could be
by giving joy to friends and letting joy flow back to me.

I earned a lot of money, since I worked more than the rest.
I loved my corporate life as I competed with the best.
I bought a lot of things. I had most every kind of toy.
I thought that what I had would surely fill my life with joy.
Accumulating stuff, galore; that's what my wealth would bring.
Forgetting that to give is more divine than anything.
In all the fuss I lost the happiness I'd had before.
Like pieces to a puzzle, I had lost my blissful lore.

And then it happened, just like that; I lost all of my wealth.
While physically I felt okay, I'd strained my mental health.
My psyche had been wounded; my emotions had some scars.
My toys were gone and worse than that, I'd even lost my cars.

Now happiness does not relate to things I used to own.
It didn't help to feel remorse or sit around and moan.
When I was on the bottom of the ladder of success,
it didn't help to sit and cry or dwell on feebleness.
I knew from all the living that I'd done before this time,
that happiness is mine to choose; there hadn't been a crime.
Just make a quick decision; it is mine to take or leave.

Then I'll rejoice in happiness and never have to grieve.
I cannot be concerned about the things I had before.
The problem's clear to me and it is one I can't ignore.

For I decide each day exactly how I want to feel!
If I decide on happiness, all pain will quickly heal.

So what is happiness to you? What fills your life with joy?
And does it matter if you are a girl or you're a boy?
Does happiness relate to whether you are young or old?
Is it a different thing if you are timid or you're bold?
There's something good in everything that happens in your life.
It may not seem that way right now, if it's creating strife.
But problems are the stuff that makes creative juices flow.
The more you have, the more you'll solve, and then the more you'll grow.

The attitude you bring to every thing you're asked to do.
Determines who is on the top, the other guy or you.
And who ends up on top may just affect you, more or less.
Your attitude achieves your goals and also happiness.

While in defeat you ponder just exactly what you've done.
Yes, losing may enhance your soul but losing isn't fun.
You learn a lot from losing for you analyze with care,
identifying every cause, what's right and what's unfair.
With knowledge that is new, you'll be much better than before.
You'll understand the rules and maybe just a little more.
So then you'll be positioned so your chances to succeed,
are better than you've ever had, and that is good, indeed.

Success in what you do will make you feel you're in the pink.
And happiness will fill your life before you even blink.
The challenges of life are the precursors to so much.
You'll never need excuses to support you like a crutch.

I've lived a long and happy life; each day gets better, still.
An attitude that's positive gives me a stronger will.
I'm happy every day and that's the way I'm going to stay.
In loving bliss, I'll live this way, till God takes me away.

FACE TO FACE WITH GUILT

You feel ashamed, and then you keep the shame a secret, too.
You feel regret and let regret take full control of you.
You wrong a friend and then you feel some sorrow that you did.
When you internalize your guilt, then you're an invalid.

Now I was young and little when I first discovered guilt.
At school I bragged to friends about a kite that I had built.
They told my mom; she asked how I had bought all the supplies.
I couldn't tell the truth; I told my mom some 'small white lies'.
I didn't have the money so I'd taken fifty cents.
I quickly learned that this was worse than fatal accidents.
My mother's purse was not the kind of thing that she would share.
She had me drop my pants and switched the spot that I'd left bare.
But worse than that, I had to tell my siblings what I'd done.
I think I might have hurt less if she'd shot me with a gun.
I kept that guilt inside me every day, for years and years.
It's one of several incidents that added to my fears.

Each Sunday when I went to church they said what God would do
if I broke a commandment, then I'd end up in a stew.
It seemed that most the things I liked were not within God's rules.
You break the rules; you go to Hell and join the other fools.

I lived my youth like I was in a house that's made of glass.
No other way would work for me, for I am not that crass.
It wasn't all that hard to do till I got in my teens,
like eating, with the habit of just cleaning up your greens.

And just like that I noticed girls; then felt a small desire.
It wasn't long until my feelings really caught on fire.
I held their hands and danced a bit, like all the other guys.

I didn't want to do a thing where I'd be caught in lies.
Temptation's great, but I can only fight it for so long.
I touched a girl one evening in a way I knew was wrong.
I left the girl right there, as I could feel the guilt begin.
I felt remorse; I felt the fear; I knew this was a sin.
In just a few short days the guilt was all that I could see.
The guilt consumed my life and there was nothing left of me.
It locked into my mind, like it would stay up to the end.
I couldn't shake it loose until I shared it with a friend.

The guilt I carried those young years served me quite well, I guess.
I lived my life so purely there was little to confess.
Yet guilt had taken more than just suppressing sinful acts.
It stifled all my dreams; I learned how much that guilt subtracts.

Without imagination and a dream to make come true,
you'll feel you're less than human, so if this occurs with you,
it doesn't matter what you do or thoughts that you may have,
just cleanse them from your mind the way you'd use a healing salve.

Guilt's not just non-productive; it's a whole lot more than that.
You may be domineering or a gentle pussycat.
If you're obsessed that you've done wrong; an act or just a thought,
it doesn't matter who else knows, or whether you are caught.
Your mind will harbor guilt until you look it in the eye.
No need to make excuses or to find some alibi.
Let your guilt live where it belongs. It's history to you now.
You bury guilt deep in your past and keep that as your vow.
You learn from what you do; sometimes it's wrong and sometimes right.
Just learn your lessons well; one doesn't need to be that bright.
Let guilt pass through your mind and learn the lesson every time.
Then use what you have learned; expunge the guilt; it's not a crime.

Now if you feel guilty for a sin or something worse.
Go back and read these words; commit to memory every verse.

Look forward to the future, to the dreams you want to live.
And then throughout your life, you will receive more than you give.
A curse that lasts forever; that's what guilt once meant to me.
It took a lot of living, and much more for me to see
that guilt's my friend if I just learn, then let it pass on by.
I tell the truth to everyone; I have no need to lie.
Let thoughts of guilt guide you to do the things you know are right.
Then let go of each thought of guilt; remove them from your sight.
And if you ever do a deed for which you feel some guilt.
Express your sorrow; move ahead, your life will be rebuilt.

Don't carry guilt along with you; you'll live more happily.
Guilt's more than non-productive; it's a "negative", you see.
So look guilt in the face and use what guilt can teach to you.
Remove guilt from your memory and there's little you can't do.

ENDURING PAIN

I've always thought of pain as something I just had to bear.
At seventy I'd say I've felt some pain, most everywhere.
A hurt in the left shoulder, then an elbow with a pain,
and even when I sit and type, my buttocks feels the strain.

A connoisseur of pain is what my father was to me.
He had one more than you, no matter what your pain might be.
At forty there was pain inside his head, his legs; his heart.
At eighty it got even worse, with pain in every part.

If you have never had a pain, you're one of very few.
For pain hurts not just body parts, but creates anguish, too.
The first pain I remember was a self inflicted hurt.
A butcher knife, I cut myself and how the blood did squirt.
I walked into the house where Mom was busy baking bread.
She turned and saw the blood; she screamed; she almost lost her head.
I'd cut my wrist, an artery, I'd severed very clean.
The bursts of blood splashed on the floor and covered the back screen.
She made a tourniquet from an old towel that hung nearby.
The bleeding stopped; then I felt pain and I began to cry.
It took us only minutes. To emergency we flew.
The doctor sewed me up and I was just as good as new.

More grievous pain was yet to come. It wasn't very long.
I didn't put my dad's new tools away where they belong.
When he got home and saw his tools there lying on the floor
I took it in the britches till I couldn't take much more.
Now that's a pain that hurts your butt; it stings for quite a while.
But even worse, my psyche hurt; it was a mental trial.
My siblings knew what I had done and why I got the belt.
They laughed, but didn't know the mental torment that I felt.

The phone rang and I took the call, my daughter's girlfriend.
A car had struck my daughter's car as she drove round a bend.
Three hundred miles away, her back was broken in the crash.
And no one knew how bad it was, it happened in a flash.

Just how much anguish can I take? Uncertainty's the worst.
The torment racked my mind more than an agonizing thirst.
With desperation as I drove, great sadness filled my mind.
Would she be crippled all her life; or would the Lord be kind?
My body wretches; God what pain, unbridled agony!
What can I do; when will I know how my daughter will be?
My child in pain, it hurts within, there is no greater grief.
I'm on the rack; it's torture and for me there's no relief.

The worst is past, I hold her hand; she opens tired eyes.
She'll be okay, a finger moves and after that she cries.
She'll live in pain for months to come, and then the pain will pass.
Some therapy she'll have to take, but then she'll be first class.

When I was twelve, my uncle was just thirteen years of age.
He worked like an adult, yet there were things he couldn't gauge.
He drove a truck across the tracks, my grandma by his side.
It stalled; broad sided by a train; that day two loved ones died.
The engineer was blameless and there wasn't any crime.
The pain I felt was deep; it didn't disappear with time.

Why did they have to die that way? They should still be alive.
I'll wait till I am old enough before I start to drive.

Perhaps the greatest pain is the "if only I'da" ache.
It doesn't make you sick at night and bones it will not break.
There isn't even any blood or broken skin to show.
But you will feel some sadness, and you'll also feel sorrow.
"If only I'da" told my dad I loved it when we played.
"If only I'da" helped grandma when in her house we stayed.
"If only I'da" hugged my son before he left last fall.
"If only I'da" represents the greatest pain of all.

SATAN'S SALE—THE PRICE OF DOUBT

The Devil has a sale and he invites both you and me.
I don't believe I want to go; you get me to agree.
He isn't up in Heaven, so we do not have to fly.
We slide way down to Hades; we are not required to die.
Now Satan meets us at the door; he lets us both inside.
The room is large and dimly lit; we take it all in stride.
We look around to see what Satan has that is on sale.
We hope we'll find some real cool stuff, perhaps the Holy Grail.

We walk through coals of fire and we are getting kind of hot.
"PROMISCUITY'S" displayed; it doesn't cost a lot.
This type of thing does not appeal; it's not the way we are.
We pass it up and walk some more; it isn't very far.
Then in a corner hanging high is "LUST", right in full view.
Now what does something like this cost? We haven't got a clue.
Then Satan says, "It's just a buck," for that's what "LUST" is worth.
We laugh a bit for that's not much; it fills our hearts with mirth.
While walking we observe some empty spaces are for rent.
Then on the shelf we see "DECEIT" for sale for just a cent.
We ask the Devil why the price for "LUST" is so much higher.
"DECEIT" gets you a warm spot but with "LUST" you make the fire.

We haven't found a thing to buy, but just ahead we see,
there hanging from the ceiling is a sign; it's "JEALOUSY".
The price is right; it only costs a dollar forty-four.
We've had about enough of this; we don't need any more.

But then we see "DISTRUST"; it beckons both of us to buy.
That's not for us, for without "TRUST" we'd never want to try.
"DISTRUST" is only fifty cents; that isn't much to pay.
Some people use "DISTRUST" a lot, like almost every day.

We enter a small room without a window, anywhere.
A box marked "GREED" is on a desk, and nothing else is there.
The price tag lists the contents for a dollar and a half.
And with the purchase you receive the Devil's autograph.
Then as we turn to leave, we see there standing by the door.
A lady dressed in skirt and blouse so we'll know she's a whore;
The sign around her neck says that she sells "ADULTRY".
The price is right, there is no cost; her services are free.

We turn to leave and listen, for there's music we can hear.
It seems to come from down the hall, behind a sign marked "FEAR".
Now "FEAR" is not expensive and in fact it's very cheap.
For twenty cents it's yours and it is something you can keep.
We're starting to dislike this place when "HATRED" fills the air.
We try to find the sale price, but there's no sign, anywhere.
Then Satan laughs and tells us hatred permeates the earth.
He sells it for a penny and a penny's all it's worth.
We tell the Devil we are done; there's nothing we can buy.
In fact we feel lethargic; we don't even want to try.
He says. "PROCRASTINATION" has a little hold on you.
It only costs two cents and you can take it with you, too.

We're wondering if Satan has a thing we might desire.
As we go on it seems we're getting closer to his fire.
We walk into a large room; it is bright; the sun shines through.
And in the middle there's a package all wrapped up in blue.
The price is listed on the box, quite evident to read.
It's priced so high we know it's something everyone must need.
Two thousand bucks! That's more by far than anything down here.
We just can't wait to look inside; its value should be clear.
To our surprise the Devil says, "The box contains some 'DOUBT'".
"Now come on Satan, something's wrong; what is this all about?"
For "DOUBT" is just a little thing, you barely know it's there
It's nothing like those great big sins; of that we're all aware.

Now Satan is no dummy, and he really knows the score.
He takes the box down gently and he puts it on the floor.
And through a hole right there on top, a little trickles out.
It isn't much but just the same, I quickly feel the "DOUBT".
It only takes a passing hint, a feeling very small.
To stop you in your tracks and you make no progress at all.
No matter what you want to do, if you've the smallest "DOUBT".
You won't even get started, for that's what it's all about.
Your will is great; you may be strong and omnipotent, too.
If you harbor a wisp of "DOUBT" you simply lose the glue
that holds your thoughts together, as you seek to reach your goal.
No matter what you try to do, you'll see "DOUBT" take its toll.
There's little wonder "DOUBT" costs more than any other thing.
It leaves you helpless, without goals, a puppet on a string.
You can't accomplish anything when "DOUBT" is in your mind.
You may as well not even start; it's worse than being blind.

If you now "DOUBT" that I am talking straight from my own heart,
and you have something in your mind that you may want to start,
then think of just one reason why it may not work out right.
You'll find it never does get done; with "DOUBT" it's out of sight.

So give the credit where it's due, to Satan and his staff.
If you don't listen to their words, then they'll get the last laugh.
The largest obstacle you face, no matter what your clout,
is just a tiny mindset, that emotion we call "DOUBT".
If it's your plan, and you have goals, and some objectives, too,
Let affirmations fill your mind; some firm, strong words will do.
Don't leave the smallest space for "DOUBT"; stay focused on your goal.
You'll reach your dreams, accomplish much, and glorify your soul.

FROM HOPE TO ACHIEVEMENT

My body needs some food to live; some every day is best.
It has to have some water too; it also needs some rest.
But hope's an even stronger need; it's just as great as air.
Without some hope I'm lost and broke; I don't have any flair.

Hope comes in many forms for me; it helps me start each day.
Hope adds some sunshine to my mood when life is dark and gray.
And sometimes when it's really bad, life turns from gray to black.
My train of life is running wild; it cannot find the track,
I count my blessings; list them all, review them, one by one.
The darkness seems to melt away; I see the bright, warm sun.
I realize my mood swings are so delicate and frail.
Success requires the best I've got; it's easier to fail.

We all have setbacks now and then; don't you agree we should?
But failure is a state of mind; it's when we've quit for good.
That's when we've reached the bottom; it's the last strand of our rope.
Life's challenges have grown too large; there isn't any hope.

I miss my friends; my family and the emptiness is great.
The warmth I feel is incomplete; now where is my soul mate?
My mind is split like I have two, each fighting for a place.
The struggle hurts; I feel the pain; it's like an endless race.
Is there a way for me to fill this void, this empty space?
To quell it for a little while, can I just pray for grace?
When there's a winner, must there be a loser in each game?
Can't I compete where everyone receives a little fame?

Each time I try to shake this mood, to make it go away.
I sink more deeply in the mire; I'm just a hopeless stray.
A sheep that's lost, I've wandered off; I'm down a deep ravine.
The shepherd's staff is just too short; there's too much in-between.

Can someone please, a friend of mine, a family member, true,
reach out with love, a helping hand, and bring me back to you?
How can I rise from down below, alone in deep despair,
to find a soul, find anyone, a person who will care?
When hope is gone my mind is blank; I feel so all alone.
And nothing has a value now; my life has turned to stone.
What can I do? Where can I turn? There's nothing left for me.
Frustration filled with sadness; will I never laugh with glee?

I need a goal, a new mindset; a dream that I can feel,
that's in my brain, and in my heart; I must know it is real.
The vacuum that exists in me is like an endless hole.
But it will disappear when it is replaced with a goal.
So many ways to fix my mood, to give my life a boost!
I simply have to open up, let joy come home to roost.
Though hope is fragile it won't break and shatter everywhere.
It's still right there to help me, if I say a little prayer.

Sometimes I need to realize the happiness I'll find
here in God's world, He watches me, for He is ever kind.
My faith is all I sometimes have, and faith will be enough.
Just face each day with prayer and hope; life's really not that tough.
With focused goals, each written down, they keep my dreams alive.
I'll feel rich happiness within, and more than just survive.
With plans in sand adjusted so that I can reach each goal.
I'll never find myself again in life's dark, hopeless hole.

I have a new perspective and the sun is shining bright.
Each night I hear the crickets chirp. My whole life feels just right.
For I have goals; they turn me on; each day I must achieve.
I feel fulfilled; I'm full of hope, no longer need I grieve.
My dreams are mine alone to view; it doesn't matter, now,
if anyone agrees or not, the sweat drips from my brow.
I haven't time to stop or care what others think is right.
I work with hands; with head and heart; I work with all my might.

I'll never stop and sit around to watch TV and sleep.
I won't let hope just slip away; I'll stop those thoughts that creep
into my mind when I relax, then turn my joy to rage.
I want to live a life complete, no matter what my age.

There's nothing more that I must do; my dreams are in my heart.
My life is filled with love and hope; I don't need help to start.
There's no more need for sympathy or words or helping hand.
Hope fills me full of happiness; life's more than great, it's grand.

NOT RIGHT OR WRONG—JUST FEELINGS

When I was young I learned to bite my lip and never cry.
My father said, "A boy is strong, just suck it in and try".
Like boys and young men everywhere, I felt a little pain.
Yet, I'd take a deep breath and walk away, or try again.

I never hugged a sibling or my mother or my dad.
The show of feelings wasn't right; my dad said, "It is bad.
You won't amount to anything unless you're brave and strong.
Just fix it, don't apologize, when you do something wrong".
He even said, "Don't laugh too much, or you'll be seen as weak".
But he forgot God's word, that to inherit the earth, "Be meek".
Just like my dad I buried all my feelings in my soul.
To be perceived as a strong man was soon my major goal.

In part we're all the product of the parents that we draw.
We can't control their actions or remove a basic flaw.
They're part of who we are and they influence whom we become.
It seems to work for most, although it may be tough for some.

Yes, I'm a man who learned quite young, my feelings I can't show.
Most other men explained that this is something I should know.
A man is strong and doesn't show the world the way he feels.
He lives with pain and if he's cut, his blood quickly congeals.
Impervious to pain, a man should never shed a tear.
And even more importantly, should also show no fear.
When children come to him for comfort he turns them away.
And points them toward a woman; his emotions cannot sway.

From youth till I was married and had children of my own,
I'd not display my feelings, lest a weakness I'd have shown.
No matter what the problem, I'd remain aloof and stern.
When my kids needed comfort, to their mother they would turn.

I grew into adulthood with this vision of a man.
"Be more like a barbarian than a Samaritan".
A taskmaster beyond compare; I worked much like a slave.
A Mentor finally saved me or I'd now be in my grave.
My Mentor was my boss; the kindest man I've ever known.
A gentleman, he reaped all of the seeds that he had sown.
He had a staff five thousand strong; each loved him, totally.
At first I simply envied him; why couldn't that be me?

He took the time, for months on end, to help me understand.
I didn't have to use a "whip", just give a helping hand.
"Give love and understanding to your staff and you will find,
they'll all reciprocate and they'll return your deeds in kind."
My Mentor said, "There's nothing weak in loving everyone".
He said, "Love makes you stronger and it makes each life more fun.
Let every person know the way you feel, deep down inside.
And though your soul is naked, you will never want to hide."

I let my feelings show a bit, to just a few close friends.
We'd had some problems in the past; we quickly made amends.
They started sharing things with me I'd never known before.
It's like I walked into a room and God opened the door.

At almost fifty years of age I woke up to these things.
I let my feelings show and found the happiness it brings.
Not just for me, but to each one that I had called a friend.
With feelings and with love, there is no wound that will not mend.

I can't control the feelings that I have from time to time.
It doesn't matter if they hurt or make me feel sublime.
I do not judge each feeling, whether it is wrong or right.
These feelings permeate my soul; it's something I don't fight.

I went to an "encounter" where communication reined.
It challenged everything I'd learned; emotions I'd ingrained.

They said that holding feelings in was not what made me strong,
for feelings just exist and they are neither right nor wrong.
You share the way you feel with family and with all your friends.
For when relationships are strained, that's how you make amends.
If you don't judge the feelings others share each day with you,
they'll not apply their judgments to the feelings you share, too.

It takes a good self-image to let feelings show to all.
Just cry when you are sad. If it's a tragedy then bawl.
Or laugh with glee when you are happy. Let your feelings show.
You'll live a life enriched with love and the whole world will know.
Great happiness will come to you when feelings let it in.
And love you share is all about the way you feel within.
If you let tears flow down your cheeks, next laughter will abound.
Then you'll be "strong" and "manly" with the "feelings" that you've found.

IMAGINATION'S POWER

With my imagination I can travel anywhere.
Yes, I can be a pauper or a "multi-zillionaire".
It only takes a thought and pictures come into my mind,
of everything I'll ever want, of things of every kind.
When I use my imagination I don't really care,
if it's a fantasy that's neither just nor really fair.
For my imagination is a special gift for me.
It doesn't hurt another soul, and it makes me feel free.

When I was just a boy I often traveled to the stars.
I had a rocket ship; an orange crate with three crossbars.
I'd sit there in the cockpit holding on with all my might.
Then landing on a distant star, the enemy I'd fight.
I'd ride my bike all over town; some "wheelies" I would do.
Then backward on the handlebars, with little ballyhoo!
I didn't care what others thought for I was riding high.
My bike had wings and like a plane, it flew up in the sky.
I bought some little trucks and cars with money I had made.
A friend had some cement and so we made a little trade.
A city I designed with lots of roads, a bridge or two.
Cement and sand, a little dream, there's nothing I can't do.
My friends and I played games in this 'big city' I'd designed.
For we were in a distant land! Our world we'd left behind.
In our imagination we could travel anywhere.
Adults would tease us now and then; we didn't really care.

With my imagination I can win; I never lose.
I climb the tallest mountain or I take a river cruise.
And I can be more handsome than I've ever been before.
With sparkling personality, I'll never be a bore.
There isn't anything I can't accomplish, when I dream.

Awake or fast asleep, imagination rules supreme.
My eyes reverse directions when they're closed and can't see out.
They look into my mind for that's what dreams are all about.

I lost my house; I lost my car; I even lost my wife.
I lost all of the money I had made throughout my life.
Yet, with imagination I was able to survive.
A half a decade later, I am even more alive.
I look into the mirror and I see a driving force.
The glow of life reflecting helps to keep me on my course.
With my imagination there is nothing I can't be.
The person I become is what my life now means to me.

I'm older than the hills and I have traveled lots of roads.
My friends tell me to do my thing before my mind corrodes.
But I have barely started all the things that I must do.
Some poetry to publish; I must write a book or two.
My past is filled with lots of stuff and some is not too clear.
Selective memory is something I hold so very dear.
For as I tell the stories of life that I have lived to date,
imagination fills the gaps; the stories are all first rate.

Each day as I perform my tasks, imagination reigns.
My soul mate is here with me, with a love that never wanes.
In fact as every day goes by, and every night arrives.
The dreams we share ignite the fire; the lust of our sex drives.
Imagination plays a part, we feel like teens in bed.
I see the beauty of the girl I know I should have wed.
And she tells me she sees the boy she dated long ago.
We're still teenagers; life stood still, a magic status quo.
Imagination adds a bit to everything we do.
At breakfast we trade kisses and we each say, "I love you".
And as each day begins we know there isn't any doubt,
we'll love each other more tonight, for that's what life's about.

There are no limits to the dreams the two of us now share.
It doesn't matter if we're broke; the cupboards may be bare.
Imagination augments all the hopes we've ever had.
Perception is reality, and that's not all that bad.
We've started making plans to celebrate a big event.
We've talked to friends although no invitations have been sent.
Our silver anniversary; we're almost ninety-five.
We know imagination will keep both of us alive.

I pray you now agree, imagination is required
to fill each day with energy so you will not be tired.
And with imagination everything that you may try,
will fill your heart with happiness; there'll be no need to cry.
No one has found a substitute for goals to fill each day.
They're equally important for our work and for our play.
Imagination is the fuel that feeds each goal and dream.
And sharing goals with others makes us "captain of our team".

Today I'm "twenty-five" and my imagination works.
I'm healthy; I'm in love and those are just two of my perks.
And Aphrodite's love falls short of all the love I give
to my beloved soul mate, she's the dream with whom I live.

PROBLEMS, CHALLENGES OR OPPORTUNITIES

They come in every size and shape; they come in every form.
You have them winter, fall and spring, in summer when it's warm.
You never have a time when they're not lurking to come in.
When finishing a task or getting ready to begin.
For problems seem to be there with each job you plan to do.
They may be little teeny ones or big as mountains, too.
They stand right there and taunt you as you try to do your best.
It isn't funny when they put you to your utmost test.

When you're a little baby you have problems, everywhere.
You're hungry or your diaper's wet; they lost your teddy bear.
The food's too hot; it's runny or it's much too cold to eat.
You haven't had dessert yet and there wasn't any treat.
Then as you grow the problems seem to increase right with you.
For now you've got to think of all the things you need to do.
They send you off to school with lots of other little kids.
You learn of ancient times and how they built the pyramids.
And then they give a test to see that you know all this stuff.
You answer half the questions and that seems like it's enough.
The teacher writes a note for you to take to Mom and Dad.
It's not a compliment; in fact it says that you've been bad.
You're grounded for a day to study what you need to know.
No play with other kids; you miss your favorite TV show.
You learn that problems are not good; you don't like them at all.
It's much more fun to hang around or play a game of ball.

You thought that this was bad and didn't need a darned bit more.
Your teens arrived and then with much chagrin you learned the score.
It didn't seem to matter what you did or where you went.
For if you did not break a rule it was severely bent.
A term called "sex" creeps into words and phrases that you use.

From what you've learned it may just be a "problem" to abuse.
Your mother finds a condom in the pocket of your pants.
This problem isn't small like all those minor irritants.
She almost faints and then she says that Dad will talk to you.
Then you are grounded for a week; there's nothing you can do.
You meet with Dad and he explains what sex is all about.
The "birds and bees" don't make much sense; he simply feeds your doubt.
You ask a teacher at your school to give you some advice.
She asks if you've had sex and you respond, "Just once or twice".
You've never seen a teacher lose it all before your eyes.
It seems there are no answers irrespective how one tries.

You've learned one thing that stays with you and you have learned it well.
When speaking to adults there are some things you do not tell.
For grownups won't take time to hear a lot of what you said.
Some problems rest much better if they're left inside your head.

At last you make it through your teens; it's not an easy trip.
You somehow weathered every storm much like a battleship.
At twenty you are ready to attack the world at large.
There are no problems big as you, you're poised and you'll take charge.
You find out rather quickly that it takes all that you make
to buy your food and clothes; pay rent and take a coffee break.
The problem now is serious; you cannot live this way.
All work without the money or the time you need to play.
Your folks come through, for they want what's the very best for you.
They help you pay for night school with some extra money, too.
You're now determined you will learn, you'll be the best, they'll see.
You'll work each day and study nights till you earn your degree.

The pretty little girl next door is helpful as can be.
She's training as a cop at the police academy.
You meet her almost every night, just after classes end.
She's helping with your studies, but you know it's just pretend.

It isn't long till she has you in bed most every night.
She may have coaxed a bit, but you did not put up a fight.
Before the quarter ends she lets you know what you have done.
In olden times you'd get to meet her father with his gun.

Now here's a problem that involves more people than just you.
There isn't anything you've learned that tells you what to do.
Do you continue now with a new baby and a wife?
Or do you disappear and make a new start with your life?
Some problems are much bigger than the ones when you were small.
But you have learned your lessons well; it is not optional.
It took two people to create a problem such as this.
It could be opportunity to find eternal bliss.

You have a loving wife and a small boy to call your own.
You'll work each day and study nights until your son is grown.
And somehow every morning when your son is still in bed,
you feel the strength of father's love just kissing his small head.
You learn to love your wife more than you've ever loved before.
And opportunities appear when you walk through each door.
Somewhere back in the distant past your problems were resolved.
From stumbling block to stepping stone—that's all that was involved.

You think about the problems that have been your bane of life.
The greatest brought this lovely girl, who then became your wife.
And even all the little things you had to suffer through.
Made you a better person as, into a man you grew.
Your problems are not problems if you look at them just right.
They open doors to walk through, if you keep your goals in sight.
Each problem is an opportunity for you to be
a better person if you want; but there's no guarantee.
You have some attitudes; they're right there with you every day.
Just keep them positive and you will never go astray.
For no one else can do a thing to make them right or wrong.
They're in your head exactly where your attitudes belong.

You need your head screwed on so it will work just right for you.
Then opportunities will take the place of problems, too.
Each morning you'll decide the way you want your day to go.
And every day you'll see, a stronger attitude will grow.
You'll never have a problem if you only realize,
a problem can be viewed as an idea in disguise.
Then opportunity will knock each time you're at the door.
You're in control; you'll never have a problem any more.

I HAVE TO GIVE A SPEECH!

It's easy to communicate when I am one on one.
I talk to friends or strangers; it is casual and it's fun.
But in a crowd it's not so cool; I seem a little shy.
And speak before large groups, oh no, I think I'd rather die.

When I was just twelve years of age, I had to give a talk
before the church assembly, I knew everyone would gawk.
The speech was short, two minutes long, that isn't very much.
I thought I might just skip the talk, but then I'd be in "Dutch".
I worked and sweat; I wrote the words and memorized them all.
I practiced morning, noon and night, each word I could recall.
On Sunday I walked to the front; my notes were in my hand.
I saw the crowd, with trembling legs, God I could barely stand.
I knew the congregation, every woman, man and child.
They stared at me; I looked at them, my mind completely wild.
I couldn't breathe; I couldn't talk; I couldn't even hear.
I ran away, the victim of this total, utter fear.

I made good grades in school so I was asked to give a talk.
They said that I could even use a blackboard and some chalk.
The audience will be the population of the town.
My grade school graduation, so I couldn't let them down.
I made some notes on little cards and held them in my hand.
I walked up to the stage behind the lectern where I'd stand.
I looked out and I saw the crowd; it more than filled the room.
Alone on stage I stood there as I felt this awful gloom.
I spoke; I checked my notes and then I spoke a little more.
My hands were shaking; God, I dropped my cards down on the floor.
Without a thought my mouth stepped up and right into the mike,
I said, "Oh shit" and that remark completely killed my psych.
The crowd responded with a laugh and then they laughed some more.

I carried on although my notes were scattered on the floor.
I finally finished with the speech; it tested all my grit.
And in that little valley, some folks still call me, "Oh shit".

I joined a bank, the leader in business technology.
Computers came into my life with no apology.
I soon became the manager, the boss of a huge staff.
When asked to give a speech, I'd just decline with a short laugh.
I thought I'd never have to talk; accept a speech request.
My boss insisted I go out and simply do my best.
Without a choice I took the step; I made a noble try.
For days before I gave a speech, I felt I'd rather die.
My body shook; I quaked with fear before each speech I made.
I did it, though to me it was a horrible charade.
I found a speech consultant and we worked one day a week.
She tried to fix my "crowd psyche" so I would want to speak.
I helped form a toastmaster's group; I'd do most anything.
I'd even take up singing, if some comfort it would bring.
I went to public speaking class, and then another, too.
But nothing seemed to quell my fear; now what was I to do?
I read the books; they didn't help; each speech was getting worse.
In my own little speaking world, I lived beneath a curse.
Throughout the country, overseas, to groups both large and small.
I stood behind the podium, my mind hysterical.

And then one day I read a book that dispelled all my strife.
Authored by Dale Carnegie and published by his wife.
Right in the introduction, there it was, beyond belief.
The secret I had searched for, oh my God, what a relief.

"Forget the thoughts inside your head; forget mechanics, too.
Just share the words inside your heart, for that's the real you."

Fear disappeared, as from my heart the words flow to my mouth.
The feelings gushing from my heart ended my speaking drouth.

Desire embraced each speech I made, how eloquent, how strong.
Then suddenly I'm in demand; I now can do no wrong.

My final wish is give a speech to groups throughout the nation,
and when I'm done, they stand and give a lingering ovation.

I'm at Masonic Hall where speakers come from far and wide.
Ten thousand bankers mill about then sit there, side by side.
I follow the bank's president; he did the keynote thing.
When I am done, they stand and cheer; I'm now the "Speaking King".

WHO DECIDES?

I wake up in the morning; snow is falling to the ground.
It's covered every thing in sight, but hasn't made a sound.
What kind of day will this one be? It's freezing cold outside.
Now that's a question I will ask and one that I'll decide.
It doesn't matter what's outside, how deep the snow may be.
Or what the temperature may read, it's there for me to see.
For weather is just weather; it is neither good nor bad.
I'll be alive, enjoy the snow; now that's what makes me glad.

My attitude does not relate to clouds or wind or rain.
I don't let these affect my mood; I've learned how to refrain.
For how I feel and how I act, the way I want to be,
is my decision, mine alone, that's how it is for me.

I meet a person on the street; we greet and then we talk.
I didn't know we'd meet today; I just went for a walk.
But people come into my life; that isn't any crime.
To make a friend, or walk away, that's up to me each time.
The friends I have, I didn't know at some time in the past.
How quickly do I make new friends; do I decide how fast?
It doesn't matter who they are; we talk and have some fun.
And I decide how I'll relate, to stay and talk, or run.

The people who make up the groups in my society,
the loved ones and acquaintances and everyone I see.
Affect decisions that I make; the way I feel inside.
And how we may relate each day, is something I decide.

It's my decision how I act; it is not up to fate.
When people are around me, do I help them all feel great?
It is my choice to do what's right, so I'm in charge, you see.
It's a decision that I make; the whole thing's up to me.

Is "Have to" something I have said? It has a lousy ring.
Is there ever a time when I just "Have to" anything?
As long as I remember, every night and every day,
each choice I've made was optional; "Have to" was not in play.
From almost all who speak to me, these words come clearly through.
I "Have to" this; I "Have to" that, is any of this true?
Am I the only one who knows with every choice I make?
I do not "Have to" anything, the consequence I take.
"Have to" is just a crutch to most, a lame excuse they use.
It mitigates a lot of things, so friends they will not lose.
I "Have to" has authority; it's used with perfect poise.
For who's to blame when I "Have to"? There isn't any choice.
I can't do this for you today; I "Have to" something now.
Have you sometimes felt there's a choice; it can be done, somehow?
To have the option to decide, for me it's worth a fight.
I "Have to" is a lame excuse and that my friend is right.

Yes, I decide to be with you or simply walk away.
It's my decision; my response, I go or I may stay.
It's not what I encounter as I walk along life's path.
For I control how I respond, with happiness or wrath.
I guess that I can just give up; my sorrows I'll drown away,
for that's a choice we each can make with problems every day.
We end up in the gutter; we're a homeless soul, at best.
Or face each challenge, fix it up, and rise above the rest.

Decisions do not have to be the big and monstrous kind.
Just look around each day, each night, there's lots that you will find.
Decisions stop a family fight or fix a thing that breaks.
Find harmony with little things, it's worth the time it takes.
You're friendly because that is a decision you have made.
You're kind to everyone you meet, like it's a game that's played.
You're grateful to the people that have shared their life with you.
And each is a decision; these are things you want to do.

Yes, things may happen that are really hard for you to take.
You look around chagrined and say, "Oh God, give me a break!"
Yet, it is your response that makes the difference, you will see.
A positive response, you win; a better man you'll be.
Who you become is most of what decisions are about.
Make negative decisions and become a useless lout.
Or you can be more positive and pretty soon you'll see,
your life's become a dream and you are living happily.

Decisions are the stuff that gives you personality.
Without them you're a sheep, no individuality.
So cherish each decision, every one that you can make.
Be proud of each decision, for it's your life that's at stake.

AM I AN AMATEUR OR A PROFESSIONAL?

Are dentists all "professionals"? They're "practicing" on me.
My doctor "practices" when he performs a surgery!
Is "practice" like "rehearse"? Am I a human specimen?
And when they're fully qualified, what should I call it then?

My father was a minister; he studied many years.
Belief in God was his forte. It wiped away his fears.
No "amateur" could ever do the work my father did.
It can't be "superficial" for he did what his God bid.
The dictionary says art "amateurs" are dilettante.
My father's years of study cannot be termed nonchalant.
A master of his trade he knew the Bible, every page.
"Professional" or "amateur", just how do people gauge?
He never got a check for all the teaching to his flock.
He went to work each day, although he didn't punch a clock.
Is he an "amateur" because he didn't earn a dime?
To classify my dad like that, to me would be a crime.

Jim Thorpe ran the Olympics and a gold he won for that.
Then someone found that he'd been paid to use a baseball bat.
Jim Thorpe was a "professional" for money that he took.
He got his medal back when they finally rewrote the book.

I play a little golf and I make bets with everyone.
The purpose of my game is just to have a little fun.
But I play hard and when we're done, I've won most every bet.
Am I "professional" because of money that I get?

If in a tournament a golfer doesn't make the cut.
It may have been his driving or he couldn't make a putt.
It really doesn't matter for when all is said and done,

he doesn't get a check; his golf this week was just for fun.
Was he an "amateur" because he wasn't paid this week?
To be "professional" must he always be at his peak?
It doesn't make much sense to classify golfers this way.
Yet "amateurs" that win get shiny trophies, but no pay.

Sometimes I get confused by definitions that I've read.
I don't quite understand what my big dictionary said.
The book says prostitution is the "oldest profession".
The working girls are "pros" for it reflects the work they've done.
They're paid for what they do and it is said they do it well.
If they're not competent they haven't got a thing to sell.
In Amsterdam they're licensed, which is what a "pro" must be,
so there's a small dilemma that I'm sure that you can see.
I grant you that a working girl is trained, if on the job.
For them the definition of an "amateur" is "slob".
So they cannot be "amateurs". But can each be a pro,
when servicing their customers and having fun, also?

"Professionals" are trained and masterful at what they do.
They're qualified, proficient and they're seasoned experts, too.
I only know from what I've read; I don't know any more.
For in the world in which I live this type of girl's a whore.

I played a little basketball when I was in high school.
I played in a pro league also; I didn't know the rule.
The high school coach said I'd become a paid "professional",
so off the team with me and no more high school basketball.
I did not earn a cent for all the basketball I played.
I didn't want my actions to affect my PE grade.
It didn't matter that I'd made an innocent mistake.
The coach refused to help me and for me there was no break.

In this case money wasn't what defined "professional".
The "pro league" didn't pay me, not a dime, nothing at all.

So what determines when an "amateur" becomes a "pro"?
The coach would not enlighten me and so I still don't know.

My son's a biochemist for he studied many years.
His wife's a biochemist; she knows more than it appears.
They live on a small farm in a remote location, too.
Their son is schooled at home; that's the most vital work they do.
They've got diplomas and degrees to hang on every wall.
They're educated, trained and skilled. Are they "professional"?
He drives tomato trucks to earn the money that he makes.
And she teaches her son so he'll avoid life's big mistakes.

My friend, an Oakland cop, returned to school to study law!
He graduated, passed the bar; a new career he saw.
He hung his shingle out and formed a legal firm one-day.
He'd been an "amateur"; now a "professional" he'd stay.
He did some things that others thought that he should not have done.
He made some money, helped some folks and had a lot of fun.
But legal ethics can be strict; he went before the board.
With just this one exception, he'd amassed a strong record.
The board referred him to the court; he lost on his appeal.
He wouldn't stop; he took it higher with a renewed zeal.
He lost again and now he knew his record would be marred.
The court threw him a fine and then he found he'd been disbarred.

Without a license was my friend an "amateur" once more?
Or was he something less than he had ever been before?
He paid the fine and did the time, then pleaded with the court.
He got his license back for he had now resolved the tort.

I've known him as a cop and as my own attorney, too.
He's better than he's ever been with work that he can do.
So does it matter whether he's an "amateur" or "pro"?
He's more "professional" to me than anyone I know.

I'd hoped by writing down some facts and sharing just a bit,
that I would understand much more before I choose to quit.
I've learned it isn't proper to apply these tags to friends,
for you cannot be sure about the message that it sends.

So while this paradox continues, ad infinitum.
I'm keeping quiet; not a word, I'll literally play dumb.
And someone else can argue what's significant, you see.
I'll just ignore it all and it'll mean nothing more to me.

If you're an "amateur" and you're content to be this way,
or you're "professional" and that's the way you want to stay;
don't bother me with what it means; these labels you require,
for I acknowledge it's your right to be what you desire.

For me, I'm now retired; tags don't mean much any more.
A working girl—"professional"—an "amateur"—or whore!
My friends are most important and I don't care who they are.
It doesn't even matter if they're near or if they're far.
I love the people in my life, each person I have known.
Each one has added something to my life as I have grown.
If they're "professionals" or "amateurs", I do not care.
I want them all to know my friendship's valid; everywhere.

ACCIDENTS LARGE AND SMALL

The news reports the accidents; they do it every day.
On TV screens, on radio, newspapers, every way!
I don't much care, for all this stuff is negative to me.
I'd rather dwell on positives. I think you might agree.
But when it happens to one's self, or friend or family,
what really matters is how bad; that's what I need to see.

For accidents will happen whether large or very small.
And most the time when I'm involved, I don't like them at all.

My puppy had an accident; he pooped there on the rug.
I scolded him and cleaned it up and then gave him a hug.
These little things will happen; they should not affect our mood.
It's not a big catastrophe where everyone is sued.

My son dove in the swimming pool; it wasn't very deep.
He went up high and then came down; the angle was too steep.
Right through the shallow water, to the bottom that he hit!
He broke a tooth; his front one and his sisters threw a fit.
A little blood, a broken tooth, it wasn't all that bad.
(But when the dentist sent his bill, it made me kind of mad.)
A tooth implant, he's just like new; then back he goes to swim.
It only took one day to fix; it doesn't bother him.

These little accidents occur; they happen all the time.
They're part of life; it's no big deal; it's surely not a crime.
But sometimes things will happen and they take you by surprise.
And they may impact health and life, no matter how one tries.

I had a drink; I had one more, and then I had a bunch.
About a dozen I consumed while I was having lunch.

I had a meeting at a place that wasn't far away.
I missed a turn; I drove my car right out into the bay.
I said it was an accident; that's not what I had planned.
Sharp curves like this one that I missed should certainly be banned.
The cop did not agree with me; he looked me in the eye.
He had me walk the line and then I got a DUI.

If it's a fluke, a happenstance, a little incident,
it may be true that you have had a real accident.
But it's no accident when you, with malice or a plan,
smoke Pot or sniff some Coke and then you wreck your brand new van.

When you are in your teens, you like to go out on some dates.
You get a little cozy; after all you're all schoolmates.
You hit the sack and soon you've gotten in each other's pants.
It isn't like the high school prom where all you did was dance.
It's just a little while till you find out the consequence,
of what the two of you create with sexual malfeasance.
Was it an accident that you're as pregnant as can be?
Deliberate; the act was planned; I think you will agree.

For it's no accident when you, without or with forethought,
do something that is simply wrong because you won't be caught.
The truth resides within your mind; it's there each day and night.
You live with the results, if they are wrong or if they're right.

Your child may wreck a car; your husband may fall down a step.
It may have happened late at night, as quietly you slept.
They're simply little accidents; they're part of every life.
Accept them as they are and they will not cause you great strife.

Some accidents are better than the best plan you can make.
My fondest dream came true for me and that was no mistake.

I got an invitation to the high school where I went.
It came by U.S. mail; oh yes, to me the card was sent.
I had an accident that day; I met a friend of mine.
I used to date this friend way back in nineteen forty-nine.
I looked at her, and she at me; she wore a pretty smile.
We soon had thoughts that we would like to talk for just a while.
For her and certainly for me that meeting was the start.
I felt the love I'd had for her; it lingered in my heart.
It only took a few short weeks; I knew that I would fall
in love with her; now she's the nicest accident of all.

PREPARED FOR AN EMERGENCY?

What happens when you suddenly are taken by surprise?
Does your mind reason logically or do thoughts polarize?
If something unexpected happens quickly as can be,
do you take action best when it's a real emergency?

You sit there in the evening and you watch your favorite show.
It's warm beside the fireplace and outside it starts to snow.
You're pooped so you relax and put your feet up on a stool.
You've got the kids in bed and now you're feeling pretty cool.
Your wife is in the kitchen doing just what good wives do.
She'll finish up the dishes; then she'll watch TV with you.
She has your lunch prepared before you go to bed at night.
For breakfast you just have some juice; you like to keep it light.
The day has been a long one, for you work from dawn to dark.
Before the rooster crows off to the office you embark.
With one income you've got to take a lot of overtime.
It isn't easy; it's a rugged mountain that you climb.

Your kids need Mom at home to supervise the things they do,
to take them on planned outings and prepare their meals, too.
She works from dawn to dark and maybe just a little more.
You love your time together; she's the girl that you adore.
Relaxed and half-asleep you barely see the TV screen.
Your mind drifts back ten years to when your wife was just a teen.
It's like another world as youthful thoughts drift through your mind.
You almost fall asleep as you now totally unwind.

Then without warning there's a sound; it's very loud, indeed.
Familiar to your psyche, it's a sound you can't misread.
The crackle of a fire and it is not that far away.
You've got to move and quickly; any fear you must allay.

Adrenaline flows through you as you jump up off the couch.
You feel the sharpness of a pain; you don't stop to say "ouch".
You're up the stairs in seconds; both your kids are sound asleep.
Their clothes are scattered on the floor; a few are in a heap.
The smell of smoke gets stronger; you can feel it in your eye.
If you don't do this quickly there's a chance someone will die.
You grab each child around the waist; then you turn to the door.
The smoke has filled the room; you've got to crawl along the floor.

With kids in tow you struggle to get out into the hall.
You can't see now; it's like you're lost in some huge shopping mall.
You hear the flames behind you as you scramble to your feet.
Without a thought you move ahead into the intense heat.
Your children cry as they attempt to free themselves from you.
To keep the kids locked in your grip is all that you can do.
You see the stairs; they're just ahead; your strength begins to wane.
Like an explosion flames jump up; you know you're trapped again.
You faintly hear your wife; she's shouting from outside, somewhere.
The sound of sirens tells you that the fire trucks are out there.
It doesn't really matter for you can't get out from here.
In all the heat you feel cold sweat; you realize it's fear.

Your children cough and pull against your grip as you hold on.
You try to think what you should do before the air is gone.
The floor is getting hot beneath the bareness of your feet.
You can't go down the stairs and there is nowhere to retreat.
You know you should have had a plan, a practice fire drill.
Just thinking of it makes you feel more than a little ill.
There isn't time to think this way; you've got to move, right now.
You think of God; you're angry; any faith you disavow.

The bathroom door is straight ahead; it's opened just a bit.
Your senses tell you it's not hot as your hand touches it.
With kids in tow you get inside and quickly close the door.
The three of you drop down and lie there flatly on the floor.

You hear the crackle of the flames from somewhere down below.
The world seems to be standing still; your thoughts are even slow.
Your children move and cry out loud; and then they try to stand.
You rise a little, look around and take them by the hand.
There's noise outside beyond the wall; you hear a male voice.
Although the smoke is thick you stand; there isn't any choice.
The window's stuck; it will not budge; you need a heavy shoe.
There's nothing here for you to use; you don't know what to do.

The heat is getting more intense and smoke is seeping through.
You're getting kind of dizzy and the whole world seems askew.
The kids are now hysterical; they're kicking, screaming, too.
You squint through watery eyes and see a bottle of shampoo.
A mighty throw; it breaks the glass and sails right through the hole.
You hear the ladders hit the wall; each fireman knows his role.
Another crash; the window's gone; you see a fireman's face.
Then one by one, you squeeze your kids out through this tiny space.
With axe, a fireman makes a hole that's big enough for you.
You falter as you realize, you need assistance, too.
Strong hands around your waist and water spraying on your face.
You're thankful for the help; there's not a vestige of disgrace.
The ladder swings around as you hang on with all your might.
You know that you are safe, but you still feel a little fright.

You take a breath as finally you are standing on the ground.
You feel relief as there you see your family all around.
The house is gone; there's nothing left; the fire was very hot.
A fire truck stays with hoses out in case there's a hot spot.
You hug your wife and then your kids; you want them close to you.
With just the clothes you're wearing, you now wonder what you'll do.
And just like that a neighbor says that you may stay with him.
You look at what's left of your home; the scene is pretty grim.
With help from friends and neighbors, everything will be okay.
While thankful for their help, you know you'll pay them back someday.

Emergencies occur; it doesn't matter who you are.
Just exercise your plan and you'll avoid a mental scar.
Like good Boy Scouts, just "Be Prepared" and know what you must do.
Then you'll take proper action and avoid your "Waterloo".

You take a moment to reflect; you hold your family close.
For it was more than luck you didn't end up comatose.
You finally say a silent prayer of thanks to God above.
You may have lost your house, but you believe now in His love.

JUST WALK

In high school I ran distances, a mile was what I did.
Sometimes I'd do a couple, for it's nothing for a kid.
As I matured I changed my pace; I jogged a mile or two.
Sometimes I'd sprint for just a while to see what I could do.

Then as the years rushed by I felt that I should make a change.
It happens to most everyone, your goals you rearrange.
Instead of running, sprinting or just jogging for a mile,
you get good exercise by simply walking for a while.
It takes a little time to get your exercise each day.
If your work isn't physical, you need some time to play.
But more and more your play is sitting, staring at a screen.
You exercise your butt and eyes but not much in between.

The gym is a great place to get the exercise you need.
They have enough equipment they can serve a centipede.
I've found it kind of lonely in most gyms where I've worked out.
The members lose commitment and the bulk of them dropout.
Like everything in life, it isn't what one thinks or tries.
What really makes the difference is, just getting exercise.
Most everyone can walk to do a little job or chore.
You get some exercise and then you may just walk some more.

Each day when you awaken think about what you must do.
For you can do some tasks and exercise your body, too.
If you'll just walk whenever it is just a little way,
your body will say thanks; even your mind will feel okay.
The experts say that you should walk about three times a week.
It builds your attitude and it is good for your physique.
Just thirty minutes at a time, that's not a lot to do.
Your friends who see what you have done may take up walking, too.

Another reason you should walk is not for exercise.
But it can help your body and relieve your burning eyes.
The fossil fuel that you don't burn when walking to the store,
reduces the pollutants in the air and may do more.
You know that the reserves of fossil fuel are getting low.
Some more will be identified; the finding may be slow.
But sometime in the future fossil fuel will all be gone.
With energy alternatives, you'll need to carry on.
Each time you walk and leave your car parked anywhere at all.
You save some energy; it's more than philosophical.
For every little bit that isn't used each day you live
will benefit your heirs and of that fact we're positive.

The experts all agree how walking helps longevity.
It's true and it's borne out with facts; it isn't witchery.
For every hour you exercise, no matter what it is.
You'll add at least an hour to life; and that you can't dismiss.
But more than that, another thing on which experts agree,
it's more than just longevity; it deals with quality.
For when you walk, your health improves as every muscle tones.
You now have more endurance; walking also strengthens bones.
The quality of life each day is better than before.
You do the things you've always done and you can do some more.
It doesn't take a genius to decide on what to do.
You're going to live a longer life; you'll feel much better, too.

If every corporation, every business in the land,
would each adopt a policy; now wouldn't that be grand?
That just one hour of every day would be for exercise.
It may seem dumb at first but it is really very wise.
For studies prove another fact and one you know is true.
The body's not the only thing; the mind is better, too.
For exercising stimulates the flow of blood, you see,
and this increases energy, I think you will agree.
So you and I would benefit if this were only done.

The benefits would spread till they affect most everyone.
And every corporation, every business, everywhere,
would have grateful employees, almost no one would despair.

So take a walk down to the store; walk over to the park.
Walk in the morning, after lunch, or evenings when it's dark.
Walk up the street to see a friend. Then walk around the block.
Just walk and don't give up; you'll be as solid as a rock.
And if you're old as I and exercise is hard for you.
Start walking up and down the stairs; a little bit will do.
Expand it just a little as each day goes passing by.
Your life will be much richer up until the day you die.

LIFESTYLE CHOICES—LIFE OR DEATH

Two hundred twenty pounds of weight, that's quite a lot of me.
At six foot tall that's not the kind of man I want to be.
I measure just about the same from hips to chest to waist.
Yet every kind of food I see exactly fits my taste.
I've never been this over-weight, a pound or two at most.
I kept my weight where it should be; of that I'd always boast.
Now there's not much that I can say, I'm more than over-weight.
With all this fat I'm now obese; is this to be my fate?

To play nine holes of golf now is much more than just a chore.
I used to walk eighteen and then have energy, galore.
My knees have aches and pains as I limp slowly to each green.
It changes my whole outlook and sometimes I'm downright mean.
At sixty-nine I feel like I am eighty years of age.
When snacks are there I eat them all; my body has no gauge.
I eat till I am full and then I eat a little more.
For when it comes to eating, I don't try to keep a score.

I got a wake up call when I had my cholesterol done.
With risk factors this high I might as well have used a gun.
It's not a whole lot different when you eat yourself to death.
Or kill yourself from overdosing heroin or meth.

I know I've got to change the way I eat, and right away.
Or I am going to die, and dead as hell is how I'll stay.
I don't have any willpower. I know I need desire,
for that is what it takes to set new lifestyle goals on fire.
I started to communicate with friends from "way back when".
I'd send each one an e-mail. Then I'd e-mail each again.
We talked about the past, about our families and our lives.
These messages tell stories of how each of us survives.

Then in the mail I get an invitation to attend
a reunion of schoolmates at the home of a close friend.
I wasn't sure that I should go; so much has gone so wrong.
To face my schoolmates from the past, I'll have to be quite strong.

I know one of my closest friends from school is very sick.
We'd played all sports together, Jake and I with Bert and Dick.
The four of us were family in a loving, friendly way.
Like brothers we did everything together; work or play.
The years have passed; we've grown apart; yet memories are still strong.
To pass this chance to reunite would be so awfully wrong.
I suck it in and with determination more than guts,
decide that I'll attend, although I feel like I am nuts.

Two hundred twenty pounds of me attends this small affair.
Yet every one I meet seems very happy I am there.
I get to meet some ladies that I dated when in school.
There's one I should have married had I been a bit more "cool".

She sends some pictures of my friends to my e-mail address.
How she could know I wanted them, I really couldn't guess.
She had some more and asked if I'd like copies of each one.
She didn't know to get such pictures I'd have used a gun.
We correspond and soon became good friends, within just days.
And neither knows where this will lead; life has so many ways.
Each day we write and learn some more about the other's past.
I even start to hope that this new friendship may just last.

The rest is history now, for we became more than good friends.
We fell in love exchanging words only a lover sends.
And just like that, I realized my lifestyle must be changed,
or life with my new love would end up totally deranged.
I've never felt this way before; I didn't know I could.
My world is filled with love to give to her, the way I should.
And she is now my reason to become the most I can.
I'll shed this obese body and I'll then become 'her man'.

Romantic love, it motivates, it motivated me.
Each time I open up my mouth I count each calorie.
And every day I exercise; aerobics for a while,
and every morning toning weights is part of my lifestyle.
Yes, exercise becomes a part of every single day.
I walk around the neighborhood; a little golf I play.
Without exception, every day, I exercise a bit.
I'll do it every day until I know I cannot quit.

Since starch and sugar turn to fat, I cut way down on those.
Each time I lose a pound or two, I fit into more clothes.
This motivates me even more to stay on this lifestyle.
I just pretend I have to do this for a little while.
Then day-by-day, I add these habits to my repertoire.
I climb this mountain step by step; it doesn't seem that far.
I know I'll reach the weight I want, and then I'll celebrate,
by making a commitment to continue feeling great.
Routinely I work out by alternating every day,
between aerobics and some weights, it's like a game I play.

I feel like I'm a young man now, for that's how far I've come.
The way I was before now seems so fruitless and so dumb.
I've energy like I've returned to when I was a youth.
And if I never pass a mirror, I won't know the truth.
For if you do not know your age, it's just a mystery!
Your age is how you feel and that's the way that it should be.

My life is full of dreams, with new ideas all around.
They fill my every thought; from every corner they abound.
And I've a goal for every one; each goal I must achieve.
And every time I reach a goal, it helps me to believe.

I live here with the reason that my life is now so great.
It may have taken fifty years, but it was worth the wait.
I've never known romantic love; this love is new to me.

She gives me all her love; I give it back, wholeheartedly.
She's changed me from a person that I didn't like too well.
And thrust me into Heaven, after lifting me from Hell.
I'm living in a dream; I'll never wake, so here I'll stay.
We share a Paradise on Earth, each night and every day.

Yes I have made a lifestyle change; I feel I've been reborn.
Her love fills me with joy, and now I'll never be forlorn.
If there was any sacrifice, it's in the distant past.
We share romantic love so strong we know that it will last.
I'm more in love right now than I have ever been before.
I give her all the love I have, yet I will give her more.
She's changed me from the man I was to all that I can be.
My love for her is total; she is everything to me.

RUN AWAY—RUN TOWARD

I think I'm running toward my goal; that may not be the case.
I'm moving fast so I believe that I will win the race.
No looking back for me for I have things that must be done.
I'll finish all my work before I ever think of fun.

I'm always in a hurry and I run from morn till night.
My running starts before it's dawn and it lasts to twilight.
I rush with everything I do, and work long hours each day.
I'm running fast right now so in the future I can play.
The pace of life is fast and it is speeding up a bit.
I've got to keep on going; there is no way I can quit.
Yet, as I hurry to and fro, I don't have time to think.
For everything occurs so fast, I cannot even blink.

I don't have time to analyze the many things I do.
I finish one, up pops the next. The whole world is askew.
There's got to be a way to have a moment now and then,
to sit back in the saddle, a relaxed equestrienne.

I leave the house at five a.m. and get into my car.
My family is all still asleep. They know I travel far
to make the money so they have the many things they need.
I'm running to my workplace where I struggle to succeed.

Kids ask me why I have to leave before they wake each day.
Can't I just take a little time—it's not a big delay,
and share their breakfast time so they can tell me what they've done,
a test they took at school; a competition they have won?
I tell them they don't understand; the world is rough out there.
If I don't stay on top I'll have to find a job elsewhere.
Yet as I say these words I hear a voice deep down in side.

It whispers in my ear and lets me know that I've just lied.
I don't run to my work at this ungodly hour each day
to just support my family so their lives will be okay.
It's just a weak excuse so I avoid what I should do
to demonstrate the way I love my wife and children, too.

At work I am a big shot, people bowing all around.
I'm in my comfort zone and I'm attuned to every sound.
For sixteen hours a day I work; I'm indispensable.
Yes I am Mr. Big; I'm at the corporate pinnacle.
At home I'm just another dad, like every other guy.
I'm just a husband with a wife he tries to satisfy.
I don't receive the kudos there, like when I'm with my staff.
My kids are there in second place, as is my "better half".

Then finally when my kids are grown and gone away to school.
And married with kids of their own for whom they set the rule.
The youngsters at the office say that I'm too old to learn.
They're gone forever, good old days; the times for which I yearn.

I work to hold my own but there is nothing more to try.
So I retire early as the young ones pass me by.
My wife has other friends and many interests to pursue.
The work that got me what I have is now a residue.
I'm all alone in this big house; there's not a soul around.
It's quieter than sin, no wife or kids to make a sound.
I finally realize while speeding through my daily life.
By running toward my work, I ran away from kids and wife.
It's even worse to realize I missed my only chance
to be a father to my kids; they barely got a glance.
As I ran toward my work each day, I ran away from them.
Priorities reversed, that's a fallacious stratagem.

It's too late now for me, but I can help some other guys
to live their lives with balance and to do so without lies.

To differentiate between "run toward" and "run away",
and put into perspective when to work and when to play.

You "run away" when you don't want to face the consequence.
You "run toward" when it's your wish to gain experience.
You "run away" from things that you have never done too well.
You "run toward" accomplishments on which you like to dwell.
You "run toward" the things that fit into your comfort zone.
You "run away" when you believe that you'll be all alone.
You "run toward" when you are recognized for what you've done.
You "run away" when you discover something isn't fun.

So, "run toward" and "run away" don't coexist in time.
You cannot reach the mountaintop if you won't make the climb.
If you've lost friends and family as you clawed your way up there.
The cost is much too great, though you may be a millionaire.
Yes, running fast you may acquire a lot of stuff and things.
You may enjoy a lifestyle that the money you earned brings.
But when the clock runs down and you are very near the end.
The loss of friends you left behind, you will not comprehend.
You'll look around to see what is important in your life.
Is it the things you've bought or could it be a loving wife?
For who you have become is what your life was all about.
Who now loves you is who you are; of that there is no doubt.

WHAT IS "OLD AGE"?

The world is getting older with more people in the game.
With "baby boomers" everywhere, they're old and some are lame.
How old am I? What do I say when asked by all that care?
Do I just give a number, or are numbers really fair?

Some folks are old before their time; it's in their state of mind.
They make their way through life, although it's sometimes a tough grind.
They limp and they throw up on you, with every word complain.
They sap your strength; to be with them is such an awful drain.
Sometimes it takes some pictures; just snapshots, it's not show biz.
They're taken some ten years apart; they tell it like it is.
In one you see the long brown waves and skin so soft and smooth.
The other has gray hair, with wrinkled skin and missing tooth.

How come that picture's changed so much? I feel about the same.
Has life been passing by too fast; my God; am I to blame?
What happened to that youthful look? What happened to my hair?
I've looked in mirrors every day; sometimes I'd even stare.

It's like a wakeup call we get; we finally realize
that life is what is happening, and right before our eyes.
So starting now, without delay, my life I'm going to live.
And that's what's called "the change of life". It's like a holey sieve.
Instead of acting out our age, behaving like adults.
We change to when we had our youth; we even might join cults.
Fast cars and smokes, some booze and drugs, a bit of this and that,
our family, friends and coworkers; they see a spoiled brat.
With luck and patience, help from those; the one's we used to love,
somehow we make it through this phase, with maybe just a shove.

So we return to be ourselves, to face the way we look.
We put the final touches on this chapter in our book.

We're not the kids we used to be; we don't run quite as fast.
We can't stay out as late at night and have a drunken blast.
When golfing we may take a cart, or maybe walk for nine.
For when we're finished with the round, we want to still feel fine.
We've learned to be the loving mates we'd hoped we were at first.
Now making love builds gradually, it's not a wham, bam, burst.
There's compensation for these things that slowed us down a bit.
We both enjoy the pleasure long before we have to quit.

Now, I'm not old and you're not old; we're at the perfect age.
We've neither lived for long enough to be an ancient sage.
To classify as old you've got to be at least fifteen,
that's fifteen years my senior and not one year in between.
The same is true for youngsters; they were born long after me.
They're fifteen years my junior; they are young, you must agree.
So all my life I've been around some folks both young and old.
Yet, my age is just right and that's the age I'll ever hold.

No matter what the clock may say, I don't need any deal.
I'm at the age that I decide and that's the way I feel.
In fact I am reminded I feel great most every day.
I work a little; read some books, I even get to play.
I know my life will be this way for years and years to come.
For that's a choice I made when I quit being so damned dumb.
It takes perspective, maybe an enlightened worldview.
For you to be the right age all your life; it's up to you.

I'll never be an old man; it can't happen, for you see,
as long as there's a soul on earth that's old enough to be
just fifteen years my senior and I don't need any more.
My age is just a concept and there isn't any score.

I won't accept the talk of those; old age is all they've known.
Their life's a still fixation; it's as if they've turned to stone.
For me, I'm going to live my life completely every day.
I'm now alive; when I am dead; I'll be with God to stay.

LAST DAY

If I could live forever, then I wouldn't change a thing.
I'd travel all the highways and just see what life will bring.
But there is lots of evidence that I will die someday.
It doesn't matter what I do, to whom or how I pray.
I know it's going to happen so I might as well prepare.
I know I'll have more things to do than I am now aware.
So giving this a little thought while I am still alive,
prepares me to accept it, for my last day will arrive.

Is there a legacy that I will want to leave behind?
Is there a thing I've said or done to benefit mankind?
Have I completed everything that I set out to do?
If everything is done, can I now face my "Waterloo"?

My weight is right for I have eaten only healthy food.
It's been a little sacrifice; there's been no latitude.
Who cares how healthy I may be the day that I depart?
I'll eat smoked salmon till I burst; I'll eat it a la carte.
A little wine I'll sip and have a drink of scotch that's neat.
And for desert I'll have a pie that's made from real mincemeat.
To top it off I'll have a shake so thick it will not pour.
I'll drink it with a spoon until I can't hold any more.
Espresso after such a meal is perfect for the soul.
It's black and thick and hot and it's served in a tiny bowl.
And then I'll have a cigarette, or maybe two or three.
I haven't smoked for forty years; I'll do it joyously.

When food no longer tempts me for I've had enough to eat,
some cold booze and hot coffee; both a very special treat;
and I have smoked my cigarettes; inhaled till I can't breathe,
with smoky breath and fuzzy tongue, a film now on my teeth,

I'll work to stay awake, for it's my last day on this earth.
I've got to organize to use this day for all it's worth.

My children are a very special gift from God above.
Somehow they need to learn of the abundance of my love.
I know I cannot visit them for they are far away.
It's terribly important they know what I have to say.
The telephone is going to have to be the way we talk.
If I could only hold their hands and take them for a walk!
Before this day has ended, I will make a video.
I'm not a Cecil B. De Mille, but it will be a show.
The words will send a message to my kids of how I feel.
The video I know will make my message much more real.

And if I do it right my children's kids will also know,
how much I'd like to be with them, to help them as they grow.
They'll have a lasting memory and a vision they can see.
So as they each become adult, they may remember me.

On my last day I'll want to share some thoughts with friends I love.
There'll be no "see you later", not from Heaven up above.
For I'll be there awaiting the arrival of my friends,
to welcome into God's own house, when their life finally ends.

The legacy I want to leave is knowledge I've acquired.
For knowledge just keeps helping even though I have expired.
And I believe the most important law of man and God,
involves the "Law of Giving" though to you, that may seem odd.
How many ways I've learned that what you give is what you get.
It works with family and your friends; it works with your house pet.
A smile begets a smile; an angry word makes someone mad.
So compliment good deeds; avoid behavior that is bad.

Now, everybody has something to give to those they see.
It may be just a smile, a word, a handshake; they are free.

I never feel as good as I feel every time I give.
This "Law of Giving" chronicles the kind of life I live.

If there's to be a legacy to mark the man I've been.
I pray I'll be remembered for my giving, not my sin.
I've not accumulated things to fatten my estate.
And love has been my greatest gift, especially to my mate.
So on this day that I now know will be the last for me.
I plan to give my love again to my mate, totally.
For she returns my love and then she gives me even more.
So we'll make love, then once again, then once for an encore.

I'm ready God; I've finished everything I need to do.
I'll leave this earth a happy man and come on home to you.
What's that? You say I'll stay here for a year or two or three.
The man I've been this "last day" is who you want me to be?

I'll form a heritage of love like no one's done before.
There isn't any limit to the love I have in store.
I'll share this love with everyone then give it all away.
A legacy of love endures beyond one's final day.

WHO'S THE BOSS?

It started as a boy when I was wet behind the ears.
Grandfather's farm was where I spent my summers through the years.
His name was Pop, George Rodney, and grandfather to me.
To all the big folks he was "Boss"; that's how it had to be.

As I grew up, I worked and played; I've answered to a few;
to people all around me; coaches, parents, teachers, too.
I sometimes wondered, would I ever feel I had the nerve,
to be the boss, to be the one that other people serve.

At twenty-four I married, forty-five years with my wife.
I think I finally understand; it's taken most my life.
I now believe the ones you serve are supervising you.
It's not the ones called "Boss" who wear their suits of pinstripe blue.
Each married man has his own list; it's called a "honey do".
It interrupts his day at work; it screws up golf dates, too.
So who's the boss when couples wed? It's awfully clear to me.
The man does what his wife requests, he's "Drone" and she's "Queen Bee".

I went in business for myself; the boss I want to be.
The guy who works for someone else; he never can be free.
I handle products; lots of them, for people far and wide.
As "Boss" I'm more exited than a groom with his new bride.
I set the hours when I will work; I schedule my own days.
For I'm in charge, there's no one else and that's the way it stays.
I take the phone calls, open mail and order what I need.
The profit's mine, no one to share; it satisfies my greed.

Now wait a bit; I'm up at dawn; I don't get lunch till three.
There's only seven days a week; that's not enough for me.
I never see my wife now and my kids ask, "Who are you?"

How can I get away from here for just a day or two?
When you're in business for yourself, the customer is "King".
And you're the guy who serves each one; that's what the dollars bring.
You're not the "Boss". It's turned around; a different game you see.
The customer is now your boss, and they will always be.

I was a teller at a bank, for that's where I began.
I worked hard; extra hours and all the monthly proofs I ran.
I volunteered for extra work; there was no extra pay.
I didn't care. I hoped to be the boss some future day.
I finally got promoted to a branch that was my own.
I'm "Boss" and I'm in charge; these kids will work until they groan.
I quickly found the staff arrived at fifteen after eight.
Take time for lunch and take their breaks, their life was really great.
I got into the office when the clock was striking six.
The staff-room's dark and empty, so the coffee I must fix.
I'd worked for almost half a day before the staff was there.
And I'm the boss; I ask you; is this system at all fair?

My staff served walk in customers; they came throughout the day.
And I took care of all my staff; for that's the game we play.
So who's the boss? It isn't me; I'm lowest on the pole.
The staff is next, but customers are boss, for that's their role

I took a job as chairman; yes that's Chairman of the Board.
I climbed the corporate ladder till I deserved an award.
At last I know that I'm the boss. From way up in the sky,
I look right down at everyone; I mean I'm really high.
To my chagrin a shareholder stops by to visit me.
Just how his stock is doing, that is all he wants to see.
Now who's in charge? Who is this guy? I meet his steely stare.
But he's the boss; he owns this place; it only takes one share.

I've been around in businesses from small to very large.
I've served with groups where every person wants to be in charge.

It took a while to see it through and figure it all out.
But now I know the answer, and there isn't any doubt.

Authority is there to take and that's what makes you "Boss".
You live with all your actions, or you end up on the "Cross".
Just bat a thousand every day, no matter what you see.
What really doesn't matter is the corporate hierarchy.
In any group of people there is one that's in command,
That person takes initiative. The leader of the band!
The others always fall in step; they want some place to go.
They need some help; they're like a child who's lost out in the snow.

It's who assumes authority and steps in front of you.
Who says to all, "I'll see to that", and follows it on through.
It doesn't take a lot to be the leader, be the boss.
You win by taking action; you leave others at a loss.

The corporation where I worked had groups with charts galore.
They covered almost every wall, from ceiling to the floor.
They showed each person, guy and gal; they showed each where and who.
They left no question who's the boss and who's on par with you.
The charts were great to show around, impressing every soul
with just how organized we were, a peg in every hole.
But those of us who really knew, we spoke without remorse.
The charts were so much paper; they were not the power source.

Survival in a company is not a complex game.
Go find the source of power, for it's always just the same.
Find who controls the budget and remember it's not funny.
For power follows hard fast rules, it's who's in charge of money.

At end of day the sun is low, the sky is crimson red.
I have a little quiet time; the children are in bed.
I realize when all is done and everything's been said.
What others think won't comfort me; it's what's in my own head.

So I'm the boss, or you're the boss, who really gives a damn?
It's how I feel about myself, that's who I really am.
So I'm in charge, in charge of me, that's all I need to be.
It's who I am; my soul inside that makes me feel this free.

Wherever I may find a "Boss", a wife, a relative,
a person at my place of work, a group to whom I give,
just let the power struggle flow like water down a fall,
I'm not concerned with others, when it's me who has the ball!
No one controls a thing I do, not without my consent.
It's up to me, for I'm in charge; no power have I lent
to others in my social groups, or where I work and play,
for I'm "my Boss", that's how it is, that's how I end each day.

I'M SORRY

"I didn't mean to hurt you; it was very wrong of me."
"I'm sorry Dear, for I'm at fault; and this I hope you see."
There's nothing I can do when something happens, all too fast,
before I know what caused it, the whole incident has passed.
At times I feel remorse and then I say, "I'm sorry", too.
In fact unless I'm not involved, that's what I always do.
Misunderstandings are the bane of all who are involved.
Denial may be natural, but the problem isn't solved.

It's usually an accident when "loving people" fight.
It doesn't really matter who is wrong or who is right.
So any time this happens, why not pause and take a breath.
It's not like someone's bleeding; after all, it isn't death.

"I'm sorry that I hurt you; I am sorry that's not done."
"I'm sorry I forgot our date, it would have been such fun."
Yes, I apologize sincerely; mean each word I say.
I make a friend or keep one; I'm a winner either way.

Am I a wimp; a feeble mind, a gutless hulk of skin,
if I apologize to you? Is that a mortal sin?
What kind of ego does it take to not accept the blame?
It takes a person weaker than the blind, the halt and lame.
No, it's not courage for me to ignore what I have done.
I may have hurt the ones I love, my wife, daughter or son.
It takes a stronger person to admit he's done some wrongs,
and stay to see they're fixed just right, for that's where he belongs.

If winning fights is my desire, the champ I want to be,
I'll treat my mate to silence; be dead quiet and I'll see,
there is no hatred more profound that cuts into a heart.
The silent treatment kills for sure, and then we'll be apart.

We study books; we read the words; we memorize a poem.
We get an education, some at school and some at home.
We learn to talk; we listen, too; that's something we do well.
Communication is our bag; it's just like "show and tell".
Now what's so hard when I've done wrong to speak up right away?
It's not like it's a problem, but the words I need to say.
"I'm sorry; I was wrong and I will not do that to you."
It's simple; it's a statement that I cannot overdo.
It doesn't matter who I am, a woman or a man.
Just let the words pour from my heart; I do not need a plan.
It may have been an hour, or a day, even a year.
Just let the words come out; the words that others need to hear.

False pride burns bridges that connect with friends and family.
Apology can stop those fires; the words you use are free.
Pick up the phone; pick up the pen; e-mail will even do.
We may be shocked when we find out that "they" are sorry, too.

When I'm at work I can't afford a rift with staff or boss.
Forget my feelings; it's my job and that's too great a loss.
It's not a weakness; it is strength to walk right up and say,
"I'm sorry; I was wrong; I need the work; I want to stay."
I've never met a man, at least a man that's worth his salt,
who wasn't willing to admit that he's the one at fault.
If I can help some others, that's exactly what I'll do!
I'll say I'm sorry, every time; I'll bet they're sorry, too.

They're little words, so keep them close for use when there's a need.
They make one feel much better; this is my advice, I heed.
No blame for who is right or wrong. Who cares who makes amends?
If someone doesn't do it, then the friendship surely ends.
"I'm sorry, I was wrong my friend; that's not at all like me."
"I hope you will forgive me; oh, how grateful I will be."

When it's the time, just use the words; most times they make it right,
and heal the wounds, the hurtful feelings, from that "oversight".

RETIREMENT—PURGATORY OR PARADISE

It seems like only yesterday that I was young and strong.
I'd take a crack at anything; some things I tried were wrong.
But life was filled with dreams and urgent plans filled every day.
The world was mine to conquer, where I'd work and where I'd play.
I didn't think of yesterdays, for they were far behind.
My life was filled with hope about a future I would find.
There wasn't any sacrifice too large for me to make.
I postponed living, seeking goals, all for my family's sake.
Twelve hours a day was not enough for me to do my work.
Each year I'd get a bonus check; a normal corporate perk.
I gave my family money to buy everything they'd need.
I didn't see them much and didn't ask if they agreed.

My children grew and left the nest to build lives of their own.
My wife had lots of friends so she was never left alone.
A thousand coworkers I knew; not one had I endeared.
My brown locks turned to gray and then the gray hair disappeared.

The "Golden Years" begin when you retire, or so they say.
We have a ton of time to pursue hobbies or just play.
It's okay now to stay out late and rest in bed till noon.
Or celebrate each day with "happy hour" at a saloon.

All through my business life I didn't have much time to play.
I worked from early morning until darkness every day.
Yet sometimes I would dream of all the stuff that I could do,
just brushing up on what I'd learned or learning something new.

A youngster, I was busy, there were lots of things to do.
At six I started bowling and learned tennis that year, too.
In grade school I played baseball; that's the only game we had.

A baseball game with friends each day made me a healthy lad.
In high school there were lots of sports and I played every one.
Each day was so exciting, even studying was fun.
Add poker, bridge, monopoly, some hunting in between,
my tank was full; my engine revved; a smoothly tuned machine.

Before I could retire the "corporate powers" let me know,
that I had served their purpose through those years so long ago.
Without a word of praise or a short note, a single call,
they pushed me from the cliff and gathered round to watch me fall.
They stripped me of the epaulets that I had worn with pride.
I looked around but couldn't find a single place to hide.
Disgraced before my peers the "corporate powers" were sure I'd quit.
For what they'd done told everyone that I was now "unfit".

I swallowed all my pride and "dug a trench" from which to fight.
Although it may take several years, I'd prove that I was right.
But what I didn't realize as I began this war.
A Corporation doesn't care what you have done before.
I "broke my pick" but still I tried; I simply wouldn't stop.
I'd persevered before; I knew I'd fight until I drop.
And drop I did; the fight was more than anyone could take.
I realized to fight the "corporate powers" was a mistake.

Alone and with no friends I went to work most every day.
No person cared if I was there or if I stayed away.
I didn't really have a job; I only "warmed" a chair.
And even former friends gave little heed that I was there.

But there was still a little fight left deep down in my gut.
With nothing else to do I followed all the scuttlebutt.
And I discovered I could make them pay for what they'd done.
With vigor I approached this one last battle to be won.
A secret buy-out program, like a corporate IOU,
had purchased the release of an executive or two.

The precedent was set; they would accede to my demands.
I left that corporation with their money in my hands.

Now here I am retired with time to do what I desire.
I'll re-hone skills I had, and then some new ones I'll acquire.
I'll grow a little every day and share with all my friends.
Where past relationships were strained, I'll quickly make amends.

Golf filled my days until I couldn't play another round.
Then contract bridge replaced the golf; a new love I had found.
I played the game of bridge until the cards became a blur.
How many games of bridge can any sane person endure?
I knew a bowling league would fill some afternoons and nights.
And meeting other bowlers might give me some new insights.
The balls I used before were way too heavy for me now.
I used a twelve-pound ball; that's all my body would allow.
With painful knees and shoulder aches, I couldn't roll that ball.
I'd drop it from the foul line to avoid an awful fall.
The pins just stood there laughing as the ball went rolling by.
That's it, I gave up bowling; my God, now what should I try?
I'd played a lot of tennis as a student when in school.
With all new gear I joined a senior club; I was no fool.
With men as old as I, I knew that I could win a few.
One set and I was done; my whole damned world had gone askew.

Okay I know I've aged and all my body parts don't work.
But I have got to do something before I go berserk.
There's got to be a way to find some purpose, some new goal.
As lonely as I am, there's still a burn deep in my soul.

Some fifty years of work and no one knows that I was there.
And not a soul remembers who I was; does no one care?
I've been so busy all my life I don't know what to do.
Now I'm about as useful as an old discarded shoe.

What happened to the life of goals that I have always had?
What happened to my family and my friends; am I that bad?
They're all too busy with their lives to ever think of me.
I have two brothers and a sister whom I never see.
I'm all alone, yet there are lots of people all around.
The roar of voices fills my head, yet there is not a sound.
Is there a friendly face, a caring person, anywhere?
Without a thing to hope for now is more than I can bear!

I call some "friends" but they're all out; I call my only son.
There is no answer; he's out with his family having fun.
I call each daughter, one by one; not one can speak to me.
I'm enveloped in loneliness; that's how life now will be.
I go to bed, it's only noon but that's the way I feel.
The world's a dark and empty place; my whole damned life's surreal.
With everything behind me now, there's nothing left for me.
I'll get what I deserve and nothing more, no sympathy.

A man can live for thirty days without a thing to eat.
And three days without water is not that much of a feat.
But he can't live three minutes if he doesn't have some hope.
Without a dream or goal the mind does not know how to cope.

Why doesn't someone notice me, how lonely I've become?
I can't be this unique; this thing must have affected some.
Am I the only person who has ever felt this way?
Where work consumed our lives without a moment left to play?
For years I postponed living till my goals were all achieved.
And graciously I reveled in the praises I'd received.
I'd make most any sacrifice to seek a goal I'd set.
Another goal was always there each time a goal was met.
Somehow I didn't realize that life was passing by.
Work memories are not shareable; no matter how I try.
Yes, work consumed my life without a thought of what I'd done.
My work became my God, with nothing left for anyone.

We pay the price for what we do; that's how life's story goes.
And yet for me I didn't know that every door would close.
We also pay the price for what we are; who we become.
There's never an exception, and that is not martyrdom.

Six billion people here on earth, and I am all alone,
with TV, a computer and a cordless telephone.
Yet they don't fill the gaping hole that lingers in my heart.
Is there a chance to start again before I must depart?

Each day begins and then it ends, with nothing in between.
Like darkness in the night, life's meaning passes by unseen.
I go to bed and every night I hope I'll stay asleep.
And not again awaken so that I'll no longer weep.
I do not have the guts to end my life and just let go.
Although I know for certain there's no future I'd forgo.

Without a purpose and no hope, I stagger through each day.
And ponder ways that I can help God take my soul away.
Now every waking hour, I scream out to God, "why me"?
Has my life really ended, or is this senility?
I'm healthy yet there's nothing in this world I want to do.
I'm ready God, so why not simply take me back to you?

I sit alone again today; it's like the world stands still.
The emptiness surrounds me; there is no "grist for my mill".
My children have forgotten I'm alive, that I exist.
I wallow in regrets for time with them that I have missed.
My grandchildren are growing and I don't know who they are.
In miles they're not that far away; but it is still too far.
For I've not given them the love that should have been their right.
That they don't know their grandfather now makes me feel contrite.

I cannot face another day, there's nothing left for me.
Somehow I need to leave this place; is there somewhere to flee?

No matter where I go, I look around and there I am.
That person in the mirror knows my life has been a sham.

The "wisdom of competing" I once learned from a dear friend.
Now why should I remember this as I approach my end?
When things looked bleak he'd say, "It isn't over till it's done".
It could be work you had to do or something done for fun.
These words rang clearly in my ears as I faced deep despair.
What other people think or do should not be my affair.
The game of life is mine; just mine, at times we're all alone.
If I look hard there'll be rewards for all the seeds I've sown.

A friend then calls and tells me that he needs some sage advice.
That anyone remembers who I am is really nice.
It only takes a month and I'm sucked in up to my head.
While it's not perfect, it sure beats the feeling that I'm dead.

Together we're an awesome team; our enterprise is strong.
We seem to have the "Midas touch" and we can do no wrong.
A little start-up company becomes a mammoth thing.
I'm anxious every morning to see what the day will bring.

We both made a mistake and we discovered it too late.
Ten million "big ones" we had lost; those losses sealed our fate.
For we had borrowed money from our family and our friends;
when money disappears, that's something no one comprehends.

Yes, we lost lots of money, but two million was my own.
Again I harvested the plight of seeds that I had sown.
And promises I'd made were now destroyed beyond repair.
Day after day I wanted to be anyplace but there.

We terminated all the staff and locked the office doors.
For what we'd done we both felt like a pair of worthless whores.
My friend returned back to the former life that he'd enjoyed.

For selling and financing cars was how he'd been employed.
For me the world reverted to the gray, dark hole I'd known.
The earth became a stormy place; it soaked me to the bone.
It seemed that there was nothing in this world that I could do.
Some friends who'd lost their money then decided they would sue.
The IRS and State came after me with all their might.
I owed them "corporate taxes" so I knew I'd have a fight.
A million dollar tax bill and I didn't have a cent.
I even lost my home and had to find a place to rent.

By now I'm almost seventy; my life is all behind.
The stepping-stones are stumbling blocks; that's all that I can find.
I get my things in order, or the best that I can do.
For I've now lost my wife and everything that I've owned, too.

As I arise each day I try to find a little hope.
Yet deep down in my heart I know I've used up all my rope.
The sun may shine or it may rain; it doesn't matter now.
Without a purpose or a life, each day passes, somehow.

The high school I'd attended then announces an affair.
A school reunion and all of my classmates will be there.
So with a little hope I take a trip back to my youth.
From somewhere in my early life, there must be a new truth.

A lady that I'd dated while a teenager in school.
Who'd let me know she loved me; though I left her, like a fool.
Was at the school reunion; we politely said, "Hello".
I walked away again, just as I did so long ago.
For I'd attended the affair because a friend was ill;
the big "C" finally had him. He was climbing a steep hill.
I wanted just this once to be an understanding friend,
and let him know our friendship would endure until the end.
I didn't spend much time with all the classmates that I knew.
My friend took all my time; it's something I just had to do.

So home again I found that very little had been changed,
for I was all alone and my whole world was still deranged.

And then when I had given up; I'd used up all my fight.
I didn't have a future; my whole life was just hindsight.
I got an e-mail letter from my high school girl friend.
A picture with the offer of more pictures she could send.
With just a flickering of hope, I sent a message back.
A ray of light tweaked through the dark; the world was not so black.
I didn't know if this had been pre-destined or was chance.
We'd dated while in high school; saw some movies; loved to dance.
Yet I knew she was married with a family of her own.
And both of us had children and grandchildren who were grown.
Though I was now estranged and separated from my wife,
I hungered for this friend that might come back into my life.
She sent the pictures with a note; I wrote a letter back.
I'd write and write into the night, like an insomniac.
When she responded I'd internalize each word and phrase.
The letters I received from her diminished my malaise.
We wrote about our lives; about the persons we'd become.
Our words and thoughts created a unique compendium.
She mentioned that she'd lost her husband, many years ago.
And shared the story of her life, so much I didn't know.

It's hard for me to verbalize the joy and hope I felt,
as suddenly I realized the dream hand we'd been dealt.
For we had been in love when we were both too young to know;
now after years apart our love had a new chance to grow.

With every word that we exchanged our love intensified.
Then thinking of the years we'd lost, sometimes I almost cried.
Yes, she brought meaning to my life; new hope replaced despair.
The depth of love we'd kindled, neither one could be aware.
Now hope replaced defeat, for a retired man is free.
It means that I can live with her or she can live with me.

It doesn't matter where we live; our love will bridge the way.
For in each other's arms we found our Heaven; there we'll stay.

My Paradise emerged as we embraced and then we kissed.
I knew at once I'd found the perfect love that I had missed.
She gave my life the meaning that I'd lost so long ago.
My heart's now filled with love, and still I know our love will grow.

It's hard now to remember how I felt when I retired.
That life had lost its purpose; that all meaning had expired.
Yet it's a truth; a hard one that I learned too late in life.
It almost triggered my demise; it filled my world with strife.
Each day I take a little time to let my lover know
how much she means to me; yes, these are seeds of love I sow.
And she reciprocates with a caress or loving touch.
We give love endlessly, for we can never give too much.

It's taken me a lifetime, but I've learned my lesson well.
For I now live in Heaven from a life that seemed like Hell.
Remember there's no limit to the pleasure it will bring,
if you'll love people more than you love any other "thing".
For wealth is never money; it's the person you become.
While you may not love everyone, you'll feel the love for some.
The goals that you achieve will wane to how much love you give.
And life that's filled with love becomes the life you wish to live.
I've found I have enough to give some love to everyone,
for giving love to others takes no effort and it's fun.
What goes around then comes around and makes each life complete.
Love ages like a vintage wine; it's never obsolete.

When you discover everyone on earth can use more love.
And love exists abundantly; instilled from God above.
Then give your love to someone every day; your love will grow.
And all your doubts will disappear; your life will overflow.

SURVIVAL

Survival of the fittest, it is nature's law for sure.
It keeps the world in balance, though at times it seems like gore.
A Cheetah on a Zebra's back, the Zebra always dies.
Too many Prairie Dogs and they will starve before your eyes.
The strong may win the battle; yes, the weak become their food.
A wrangler wins the fight against a puny city-dude.
When there is lots of food, the herds all multiply and grow,
then soon there's not enough for all, and some have got to go.

The system isn't all that bad, it keeps the world in check.
It's "nature's law"; without it everything would be a wreck.
It's like a pendulum that always swings from side to side.
A little left, a little right, the pendulum will glide.
These fundamental laws of nature affect most of us.
Though humans mitigate a few, there's not a lot of fuss.

When homeless, poor and hungry drop and die before our eyes,
the world may help a bit, but not enough, it only tries.
Yet, individually, each person, everyone on earth,
will give all that they have, and they will try for all they're worth;
so they and all their loved ones have the basics to exist;
a shelter, food and clothes for all, so all of them subsist.

You send a starving child into a candy store and see;
that child will take some candy, then take two or maybe three.
No matter how you watch the child inside the candy store,
there's nothing that will stop a hungry child from taking more.

Survival is an instinct and you can't measure its strength.
When faced with pain for loved ones, we will go to any length
to guarantee that they receive what they must have to live.
When all you have is love, there's not much else that you can give.

You're out of work and hungry and your family's hungry, too.
You've tried to borrow and you beg; there's nothing left to do.
You go into a store; a single thought now fills your head.
Somehow your wife and children have to have a loaf of bread.
You've never stolen anything in all your life before.
You've always had enough and never had to want for more.
The storekeeper could give you just a single loaf of bread.
He won't; he wants some money, so you steal a loaf instead.

You don't care if he calls police; you've got to have some food.
Without a job, a wife that's sick, your world has come unglued.
He calls for the police, and then he shouts obscenities.
Survival drives you now; it doesn't matter whom you please.
The storekeeper comes out the door and chases after you.
You run as fast as you can run; that's all that you can do.
But long before you make it home, you hear the sirens wail.
You've got to feed your family; this one time you cannot fail.
You hide behind some rubbish as the sirens pass you by.
The stench and filth around you makes you almost want to cry.
Then when it's clear, you make it home; you have the loaf of bread.
A grateful wife, a smiling child postpones your awful dread.

Security's a phantom; it's a state you can't attain.
Each time your life seems perfect, then it disappears again.
Your boss says, "Times are bad and I just don't have any choice".
How come the workers in this place don't ever have a voice?
Again, you're unemployed, and with credit cards at max,
you thought you'd solved the problem, now your boss has dropped the ax.
Your wife and kids are waiting for the stipend that they need.
Survival is your only wish; you've not an ounce of greed.

You pray to God for help, but help seems awfully far away.
The landlord says, "You've got to go". Is there someplace to stay?
Your wife said that she married you, "for better or for worse".
How could she know you'd be the victim of this dreadful curse?

You look around and find a place, deserted, cold and bare.
Yet, it provides some shelter, so you move your family there.
Then in the middle of the night a light awakens you.
The cops tell you you've got to move. So now what can you do?
The building's been condemned; the cops tell you that it may fall.
Your family's cold and damp and hungry, huddled by a wall.
What choices do you have? Somehow you know you must survive.
You've got to find a way to keep your wife and kids alive.
The cops escort your family from the building to the street.
It's raining with a wind chill; kids have frozen hands and feet.
You'll not survive the night unless you find a place that's warm.
The rain turns into sleet; there's going to be a winter storm.

It wasn't long ago you and your wife both had good jobs.
Both thought of homeless folks as worthless bums; some kind of slobs.
You didn't know how fragile life can be when things go wrong.
You thought that you could lick the world, but now you're not so strong.
Your family waits for you to tell them what you're going to do.
There's got to be a way, but now you only wish you knew.

Survival is an instinct; it does not know social moors.
And, it becomes the strongest when world has closed its doors.

No relatives or friends, you've got to find a place to stay.
Somehow your family has to make it for another day.
The wind-chill's below zero and the snow is coming down.
There's got to be a helping hand somewhere in this cold town.
You raise your hands to heaven, and you say a little prayer.
And, just like that God answers; you are suddenly aware,
around the corner, down the street, a shelter fills the block.
A church stands on the corner; doors are open round the clock.

You've seldom been inside a church; it's not what you believe.
Just shelter for the night, then with your family you will leave.
But, once inside you see the priest approaching with a smile.

With hand outstretched he welcomes you; "Stay with us for a while.
We're just a little Parish, and we've not an awful lot.
But you are welcome here to share in everything we've got;"
In disbelief you listen as your family huddles round.
Did God reach out and guide you to this shelter you have found?
You gather wife and children and you all kneel down and pray.
The priest kneels there beside you, for he's asked you all to stay.
Together you find peace that's been a stranger for so long.
The peace transcends your fears, and now with God, you're feeling strong.

Survival is an instinct, and that instinct is divine.
For God resides inside your soul; your body is the shrine.
Believe in God; believe in self; and then "fight one more round".
You'll stagger, even fall, but never fail, for you'll rebound.

Remember what I've told you; it's important, it's profound,
Reflect and find your God within, the God I finally found.
It doesn't take a special faith; it doesn't take belief.
Your God within is always there to spare you all that grief.
Don't wait for faith; open your heart; you'll feel your God within.
Your God defines what's right and wrong. You live your life, sans sin.
Yes, God within will help you as you go to any length,
so you'll survive, no matter what; you'll find the inner strength.

"Survival of the fittest", that's the way we've all been taught.
And you'll be "fit" beyond belief, if into God you've bought.
For God is in your brain and in your heart and in your soul.
Work hard, relax and live your life; God plays the leading role.

And, when you have some "excess", though it may not be a lot!
Your family's living well and you don't need all that you've got.
Remember those less fortunate; give them a helping hand.
And, you will be rewarded; you'll feel great; yes, you'll feel grand.

Then, should life ever play a dirty trick or two on you.
You're down and out with nothing, and you don't know what to do.
You'll find friends in your network, family; strangers you don't know,
will prop you up; give help to you, until your fortunes grow.

LONG-TERM CARE—NO MONEY, NO SALE

I called for an appointment for I did not understand
the way this long-term care stuff works; I've papers in my hand.
But they're a lot like reading Greek; it's difficult to see.
Insurance is a special field and it confuses me.

Her name is Elle. She's as competent as agents come.
A minute in our meeting and she's got me feeling dumb.
You've got to have some money and some assets that you hold.
It's not enough to dream of it; you've got to have some "gold".
I feel about an inch in height; I'm smaller than a mouse.
How would I feel if this were not right here in our own house?
I try to stay my loving self and not that "former Rod",
who's tough and treats the folks he meets as if he were a God.

My lover tries to intercede, to smooth the waves that swell.
But there's no stopping Rod and Elle; it's not going well.
Then Elle tries to let me know I'm broke; I've sealed my fate.
"Come on tell me how much it costs for me to simply wait."

Now Elle's had about enough. She's ready to depart.
I'm having fun and learning, too, so let this meeting start.
I know I'm stealing Elle's time; she cannot make a sale.
But that's her problem. Now she knows she's here to no avail.
A little coaxing; kind words too; she reaches for her book.
It isn't much but now I feel a bit less like a crook.
She calculates some numbers and she writes them down for me.
It's not a lot, but it's enough; it's what the cost will be.

She says once more, you're old and broke; you don't need LTC.
I tell her I'm a writer, and again some wealth I'll see.
Her patience is exhausted and she's tired of all this stuff.
She's finished with this meeting and her voice has gotten gruff.

I figure that's about the end, that's all I'll learn today.
One look into her eyes tells me she wants to get away.
I try to let her know, although her mind is like a sieve,
if nothing else, from networking, referrals I can give.
For sales people all should know that everyone they meet,
knows people in their office and at home, and on the street.
Each has about two hundred fifty friends and relatives.
The attitude you leave with each affects how much he gives.

I try but fail; she's deaf by now; she doesn't even care.
She thinks there's something very wrong; all I can do is stare.
She grabs her bag, her book and coat; she moves right to the door.
There's nothing more that I can do; to her I'm just a bore.
I feel just like a child that asks his mother for a treat.
She firmly answers "No!" yet the request he'll then repeat.
He tries again, and then again, he doesn't want to fail.
And then he simply walks away; he feels so weak and frail.

But maybe in the future, not too far from this day's date.
We'll meet again, I'll have some dough, not just that of my mate.
And I'll buy long-term care from her, securing life for me.
We'll both feel great; I've paid her back and that's how it should be.

NO TIME FOR CHRISTMAS (A Parody)

Christmas! Bah Humbug! How I hate this holiday!
I've work to do! Important work! No time to waste with play!
My time is too important folks, for such "frivolities".
I'll work and make a fortune that I'll share with whom I please.
It's shameful all the hours that people waste this time of year.
They spend their money like each is a wealthy financier.
I can't believe they do this; they just throw money away.
And then they find that they're in debt, beyond what they can pay.
They spoil their kids with lavish gifts; all stuff the kids don't need.
It does no good; it's wasteful and increases children's greed.

Now why is it so difficult for them to realize
that work and saving money creates wealth; that's the first prize.
Without a clue they buy a gift and give it to a friend.
He doesn't give a rip about the money that they spend.
Who really gives a damn about the gifts that they exchange?
We all get junk that we don't want; now tell me, is that strange?
Yet worse they chop down Christmas trees; they're small; they need to grow.
No thought of the environment. How little people know!
The Christmas trees are a resource for all of us on earth.
They're dead as soon as Christmas ends. Now, how much is that worth?
You'd think they'd realize the waste on gifts and worthless stuff.
And missing work to shop and party; that is not enough.
They decorate their homes till it looks like they're in a zoo.
Waste energy, more time and money; still don't have a clue.

So I've resigned the human race; I won't compete again.
My nose is at the grindstone, whether sun or snow or rain.
The Christmas holiday won't take a penny from my wealth.
I'll keep on working endlessly, until it breaks my health.
I don't need friends or family; God gave me the earth and sky.
Alone, without a friend, I'll have a fortune when I die.

SURGERY—YOU'RE GOING TO DO "WHAT"

I've always had respect for those who practice medicine.
In fact like some I've stood in awe, which may have been a sin.
For it's important for us all to know they're human, too.
Although they do their best, they make mistakes like others do.

I went to my internist for a routine physical.
He thought I had a hernia; it wasn't trivial.
But he went on vacation and put surgery on hold.
Upon return he'd call a surgeon; that's what I was told.
He made the call and after that the surgeon talked to me.
I dropped my pants so he could probe and feel my injury.
When he was done he wasn't sure exactly what to do.
He said, "I'll do a test or two and have my nurse call you".

Some years before the Army couldn't fit me with a shoe!
A fifteen foot, I got thirteen's; the best that they could do.
It didn't take too long before the shoes had left their mark.
A planter's wart on both my feet, and that was not a lark.
And to confirm that size thirteen was just too small for me.
The "scrunch" created hammertoes for everyone to see.
I lived with this for twenty years; it wouldn't go away.
I trimmed the warts to ease the pain; I did it every day.

A friend who knew about my warts and just how fast they grew,
referred me to an orthopedic surgeon that he knew.
The surgeon told me he could stop the growth with surgery.
He'd also fix the hammertoes if I would just agree.
To get it done I wanted to proceed without delay.
The surgery was scheduled then, about a week away.
I checked in to the hospital for tests they had to do.
They took some blood and asked me to pee in a bottle, too.

The morning of the surgery they doped me up quite well.
They put me on a gurney; people talked; I felt like hell.
As I laid on the gurney my "first" surgeon met with me.
He told me that my hernia would soon need surgery.
Sedation working now, I wasn't sure what he had said.
I'm in a trance, exhausted; there were cobwebs in my head.
I mumbled he could come in now and do the surgery.
He had another patient then, so he could not agree.
So he said that tomorrow he could operate, okay.
I'm half asleep, so I agree; what else is there to say?

The orthopedic surgeon did his job on both my feet.
All fixed I felt no pain and now my world became upbeat.
Then later in my room it wasn't long till there was pain.
It started in my feet and soon the hurt consumed my brain.
And then a nurse approached me and she shot me in the arm.
She said the stuff would give relief and there would be no harm.
Another nurse came in and shaved my groin till it was bare.
I'm scheduled for a surgery—my hernia repair.

I'm weak with pain that's killing me. What action could I take?
It's way too soon to operate; I know my gut will break.

My body wanted rest but there was nothing I could do.
The nurse who pushed the gurney said, "They're going to cut on you".
I can't remember what they did; I felt my body shake.
The tremors to my body proximate a small earthquake!
Recovery was not much fun; I thought that I would die.
Two surgeries in just two days, that's not something to try.
And worse than that, it took a while, but soon I knew for sure.
They may have been professionals; their work was amateur.

My feet returned to how they were before the surgery.
The orthopedic surgeon had done nothing to help me.
And soon my stomach told me it was worse than it had been.

The words from my internist were received with some chagrin.
The hernia repair had been a flop; it didn't work.
He said, "Don't blame the surgeon for there'd been some kind of quirk".
So I was told to take some time until the surgeon's cuts
had healed so they could try again, on both sides of my guts.

Another surgeon this time; he was old enough to be
my grandfather or some much older relative to me.
He took my history, word by word; his hand was shaking, too.
As old as he appeared I thought he knew what he should do.
Together at the hospital, a week from when we met,
I prayed this operation wasn't one that I'd regret.
A double hernia is not a great big deal, you see.
The surgeon simply had to make two little cuts on me.

Somehow he got me mixed up with another case he had.
He thought my name was Rogers; that's a mix up that was bad.
For Rogers had a single hernia repair to do!
I'm glad it wasn't bypass and a lung removal, too.
Before I left recovery, I knew what he had done.
Where two cuts were supposed to be, my gut had only one.
What do you do when something like this happens by mistake?
How can you find out in advance, your surgeon is a flake?

I let six months go by to see if what he'd done would heal.
It didn't, for each time I moved the pain was very real.
By now I had a friend who was a doctor I could trust.
I told him what had happened; he responded with disgust.
My friend, the doctor, was the owner of a clinic, too.
A group of specialists; each doctor knew what he could do.
My doctor and my surgeon checked me out most thoroughly.
And, neither could believe what that surgeon had done to me.

They asked that surgeon for my records from the surgery.
They thought they'd get my records with my medical history.

They got a file for Rogers; now they knew that what I'd said
was not a joke and I was lucky that I was not dead.
They wanted me to sue, to stop that doctor right away.
They didn't know that he was quitting practice, anyway.
I told them he was very old; that he would soon retire.
And I was thankful for my health; that I did not expire.

So once again my doctors took a scalpel to my gut.
The third time in a row; now I was really in a rut.
This time I took a local so that I could watch and see
exactly what the surgeon and my doctor did to me.
I'm happy to report that everything went AOK.
I checked out of the hospital for there was no delay.
With hernia repaired, I had no pain from that day on.
No other doctor ever used my body as a "pawn".

And then a little later I discovered something strange.
One testicle was twice its size—now what had made it change?
I checked the books to see what diagnosis I might find.
A tumor—the big "C"—the diagnosis wasn't kind.
With haste I called my doctor and I went to see him, quick.
Confused by what I'd read, I simply didn't feel that sick.
The book had said that by the time the swelling was this high,
no treatment was effective and the subject now would die.

I drove about as fast as that old car of mine would go.
I had one hand for steering with the other hand "below".
I thought the testicle was getting bigger with each feel.
The minutes seemed like hours. Oh my God, what an ordeal.

I died a thousand deaths just like they say a coward dies.
Sometimes the thought of death is there, no matter how one tries.
It took almost an hour for it was sixty miles away.
Although my mind was in a whirl, I even tried to pray.
I raced into the doctor's waiting room when I arrived.

I felt that I'd been comatose and now had been revived.
The nurse took me into a room; the doctor followed her.
Eyes wet with fear, the doctor and the nurse were just a blur.

The doctor checked my testicle and then he laughed at me.
He told me what was wrong, and then I also laughed with glee.
No cancer in my testicle, for that's what young men get.
I'm much too old for that and there's no need for me to fret.
The membrane's simply clogged a bit; it's nothing very bad.
He checked me head to toe so we were sure that's all I had.
The rest was very easy for the only thing I'd need,
was surgery to peel the thing; now that's good news, indeed.

I watched the surgeon as he raised the knife and made the cut.
He did it under local and it almost killed my gut.
Each time he cut I felt the pain, like someone hit me hard,
in both my testicles at once, with total disregard.
With my bare hands I bent the steel that held me in my place.
My body was contorted; agony consumed my face.
It went this way for half an hour, more like eternity.
When they were done I felt like I'd been granted clemency.

So I've got some advice for you should you need surgery.
Get more than one opinion, even though it is not free.
And if you have some doubt, just go ahead with number three.
Let one more diagnose you and make sure they all agree.
It doesn't hurt to talk to someone else who's had it done.
You'll better understand before the surgery's begun.
Your attitude's important when you have a surgery.
And make sure every person there knows your identity.

For me, I'm working on another plan that I want tried.
The next time that they cut on me will be after I've died.
For I'm an organ donor and it's my desire to give
each organ I have left so some one else in need can live.

TAXES—GOING IT ALONE

I need to tell this story and I hope it's not too long.
You'll read of things I didn't know and things that I did wrong.
I guess I broke some laws I didn't even know were there.
So as you read you'll find out if the price I paid was fair.

When I was fourteen years of age I didn't understand
that taxes are not optional; they're paid upon demand.
I worked for neighbors every day when all my chores were done.
With money in my pocket all my work seemed more like fun.
A dollar for each hour; that's the price for me to work!
Sometimes I got a meal; food for working was a perk.
My rate was paid in cash for that's the way we did it then.
I always did what I was asked so I'd have work again.

With every dollar I was paid, I kept one hundred cents.
For nothing was withheld, I didn't have to do percents.
And when the year came to an end, I knew what I'd been paid.
No taxes were withheld on all the money that I made.

At eighteen years of age I started working all the time.
I made a lot of money and did not think it a crime.
I still got cash for work I did; no taxes were withheld.
I spent my cash so fast you'd think that I was jet propelled.

With little training I became a bookkeeper one-day.
I knew to do that job okay to God I'd have to pray.
A friend gave me some help when I got totally confused.
Before I learned the rules, I felt my mind had been abused.
Just two of us drew money from the business we were in.
No taxes were withheld; we had committed "legal sin".
Yet no one seemed to care; we paid our sales tax, okay.

Before the day of reckoning, we both got called away.
I went to visit Uncle Sam; a soldier I became.
My partner fell to polio and that was a damned shame,
for everything we'd built was stolen by some guys we knew.
But with me gone; my partner sick, there's nothing we could do.

So no one ever asked about the taxes we'd not paid.
I didn't even know all the mistakes that I had made.

I went to work in banking and I paid my income tax.
I studied hard in night school so I'd know all of the facts.
And then I found out that the State wanted a piece of me.
I thought I'd paid my Uncle Sam enough to make me free.
The State said they get their cut of the money that I made.
I had to file for all the years my taxes were unpaid.

How come they didn't teach us this in high school long before?
You'd think as young adults someone would let us know the score.
But ignorance is no excuse; I paid the penalties.
It took all of the bucks I had, my first financial squeeze.

For twenty years it went okay, I paid a little more.
The more I made the more they took. Then I declared a war.
I started a home business in the spare time that I had.
Avoiding taxes is okay; evading them is bad.
In my home business I deducted everything I could.
I fought the war with Uncle Sam the way I knew I should.
I followed every rule and regulation I could find.
That I did not owe taxes was a fact I did not mind.

The first eight years went great without a word from Uncle Sam.
Then auditors descended like a giant traffic jam.
I gave them all my records and they worked both day and night.
They audited three years; then said, "Your taxes are all right".
The only thing the auditor asked me when he was done,

was when I'd make a profit, adding money to my fun.
I asked him if he'd like to be my partner selling soap.
He thought a while and then his answer was a simple, "nope".

I'd filed my tax returns but didn't have to pay a dime.
What would have gone for taxes, built my business, over time.

Retired and set for life, I got involved with a good friend.
I loaned him lots of money, every cent I had to lend.
Together in this business we made auto loans galore.
We borrowed money from our friends so we could make some more.
The business that we built became the largest in the land.
A difference of opinion and we lost the upper hand.

With corporate taxes due and without money in the bank,
the State and Federal auditors were very, very frank.
The corporation pays the taxes; everything that's due,
or they'll collect from me and take their pound of my flesh, too.

We soon released the staff and shut the operation down.
We owed a lot of money to our friends all over town.
But most of all the taxes that were due the IRS,
created lots of havoc and our lives became a mess.
And then the State pounced on us like a tiger with a lamb.
They threw their weight around at us with threats, ad nauseam.
To show us just how serious the taxes were to them,
they took my money from the bank; they didn't say, "Amen".

My friend and I both tried to let the regulators know,
we needed just a little time so we could raise some dough.
But they refused to listen; they used everything they had.
And by their actions they insured the ending would be bad.

The IRS insisted all the taxes that were due,
were personal to me as CFO and Chairman, too.

Yet they turned a deaf ear when I explained I couldn't pay.
To them the tax was black and white, no hint of shades of gray.
So I negotiated with the IRS that year.
That I had lost my wealth was something they refused to hear.
Reluctantly I then agreed to pay a small amount.
I hoped that my intentions were a gesture that would count.

I talked with State officials to work out a plan with them.
But they refused to listen; they were quicker to condemn.
The State said they would wait until the IRS was done.
They laid in wait for me, just like a sniper with a gun.

A year went by and then another year just came and went.
The IRS did little; there were letters that were sent.
They told me they were busy working with some other guys.
I couldn't know for sure; I thought someone was telling lies.
According to the Service, half a million bucks were due.
We offered fifteen thousand, from my friend and from me too.
I finally got a call from a new agent they'd assigned.
Now three years underground, I felt that I had been maligned.
The agent said that someone would contact me very soon.
We had this conversation in the latter part of June.
Then I received a letter in the fall of that same year.
Time to the IRS is something I found to be queer.

At last the agent called and then we set a meeting date.
Now finally I believed that I would learn about my fate.
We met for half a day; the only thing the agent did,
was try to find some money or some assets I had hid.
With nothing left to offer, we discussed what rules apply.
The agent let it slip about some things that I might try.
For in the regulations it was clear as it could be,
I didn't owe the taxes; there was nothing due from me.
The regulations stated that responsibility,
to pay the corporate taxes meant I had authority.

But under strict instructions from the owner of the firm,
I couldn't do a thing; I was like semen without sperm.

I withdrew all my offers and I filed a new request.
The IRS agreed to process it and do their best.
It made the case quite clear about my liability.
A compromise, the Feds called my request an OIC.
It only took six months this time for them to call me back.
The agent with my new request was totally off track.
She said that as a creditor I still was in control.
And this revealed her ignorance about my corporate role.

Again the IRS declined the offer I had made.
The whole damned scene was ludicrous, a comical charade.
Yet I had every right the law gives to a guy like me,
when regulators do some things with which you can't agree.

I gathered all my evidence, exhibits; letters, too.
I read all the instructions that described what I could do.
No money for attorneys or a representative,
I filed my own appeal and hoped there'd be a little give.

It took about a year before I heard from them, once more.
I drew a lady agent who was like a counselor.
She listened with intent to everything I had to say.
I finally had the feeling that this time, there'd be fair play.
That's all I needed, only one, who studied what was done.
It's not as though I'd robbed a bank and used a loaded gun.
The evidence was clear to anyone who cared to know.
I didn't owe a cent, but it was not a quid pro quo.

The IRS had confiscated monies they owed me.
It's like I made a loan to them; and it was interest free.
They have another set of rules to use for monies due.
It's not like I could just present them with an IOU.

It took some time and work but when the smoke all cleared away.
The sun shone through the clouds; that lady agent made my day.
She said my story was clear, and she'd approve my OIC.
And when her boss agreed, I'd have no liability.
I waited for a month and then another week or two.
She had the ball, so there was nothing left for me to do.
And then one day my mailbox held a letter she had mailed.
She'd changed her mind; I'd lost again; my best efforts had failed.

The IRS advised me they'd take everything I had.
But living underground without a cent is not so bad.
There wasn't anything that they could confiscate from me.
A broken man with nothing, that is all that they could see.

But that was not the end, for I felt they had been unfair.
I took them on again; I'd win or lose; I didn't care.
I knew I had to settle with the IRS for good.
Financially, I had to know exactly where I stood.
I filed another OIC; I offered them a "grand".
My budget showed that's all I had, so they would understand.
To my surprise, an agent called to discuss my request.
I told him I'd lost everything; this offer was my best.
He seemed to understand but said he needed two thousand,
to forward my request and put it in his boss's hand.
I said, "Okay, I'll do it", send the paperwork to me.
If I can get it done this once, I'll finally feel I'm free.

It took a lot of phone calls and all kinds of paperwork.
Enough that it would make a normal person go berserk.
But after all of this, and more, I finally got my way.
I settled for two thousand bucks; that's all I had to pay.

Six years I fought the IRS; I lost each round until
I found an agent who displayed the strength of his own will.
Like whistling in the wind, it didn't matter what I'd say.

I'm guilty till I give them proof; it doesn't help to pray.
I guess it cost the Service quite a bit to process me.
The money was from taxes that you pay; it isn't free.
A hundred thousand big ones wasted on this exercise.
And I was just one case; that's hard for me to visualize.

And worse than that, the State did just the same from the get-go.
I finally understood my black friend's words about 'Jim Crow'.
They fell in line behind the Feds attaching all I had.
Since everything I'd owned was gone, it wasn't all that bad.
Yet it was my desire to be completely in the clear.
To start my life again, without a worry, devoid of fear!
The State has its procedures, different from the IRS.
Sometimes I think they do this to create taxpayer stress.

I'll now attack the State to get their agents off my back.
With all of this experience there is nothing that I lack.
A little work, a little time, a little patience, too.
I'll win this one just like the last, for nothing else will do.
I gather every piece of paper from the last eight years.
So many piles of paper that it fills my eyes with tears!
Yes, eight long years they drowned me in their letters and demands.
With neither cash nor assets, this had been out of my hands.

With lots more gall than knowledge I contact the EDD.
I get all of their rules, the forms to do an OIC.
Three hundred thousand due in taxes; that is quite a lot!
I offer them three hundred bucks; that's every cent I've got.
Just like the IRS, they send a letter back to me.
I've settled! They've accepted! Oh my God, I'm finally free.

The IRS and EDD are history to me now.
I'll never play that game again; and that's a solemn vow.

We're in the greatest country, and I'm sure you will agree.
This tax thing wasn't easy, but the process strengthened me.
It could have taken all my life and gone another way.
And then I'd pay delinquent taxes till my dying day.
I learned a lesson and I learned this lesson very well.
And you can learn a lesson from this story that I tell.
When you have lost your money, all the things you've held so dear,
walk straight and hold your head up high; this is no time for fear.
Be proud of whom you are; forget the money you have had.
The loss of money's no big deal; it isn't all that bad.
If you still have your health and you are driven to succeed,
and friends that still surround you, that is all the wealth you need.

For life is not about the toys and other things you own.
If you lose them just give a sigh, perhaps a little groan.
It's who you have become as you proceed along life's path.
An honest, loving person will survive the aftermath.

Be sure that when you've lost your money that is all you've lost.
To lose your faith or honesty is far too great a cost.
For your integrity and your belief in God above,
is all you need to build a life, where wealth's defined as love!

REWARDS—PERSONAL, POLITICAL AND RELIGIOUS

We live in a great country with more personal, political and religious freedom than has ever been available to mankind. Among other rights, our Constitution states there will be no law respecting the establishment of religion, or prohibiting the free exercise thereof; or abridging the freedom of speech. We enjoy the right to bear arms and the right to the security of our persons and possessions. Yet, these time tested and well documented Constitutional rights do not guarantee that individuals, special interest or political groups; even elected governmental leaders, will not compromise our individual rights under the guise of their "personal ideology", a perceived "national emergency" issue or "security" threats.

As a "business representative consultant" to city, county, state and federal government agencies during my corporate career, I was blessed to view "political processes" from a business person's point of view. While I was given these opportunities to provide a "business perspective" to government, I always seemed to receive much more that I could ever have given.

And, at some point in our lives we begin to realize that there will be an end; that we as individuals are not indestructible, but like all who have gone before us, we will eventually face the inevitable of an aging body that ceases to function. With this realization, many are imbued to learn more about "the soul", "the beginning" and "the end". I am no exception. Organized religion played an important role in my young life. Finally curiosity, confusion, concern, even anxiety were replaced by a very personal, simple and fundamental "system of beliefs".

OUR JUSTICE SYSTEM—FOR ALL?

Our country is the greatest that the world has ever seen.
We may be black or white or any color in between.
It doesn't matter where we live or who our parents are,
or if we are religious or if we are secular.
We have a Constitution and it guides the way we live.
In many ways it's literal and others figurative.
But it defines the principles, for which we'll fight to death,
protecting all our freedoms right up to our final breath.

That we're assured of Justice is a fundamental right.
An adversary system in the courts where we can fight!
We're innocent until our peers hear all the evidence.
If they decide we're guilty; we suffer the consequence.
The system isn't perfect but it is the best there is.
Sometimes it gets theatrical; a little like show biz.
But we would rather let a guilty person walk away,
than to convict the innocent, because of some hearsay.

So there are rules of evidence; these rules we all abide.
The evidence the courts can see must all be bona fide.
A judge hears every case and each has sworn to faithfully
defend the law with vigor and perform judiciously.

Then why am I concerned with what the President has said
when he responded to the utter horror and the dread
of terrorists attacking at the heart of freedom's soul?
They "bombed" the World Trade Center and our Country's Capitol.

As millions watched with me the World Trade Center towers fell;
a target of the terrorists, that no one could foretell.
And then the Pentagon, that is our military brain,
was targeted and bombed by yet another hijacked plane.

So many thousands died in spite of efforts that were made.
The fear of more attacks made lots of citizens afraid.
Yet from the rank and file of firefighters and police;
these heroes lost their lives so that the toll would not increase.

A country mourns the loss of those they love and others, too.
The whole free world joined in, for that's the proper thing to do.
And while these people mourned, our country's leaders built a plan.
And all seemed to support it, every woman and each man.

The President spoke boldly so that everyone would hear.
We could not misinterpret, for the message was quite clear.
Our country is at "war" with terrorists, no matter where.
The rules of war prevail, without regard to what is fair.

A terrorist is not a nation, nor a sovereign state.
Like murderers and rapists it's our laws they violate.

Do terrorists, like us, deserve the rights we all enjoy?
A trial by peers, for that's the legal system we employ!

As hard as it may be when faced with loss of human life,
when many lost a child, a friend, a husband or a wife;
and we feel grief beyond what human beings can endure;
that's when we need to pause for just a moment and be sure,
so we don't compromise the Constitution we hold dear,
by using "acts of war" when they are really "acts of fear".

In anger we may compromise with action that is wrong.
Is in a court of law where terrorist "suspects" belong?

You're innocent until you're proven guilty by your peers.
That's in our legal system; it has been there all these years.
And there are no exceptions, whether citizens or not.
If that's not your belief then our whole system is for naught.

I'm grieved and angry; broken hearted, praying to my God,
our nation won't retaliate by doing this roughshod.
With all our friends around the world, we'll hunt down every one,
and try each terrorist in court, until "justice" is done.

As we proceed, remember all of those who fought and died,
so in our legal system every "suspect" will be tried.
This basic freedom means more than revenge will ever mean.
It's black and white; that's how it is; there's nothing in between.

SEARCH FOR GOD

Prologue

You need to have a "System of Beliefs" to guide your life.
A "Comfort Zone" to make decisions minimizes strife.
Experience; what you have learned, are "pillars" to guide you.
To help you down life's many paths in all the things you do.
You learn from others, learn from books, you learn from what you try.
Sometimes this creates happiness; sometimes it's cause to cry.
It doesn't matter, for as you gain more experience,
You grow a bit and it adds to what's called your "common sense".

At some point you will ask yourself, "How did this all begin?"
And looking back, you'll realize that you've committed "sin".
And you will wonder just what counts when life on this earth ends.
If there's a Deity, then should you strive to make amends?
Can you repent; ask for forgiveness, if you do not know
if there's a God, does God expect your life's a quid pro quo?
Must you return to God the same as God provides for you?
But what if there is not a God? What ever should you do?
We know that life on earth will end; we simply don't know when.
The world may be our playground; life is very good, and then
as suddenly as it began, it all comes to an end.
There is no help; not from a doctor; family or a friend.
And when we die, what happens to the "life" our body had?
If it is "gone" forever, then we ask, "Is that so bad?"
And if it goes on living, will we know, or really care?
What happens after "life on earth", no person is aware.

Yet as a species we have come so far we want to know
just how it all began; and when we die, where we will go!
Why can't we make that "leap of faith" that's just beyond "belief"?
And find the answer, based on facts, to everyone's relief.

An incongruity exists, for "faith" does not need "facts".
Though faith influences the many ways a person acts.
By definition "faith" involves belief that has no proof.
When facts don't count, then your beliefs are yours; you stand aloof.
For faith cannot be challenged. It exists without "support".
All facts are impotent for you're the "judge" in your own "court".

Then why is there so much debate about "Religious Faith"?
And why do Christians labor so about a Jesus wraith?
And why is God called Allah if you're from the Middle East?
Why celebrate God's holidays with a religious feast,
while others die of hunger, we live on "excessively",
enjoying our wealth, ignoring others totally?
Can you really believe that there's a God, a "Divine Plan"
with oversight from God for every woman, every man!

Search Sans Logic

Don't people have to have some evidence when they decide,
the principles they'll live by and select to be their guide?
Don't people need good evidence when they commit their life
to who will be their husband, or to whom becomes their wife?
Should evidence at least as good, not be included in
decisions about faith and God; about virtue and sin?
Does "faith" make one so blind the mind can see no other choice?
And does religion cause the mind to hear no other voice?

There are about six billion people living on this earth.
Some twenty plus religious faiths vying for all they're worth,
to add each man and woman to their tithing membership,
and grasp them so completely that they'll never loose their grip.
Though similarities exist, I find that it's quite odd,
each claims it has the only pathway leading you to God.
To follow any other faith is sinful, even worse,
you'll earn eternal death, suffer in Hell; live Satan's curse.

Is fear the motivation, the incentive for the lore,
the offer of eternal life in Heaven, even more?
You'll sit at the right hand of God, in perfect unity,
to live forever; peace and love; now who would not agree?
Yet who produced the evidence that what they speak is true?
I looked; it wasn't there; support for all the words they spew.
For every such religion there's a person who has claimed,
a Divine Intervention, yet they all should be ashamed.
For under this façade they create wealth beyond belief,
with no concern that what results, are lives they've filled with grief.
For many give from substance, limiting the life they live.
Their children do without; for it is in God's name they give.
The leaders of the church live lavish lives beyond compare.
And after life, does anyone know why, or when, or where
our soul may travel or reside, if it lives on at all?
For your belief, your faith in God, the price is pretty "tall".

I ask, it's not rhetorical, must you "belong", be part
of a religious group, a group that someone had to start?
Must you attend a service so that your belief is real?
Does having others pray with you affect the way you feel?

Why not step back for just a moment? Take a look again.
And maybe you will realign how you hear "God's refrain".

A jury in a civil case hears all the evidence.
It isn't always true and some of it may not make sense.
But legally they must decide what they believe is true.
"Preponderance of evidence" dictates what they must do.
.

A criminal case is different, there are stronger tests, you see.
Defendants are all "innocent" until proven guilty.
The Judge controls the evidence; he may throw some stuff out.
The jury is convinced "beyond a reasonable doubt"
before they can convict someone in any criminal case;
no matter the defendant's gender, origin or race.

A civil case involves a person's money, nothing more.
While money is important, it is kind of like a "score",
for how much money people earn, the lifestyle they achieve.
It's not like life or death events that cause families to grieve.
A criminal case can change one's life or end it totally.
And "life" trumps "money" every time. I know you will agree.

So evidence comes in to play in shaping a belief.
Belief without good evidence can lead to painful grief.

I've studied, talked to learned men and prayed with all my might.
I've gathered tons of evidence in search of what is right.
Yet all religions seem to ask for one thing that is hard.
Accept their teachings on blind faith; no question, no regard
to evidence that shows beyond a doubt that they are wrong.
They blindly say "Hail Mary" or get lost in "Gospel Song".

With "hope" that transcends logic and "blind faith" in their belief,
they close their eyes; their minds are prey for a "religious thief".
Each minister and priest, each man of God teaches the same,
that they are right; all others wrong; such teachings are so lame.
"Eternal life in Heaven, if you'll just believe like me",
all others die in Hell; kind of absurd, one must agree.
Yet when religious faith consumes a person, totally,
with mind snapped shut they follow, yes, they follow, faithfully.

The Search for "Faith"

A little boy, quite young, I hadn't really learned of God.
My friends were Catholic, yet I didn't think that it was odd
for them to go to church on Sunday, every Sunday morn.
I didn't go; not once, not from the day that I was born.

Our town was mostly Portuguese, so Protestants were few.
The Catholics had a lot of kids and that's how their church grew.

The Protestants were mostly old; their kids were grown and gone.
They didn't spread their gospel; they were just a bit withdrawn.
My mom decided we should go to Sunday school one day.
The local church was Protestant; we'd find out what they say.
The minister preached "fire and brimstone" and "the road to Hell".
We never did return; Mom didn't like it very well.

So Sunday stayed a day for play till I was almost nine.
While my friends went to church, I played. For me that was just fine!
And then one day my mother said, "You've got to learn, my son,
about the Holy Ghost and God and Jesus; they are one.
You need to learn the Articles of Faith, and even more,
the Bible and the Book of Mormon; all our Church's lore".

We traveled to another town, a half an hour away.
The church was new with stained glass windows cast in walls of gray.
The congregation gathered in a great room, filled with chairs.
The kids sat in the balcony, just up a flight of stairs.

The Bishop spoke of revelations in the "latter days",
of Joseph Smith, the Book of Mormon; I was in a haze.
We ate some bread, the flesh of Christ; the water was His blood.
The more I learned the less I knew; the whole thing smelled of crud.

Well, I soon learned, my family, every one was "LDS".
Polygamy and bigotry; what a religious mess!
My great, great granddad had three wives and all at the same time.
Fed twenty-seven kids; took all his money; every dime.
Then worse I found that blacks could not attend the church with me.
The church said they're "sub-human", a belief of bigotry.
The members of the church did lots of good; I didn't care.
Their treatment of the women and the blacks just wasn't fair.
I said, "Goodbye" and left the church; I'd find the truth myself.
Naïve, I thought I'd find it from a book up on the shelf.

I searched for God in churches and I studied the Koran.
I searched in Buddhist Temples on the Island of Japan.
I looked at Scientology, some good, but not for me.
Agnostic? Maybe Atheist! No, they feel too lonely.
Somehow I know that there's a God; my life is not "by chance".
I'm so confused my mind is lost inside a foggy trance.
I try to understand how "it began", so long ago.
I try to understand "the end" as though it's just a show.
The "alpha and omega", they're beyond the grasp of man.
I'll be the first to understand, for I have faith I can!

My father then changed his belief; a "Witness" he became.
For him there are no "special days", each day is just the same.
I can't say "Happy Birthday", "Merry Christmas", give a gift
to celebrate in any way creates an awful rift.
There isn't any love in his belief; there's only "fear".
His fear of sin and fear of God is all I ever hear.
I tell him I can't live with fear; my life requires love.
I need to find God's love for me, on earth or Heaven above.
Somehow "eternal life" is not a motivating thing.
I'm willing to accept whatever "earthly deeds" may bring.

I find a "Bible Study" church, a really friendly group.
The sermon's always positive; the choir's a "singing troupe".
And every member seems to understand the Bible is
the word of God; it's sacred; every word and phrase is His.
The membership believes God's word, the Bible, through and through.
I study hard for I want to believe in God's word, too.
The more I read the Bible, the more conflict comes to mind.
A bunch of stories; most are good, yet much I cannot find!
I cannot comprehend all of the killing, sin and more.
Each "Prophet's vision of his God" to me is ritual lore.
The Bible may be "God's own word" to Christians everywhere.
I guess I'm not a Christian; to pretend would not be fair,
for I don't think that God wants me to fear him, not at all.

In my life God means understanding, love is my God's call.
So I just keep on searching for the God I know exists.
A search into the unknown sometimes takes a lot of twists.

A "Course in Miracles", a little Yoga, with some prayer,
Some Judaism, name it and you'll find that I've been there.
I've searched the minds of scholars, priests and bishops, heads of state.
I can't develop their "blind faith". I'm trapped inside my fate,
for there is too much missing from their "systems of belief".
I guess I've learned a lot and in a way it's a relief.
For I know I will search up to the end of life on earth,
to find the truth of "life and death", the meaning for my birth.

At times I thought I'd found it, as I glossed over the facts.
I'd take "a leap of faith" and I'd "perform religious acts".
This gave great comfort to me for as long as I believed.
My life now had a meaning and my psyche seemed relieved.
Then I would look beyond the words, to where scriptures were born.
Behind each word and phrase there stood a man, stark and forlorn,
propounding his beliefs, beliefs without a "Divine" source.
I lost belief; I lost my faith. Faith won't submit to force.
I'm three score, ten plus years of age, before I realize,
"Religious cults", yes, all of them, are based on "wishful lies".
It's comforting I guess to know you'll have "eternal life".
Forever, live together, with your friends, family, and wife.
It takes a "leap of faith" that's beyond my reality.
To each his own; yes, that's okay, but it is not for me.

There's just one other little thing that bothers me a bit.
It has to do with wealth, how many churches denounce it.
And all the time they beg and plead for money from their flock.
They get so focused on their "tithes" they seem to run amok.
While basking in their "sinful wealth" they live with small regard
for those in need among their flock, the folk who work so hard,
so they will have the means to pay their tithes from what they earn.

Blind faith in ritual, blind with hope; I guess they'll never learn.
The membership is told; if they'll give all that they can give,
they'll earn "eternal life" and then in Heaven with God they'll live.
Meanwhile the Priests and Bishops, the church leaders, everywhere,
live lavish lives of comfort, not a thought of being fair!

God Discovered—A Little Profundity

Now in the twilight of my life, I'm totally at peace.
My doubt and fear; the searching for my God can finally cease!

I've found my God, my God within. Why did it take so long?
I've found the place; the "order", where on earth that I belong.

I share a love that's so intense there is no need for more.
My life on earth is perfect and I don't care what's in store,
for every day my God within, guides me in what to do.
God gives me hope and inspiration; every day is new.
My body may just falter and my mind may play a trick.
And I may even lose my health; but my soul can't get sick.

For God's my soul, that's how it is, yes, God and I are one.
We'll live together, just like this, until this life is done.

And if my soul lives on with God, beyond the day I die,
there's nothing further I will ever wish to justify.
Conversely, if my soul loses this earth's identity;
sans body, soul, existence, life then ends; ends totally.

That's reason, rationale enough for me to fill each day
with happiness, with joy and love, to God within I pray,
that all on earth whose paths I cross will know how much I try;
to make their life more meaningful, until the day I die.

PUBERTY'S GOD

You ask my child, "Is there a God; does he watch over me?"
You read the books; you go to church; you pray quite reverently.
And while your life is filled with blessings, all you need and more.
You ask, "Why is the world so filled with violence and with war?"
"And why" you ask, "Does God condone the evil everywhere?
With endless suffering all around, is God even aware?
Why doesn't God create a rule and make all people good?
If He's the kind of God you say, then I'm quite sure he could.
How can a God who loves his children, each and every one,
who created the earth we're on; the planets, stars and sun;
sit by while people on this earth are starving, sick and poor?
Would not a loving God reach out and do a whole lot more?"

"You taught me from my childhood to believe in God above.
You told me if I prayed to God, He'd fill my heart with love.
Does God watch over me when I am happy or I'm sad?
And does God really care if I am good or if I'm bad?
I've had an unremitting faith that God looks after me.
I've held to my beliefs when my close friends did not agree.
When I was young I needed all the guidance you could give.
But now the God I've loved seems to restrict the way I live."

"I'm now a young adult and many changes have occurred.
Sometimes the lines dividing right and wrong have become blurred.
I've prayed to God for guidance when I've not known what to do.
The urges that I feel now challenge mind and body, too.
I've known love for my siblings, for my parents and my friends.
But now there's someone special, I don't know what God intends.
We're both too young to marry, for there's much for us to learn.
But God creates desire that causes both of us concern.
Our God must know that we are young; that we're not fully grown.

Yet yielding to one urge could start a family of our own.
So why does God create so much desire it blinds our sight?
Is this temptation something God creates for us to fight?
I've prayed to God for guidance, but the feelings I receive,
are different than when I was young; yet I want to believe,
that anything I do that's done with love from in my heart,
is blessed by Him and won't cause God and me to drift apart."

My child you've asked the questions every parent wants to hear.
For God resides inside your heart, God neutralizes fear.
And God is there for you and yours as long as you desire.
God knows exactly what you have, and all that you require.
We learn when we are young, success comes only when we strive.
Sometimes the things we need may be required to stay alive.
Though there is no assurance that we'll have all that we need.
Our God imbued desire in us to try till we succeed.

The happiness that you've achieved has come from little things,
accomplishments in school or just the joy that friendship brings,
a meal when you are hungry; a warm bed in which to sleep,
a helping hand to pull you up, when you get in too deep.

Religion doesn't matter; you may go to church or not.
Attend a church and pray together if it helps a lot.
Or simply stay in touch with God whenever you're inclined.
No matter where you look for God, he's there inside your mind.
Remember, God alone is not the cause of human plight.
It takes a human being to initiate a fight.
When we reject the living God residing in our heart,
then all alone, without God's love, we tear our lives apart.
Just listen to your God, for God resides inside your soul.
Your God will guide you flawlessly as you achieve each goal.
And always be considerate of everyone you know.
Give of yourself and stretch your love, as far as it will go.
There isn't any limit to the love that you can give.

Keep giving and your love will grow, as long as you may live.
And God will guide your every act, your every thought and deed.
In every undertaking, in God's eyes you will succeed.
So do no harm to anyone and give a helping hand.
Don't be afraid to err, for God will always understand.
Request forgiveness; pray your thanks and give your God his due.
You'll have a life that's filled with love; God watches over you.

My child you mustn't wait for God to suddenly appear.
Just listen to your voice and thoughts; that's all you need to hear.
Don't judge another; judge yourself, for God is helping you.
Live life with God inside your heart; that's all you need to do.

SIN IS SIN

When born a baby's sinless, a creation of its God.
Most people will agree with this; it isn't all that odd.
Some folks believe their sin includes the serpent tempting Eve?
And Adam's fall is theirs to bear; that's what some folks believe?

It may be just our different view of who Christ may have been.
Was he simply a Jewish boy? Was he tempted to sin?
Or was he who the Bible says, the Savior for us all,
who healed the lame and sick across the land before his fall?
I guess it doesn't matter; God created everyone,
and every living creature here on earth, beneath the sun.
So whether we were born in sin, is moot for you and me.
It's what we do each day of life that tells who we will be.

I barely make it home before I fall on my first snag.
I cry because I'm hungry; to my folks that's not a gag.
It's just a little sin, a kind of misdeed, barely wrong.
A bottle keeps me quiet. I'm in the crib where I belong.

I learn to walk; it's much more fun than crawling on the floor.
While standing, I can move just great and even reach the door.
A little push, I'm out of here; the door hits my behind.
Wow, this is some big place; it's great, who knows what I will find?
I hear a scream behind me, it's my mom; I hear her run.
I take off fast as I can go; now this is really fun.
Before I'm even down the stairs she's got me by the hand.
Her yelling in my ear keeps me from feeling all that grand.

Now that was just a little sin; it wasn't all that bad.
I'm sure that Mom has sinned that much and maybe even Dad.

I grow and then I start to school with new kids all around.
A friend and I decide it's time to "pee-pee" on the ground.
My teacher is appalled at this; it's more than she can take.
She calls my mom without delay; she won't give me a break.
I can't believe a little sin like peeing on the ground
should cause such a commotion, for it can't be that profound.

Then in my teens a girl and I are walking hand in hand.
We're at the beach in bathing suits; we lie down in the sand.
She rubs my back and then my legs; she touches my behind.
I do the same to her; I know there's something on her mind.
We're hugging and we're kissing and it feels just great to me.
Then suddenly a shadow forms; it's like a giant tree.
It's Mom and Dad; they're standing there, just staring at us two.
I'd like to disappear, but there is nothing I can do.

We take a little walk; there's only Mom and Dad and me.
It seems that I have sinned again; they're angry as can be.
They get right down to cases; they hold nothing back at all.
From here on in, all girls should be placed on a pedestal.

At sixteen I'm a little bored; I'm part of a small gang.
So I decide to whoop it up, to give my life some bang.
We take a car; we drive around; we simply want to play.
We crash because a great big pole jumps right out in our way.
Now no one's hurt; the cops are tough; they take us right to jail.
My mom and dad come rushing down and soon they make my bail.
If I thought I had sinned before, I didn't scratch the scratch.
It's like I'm boxing for my life and lost the whole damned match.
I've sinned big time; I'm grounded now; I go to church and school.
It's like the only books I read contain the golden rule.

My sins confessed and with remorse, I get another chance.
And just in time for Saturday, when there's a high school dance.

I'm dating this cute girl whose parents know my mom and dad.
Her folks are nice; they talk to me; they know that I'm not bad.
Then at the dance my date and I have just a drink or two.
We hit the sack together; wow, does she know what to do.
She tells her mom what fun she had; she tells her even more.
The riff is big for next I hear my folks call her "a whore".
The words they have for me are not much better, not at all.
They say my next accessory will be a chain and ball.

If sin's so bad, how come it always feels so good to me?
From getting that first feeding to some sexual liberty!
I've looked around for I'm not blind; I see what others do.
If everyone's a sinner, is it bad that I'm one, too?

Dad's speech has changed, for I have grown and now I am mature.
My dad just never minces words; he wants to know for sure,
that I have learned the way to live; to be a Christian, too.
Confess my sins, to feel remorse, and start my life anew.
I tell him I'm just sowing oats; it's what all young men do.
He says, "Son, don't make ladies be responsible for you.
For, sin is sin; ungodliness, they're acts that are not right.
They're wrong; you've got to think; you have to fight with all your might.
Yes, all of us are sinners but we don't just sit and grieve.
We're all creations of one God, for that's what we believe.
But with the imperfections that we all have, more or less,
remember that it cleans your soul whenever you confess."

It's like a light that just came on; it's shining in the dark.
It doesn't really matter how I live; my life's a lark.
Who cares if I'm immoral or who loses or who wins?
To get the score to zero, then I just confess my sins.

I live this way for twenty years; my life's a sacrilege.
In everything I undertake I'm right out on the edge.
Six days a week I live my life exactly how I please.

Confession every Sunday, for it puts my mind at ease.
I've never thought or worried much, or cared who I might hurt.
For people are just people, like so many grains of dirt.

And then one day just like the mirror hanging on my wall.
The whole damned world collapsed on me; my God it was a fall.
The way I'd treated people for all time, eternity,
reflected in my face so bright, it damn near blinded me.
It took what I'd been dishing out, returned to me in kind,
to finally permeate my soul and saturate my mind.

Yes, sin is sin, it's simply wrong; it's not what God would do.
My story's long, there've been some bumps; I've tasted sorrow, too.
Each day when I arise I ask, "Who do I want to be?
I'm not yet perfect, yet I know, God watches over me.

WITHOUT HONOR—A KOREAN VETERAN

What happens to the soldier who has never fought a war?
He's fully trained, but he's not been on a front line before.
The war was there, but he was shipped to quite another place.
The recognition he received was just his Father's grace.
No purple heart, no silver star, no laureates from peers.
He did his work and after that, with buddies drank some beers.
His unit stood at ready; every man prepared to fight.
His body and his mind all set, he'd trained with all his might.
He may have volunteered or simply answered "Uncle's" call.
He may be shy and lonely, with a stature that is small.
Or he could be a giant, full of fight and haughty deeds,
defying all authority till someone intercedes.

It doesn't matter who he is or where he might have been,
or if he's white or brown or black, or has a yellow skin.
He gave a part of life; a life that's his alone to share.
He asked for nothing in return, to thank him for his care.
He represented lots of guys and yes, young ladies, too,
who left their families and their homes to see what they could do.
The "war" was somewhere in the east, not on his country's shore.
His obligation to his country, he could not ignore.

His education now on hold, his life was set aside.
He left the girl he loved who had agreed to be his bride.
His plans and dreams came to a stop, and there was even more.
The battle was a conflict unlike any other war.

Korea was the battleground where all his buddies went.
But he was whisked away to join another regiment.
He hadn't asked; he had no choice; he went where he was told.
It didn't matter how he felt; that he was brave and bold.

He fought a war of paper while his friends assault the foe.
He stayed warm in his office while his friends crawled through the snow.
He had his meals served on a plate, inside a dining room.
His friends ate rations in the rain; wet trenches filled with gloom.

Eventually the war was won; the servicemen came home,
returning from Korea, Okinawa; even Nome.
So many lost their lives in battles in this distant land,
while others lost their sight or lost a leg, a foot or hand.

The unsung hero also came back to the town he left.
Now older and without a job; of hope he felt bereft.
Without a medal or a friend, he made the lonely trip.
No hero's welcome, no one came to meet him at the ship.
Now older but not wiser, with a life to start anew,
he feels just like a ship that's left adrift, without a crew.
He isn't sure that he can now compete in school again.
Four years he's been devoid of any intellectual strain.
His fiancée is married to another veteran now.
It's like they'd never been in love or had a faithful vow.
His friends are all in school or working in a distant place.
Alone without a job—a stranger to the human race!

He cannot understand this thing that happened to his life.
To find a job or go to school—his mind is filled with strife.
He doesn't have a plan; he's been a soldier all this time.
Yet he can see before him, a great mountain he must climb.

Experience in soldiering is moot as it can be.
It's not the kind of background that recruiters want to see.
His soldiering he offers, yet there is no helping hand.
His buddies have degrees and now are all in great demand.
To ease the pain he takes a drink, and then he drinks one more.
He smokes a little pot to think of ways that he can score.
Some guys are pushing drugs and he decides to help a bit.

He'll make some bucks to see him through, and then he'll quickly quit.
It doesn't work that way and he is hooked right from the start.
Soon broke and then in jail, he finally knows it wasn't smart.
The school of 'hard knocks" isn't where he wants to learn his trade.
He's going nowhere fast, and that alone makes him afraid.

Where are the people back at home for whom the war was fought?
Is integrating soldiers handled like an afterthought?
Does no one care that he responded to his country's call?
Does no one feel a need to help the veterans, after all?

Friend, loyalty is not a two-way street like it may seem.
It doesn't work that way, and that may hurt your self-esteem.
Your country will accept all of the loyalty you give.
Abstractions can't reciprocate; such entities don't live.

MEMORIES OF YOUTH

A memory is a memory till the memory gets quite old.
Then everything's more beautiful each time the story is told.
I have a perfect memory for the subjects I hold dear.
And every time I tell the story, the details are so clear.
Our lives are filled with drama; we each have a story to tell.
Some people are articulate, and some don't speak too well.
But there's a story in every life, no matter who you are.
Your story could be a book length novel or a short memoir.

In Potter Valley where I lived when I was just a teen.
The high school was a special place where we would all convene.
The gym was used for movies and for dances, now and then.
The teenage girls were ladies and the guys were gentlemen.
Each function had a chaperone to see that we behaved.
And moderate a little bit, the things teenagers craved.
For we were healthy girls and boys with lots of energy!
We'd hold each other's hand and share a mental fantasy.

Outside of school there was a ton for all of us to do.
We'd work on farms; we'd fish and hunt, at times just hang out, too.
A friend who owned a car became a special friend, indeed.
Not many kids had vehicles; there wasn't that much need.
Then someone with a car would stop and everyone jumped in.
We'd travel to the city where we'd visit friends and kin.
The city was a little more than twenty miles away.
We'd go there every now and then, but we would never stay.

This city had so many folks, like bees around a hive.
The streets were way too crowded; it was difficult to drive.
We'd see a movie, have a snack and talk a little bit.
And sometimes we would do some things we'd rather not admit.
Those city kids would follow us and call us country hicks.

They'd have us two to one but didn't know about our tricks.
For we were strong as steel; much tougher than a lariat!
We'd send them back where they belong, and not work up a sweat.

I loved the many friends I made while in our small high school.
Some played around, but I worked hard, for I was very "cool".
The teachers were all helpful, and I learned more every day.
And after academics there were always sports to play.
There weren't many students, but we had enough, for sure.
We played most every sport, and then we'd all return for more.
First football and then basketball, some track and tennis, too;
then baseball ended the school year, my how the seasons flew.
In football we were county champs; we won most every game.
We beat them fair and square and they had no one they could blame.
And then we played the champions of the county, right next door.
Bi-county champs, man we were proud; we felt we'd won a war.

At night we'd do some things we thought were really lots of fun.
Like poaching watermelons from the farmers; then we'd run.
Sometimes the farmers heard us, and came to their fields to look.
We didn't waste their melons for we ate all that we took,

We'd fish at night for salmon that swam up the streams to spawn.
The fishing sometimes lasted through the night, right up to dawn.
With flashlights and our sock downs or a gaff hook on a pole.
We'd wade across the riffles till we'd reach a fishing hole.
We'd hook those salmon in the gill and drag them to the side.
It didn't take us very long; the river wasn't wide.
And when we'd caught enough, we'd clean them all along the bank.
The currents were quite strong and so the river never stank.

These memories of my youth are very special now to share,
with friends whose memories are the same, because each one was there.
And they exaggerate a bit, for they're a lot like me.
The facts are not important, and we don't have to agree.

I trained for the Korean War when I was twenty-one.
I knew I'd fight that war till all the fighting there was done.
Then I'd return a hero to the people that I knew.
There'd be a big parade where we would all march in review.
That's not exactly how it went; I didn't go to war.
You never seem to know what Uncle Sam may have in store.
I'd scored so well on Army tests I got a special break.
Assigned to Personnel, I knew this must be a mistake.
Two thousand soldiers to the front; they went there without me.
An air-conditioned office is where my war was to be.
A typewriter replaced the weapon I'd been trained to use.
With orders from my Uncle Sam, now how could I refuse?

I studied every book and regulation I could find.
The NCOs and officers were all helpful and kind.
So soon I was the boss, the Sergeant Major of the place.
The stripes and pay came gradually; I wasn't in a race.

The memories of those years across the sea are vivid, too.
This kind of soldiering was great, with lots of things to do.
I organized a bowling league; I helped to form a band.
The team I coached in basketball won the Far East Command.
And I was on the rifle team; we practiced every day.
If this was work, "okay with me"; for I thought it was play.
The Air Force, Navy and Marines competed for first place.
But I was anchor for our team; we won with natural grace.
I swam out in the China Sea with jellyfish and more.
Sometimes I'd get a sting from something called, "a man-of-war".
Although it hurt a lot one didn't die from such a sting.
The medics couldn't help relieve the pain those stings would bring.

When finally I had done my time, I went back home to live.
By now I'd lost a wife and son; I had no more to give.
So I became a banker, business suit, white shirt and tie.
I'd climb the corporate ladder now; I'd climb up very high.

At banker's school I passed each course; "a brisk breeze filled my sail".
With everything I'd learned I knew that I could never fail.
I landed on the ground floor of the information age.
A world filled with computers now had just become the rage.
As I look back I know I was a legend in my time.
Yet I was still a youngster, barely entering my prime.
I climbed up to the top and looked around to see what's there.
Sometimes the "corporate ladder" shook and that gave me a scare.
Yet every day I loved my work; sometimes a bit too much.
Like other "big executives" I used it as a crutch.
Ignoring family and the friends who'd lent their helping hands.
I basked in my success as I flew off to distant lands.

"Now watch out who you step on as you climb above the rest".
My boss's words rang in my ears as I pursued my quest.
"You may meet one or two of them as you come tumbling down.
For when the lake dries up even the strongest fishes drown.
You know the power structure shifts, for that's the 'corporate game'.
One struggles, fights and argues, but it's never quite the same".

My boss was wise as Solomon; what he said came to pass.
Like that, I dropped from "flying high" to down below third class.

You win a few and lose a few, a philosophic view.
While learning from each win, you'll learn a lot from losing, too.
So scarred and bleeding, wounded, sans the ego that I'd had,
I launched a new endeavor, so the pain was not that bad.

In thirty years I'd saved enough to see me through my life,
with plenty to accommodate the shopping of my wife.
A home worth half a million bucks; two brand new cars to drive.
Though I was called a "senior" I was very much alive.
So when a friend requested my assistance, I was there.
Elected "chairman of the board", I felt that he'd been fair.

We financed cars for people who could not get a bank loan.
Soon we were both amazed at how the company had grown.

We borrowed lots of money to accommodate the growth.
With every dollar we received, we took a sacred oath.
We told investors that the money would be safe with us.
As friends and family they knew we were fully virtuous.
In two short years we grew to be the largest in the land.
By helping people banks refused; we lent a helping hand.
But then we learned why banks would never make these people loans.
They lied and cheated; they were rotten right down to their bones.
Then just like that, nine million bucks we'd borrowed disappeared.
What came to pass was worse than any person could have feared.
And in addition, everything that I had earned and saved,
was gone forever; I'd lost all the riches that I'd craved.

How much can any person take and still remain the same?
And when another is involved, is he the one to blame?
I lost two million dollars and my home, and then my wife.
It looked like I would be alone to "squeak out" a new life.

For those who know me now, there isn't much for me to say.
They know there's sunshine in my heart as I start each new day.
Fate beckoned and I answered; there I found true love at last.
A romance kindled with the teenage sweetheart from my past.
We didn't know for fifty years, love's ember was alive.
Or after all this time, that such a love could long survive.
Now every moment is a precious gift from God above.
No person on this earth has ever felt a stronger love.
With memories of the past to be enjoyed with someone dear,
and with a present filled with love that's replaced all my fear,
I have my sweetheart by my side in everything I do.
And now together, hand in hand, we've started life, anew.

Yes, we build memories every day, my one true love and me.
We share our lives completely and there is no secrecy.
So in the future when we talk of how we met, once more.
Each telling of our story will be much better than before.

LETHAL FIGHTER

He thinks that he knows how to fight, a student young and brave.
How can he know that one mistake can send him to his grave?
It isn't fair. Who'd ever guess; the victim of a gun?
But no one said that life is fair; he might have "cut and run".

He studies with a friend, learns martial arts of every kind,
to be prepared for any type of trouble he might find.
Each leg can deal a lethal blow; each hand is better still.
He's sharpened all his skills till he is strong enough to kill.
Then as adults they part and they go off their separate ways.
His friend starts his own business; he encounters some delays.
A war has just begun and he is called by Uncle Sam.
He learns more about how to kill, and never give a damn.

Now added to his arsenals are guns and bayonets.
Strike first and live; don't hesitate, or die with your regrets.
From only lethal he is now a death-dealing machine.
They're separate, soul from body, and there's nothing in between.
Don't hesitate a moment or you're dead meat, every time.
In battle you kill first or die; war isn't any crime.
Five hundred yards and more, he hit the bull's eye, center cut.
One thousand yards, he squeezes rounds and opens up a gut.
He's ready; any distance is within his repertoire.
He'll fill the sky with tracers; they'll look like a shooting star.
No animal or man will get within his lethal range.
Or everything they've been and are, he'll quickly rearrange.

He takes some R & R; he's back behind the combat zone.
A room with running water, television and a phone!
He calls a girl he met; she wants to join him at the pool.
Together with this gorgeous gal, he's acting very cool.

An afternoon of swimming with a drink; and then some more!
She's cuter than his sister, yet he knows that she's a whore.
They take a break to dress and then they meet down in the bar.
A combat seasoned soldier with his girl—a waiting car.
Three months on the front lines and he is ready for some fun.
It's great to have a girl in hand, much better than a gun.
They've had some beers to drink and now they're off to see the town.
His girl gets in the car with him. She's in a comely gown.

Steak dinners and a drink or two; they dance a little bit.
He hasn't held a girl like this for months; he cannot quit.
A few more drinks, he starts to feel like he's been in a wreck.
The lights and noise remind him, he's now in a discotheque.
A combat soldier, stinking drunk, five thousand miles from home,
unwinding like good soldiers do, draft beer with lots of foam.
A local girl to share the fun and maybe something more!
At home he'd rather die than date a prostitute, a whore.
She takes him to her home, just like she's always been his friend.
He's far too drunk to even think that this could be the end.
Too late, she jumps out of the car, the driver exits, too.
Surrounded by a dozen "gooks"; there's not much he can do.

He hears the chatter first; then feels the burn across his chest.
He feels the blood moisten his shirt; this is a crucial test.
The AK 47's seem to tear the car apart.
He's on the floor; to live through this he'll need more luck than smart.

The muzzle of an AK 47 through the door;
he guesses God is watching him; He's always watched before.
No hesitation, one swift move, he's got it in his hands.
It's pointed at the very spot where a shocked "gook" now stands.
Cold steel is warm, indeed, when it's a weapon you can use.
He's on the ground, returning fire, a gift they can't refuse.
It's over in just seconds, bodies lying all around.
Expectantly he listens; it is silent, not a sound.

The minutes pass; he feels the blood that's oozing from his chest.
He's dizzy and he's tired; somehow he knows he's got to rest.
No medics and no buddies; he is all alone out here.
Yet he is very peaceful, not a sign of fright or fear.

The stars up in the heavens shine as bright as daylight sun.
His eyes are closed; his head lies back; it rests upon his gun.

There's something very peaceful as the blood flows from his gut.
Soft voices all around him, yet he knows his mouth is shut.

The sky begins to open and he hears the voice of God.
He's quite alone out here with Him; it seems a little odd.
He feels God's words pass through his mind and then they fill his heart.
"Your past is now behind you and your life's about to start."

You're right, a combat soldier died, there's not much more to say.
He didn't go back to the war to fight another day.
Instead he finally found his God, residing in his heart.
Yes, from the earth, this soldier was now ready to depart.

With battle wounds too great to heal, he answered to God's call.
Now finally he had found his peace, no fighting, none at all.
He let God's love become his guide; with love to give to all.
"Make love, not war; continue till you hear God's trumpet call."

DENIAL—ACCEPTANCE—HOPE

It's wrong. It can't be true! I'm doing everything so right.
I'm careful what I eat; I exercise with all my might.
I'm healthier than ever; better than at thirty-five.
And more, I'm so in love now that I have to stay alive.

I know there must be some mistake; it happens every day.
That's what it is, a mix up; I'll just wait and maybe pray.
The lab will find the error and they'll test my blood once more.
They'll find my PSA's in line; I'll have a "perfect score".

Who am I kidding? Months ago I had the warning sign.
Always the optimist I knew the worst would be "benign".
Yet Dr. Ed seemed pretty scared; excitement filled his voice.
He talked as though a biopsy is now my only choice.

I'm going to die! I'm going to die! Dear God, I'm going to die.
There's nothing I can do. It doesn't matter what I try.
The "big C's" got me now, this "mountain's" far too steep to climb.
I've always known that "someday" I would have to face "my time".

Just yesterday I felt so young; so full of love and life.
We laughed and walked together. I held hands with you, my wife.
No care, just happy moments filled with love and joyful words.
The blue sky bright above; the pleasant sound of chirping birds!
Our memories filled with "yesterdays", when our love first began.
How you are simply perfect for this lonely, grateful man.
Each day more perfect than the last, nights filled with love galore.
And yet we knew the future would be kind, bring so much more.
For five plus years life's been like that, more happiness each day.
Our Heaven here on earth, it's how we prayed our life would stay.

What's wrong with me? Old "doom and gloom", that's not what I have learned.
The love we share each day and night; yes, that's the life we've earned.
With you beside me there is not a thing I can't survive.
Yes, we will make the most of every moment we're alive.
I'll fight this thing with all my might; I'll "win a round" each day.
We'll live our lives so filled with love; in "Heav'n on Earth" we'll stay.

AT DEATH DO I PART

Today is very special; it's the day that I was born.
But that was many years ago, I wasn't then forlorn.
The nurse arrived with food for me as I awoke, today.
There isn't much for me to do; I stare at my food tray.
I'm mobile and I walk around; I even bathe myself.
A few just lie there stiffly, like a picture on a shelf.
I'm waiting for the phone to ring; my son is going to call.
I still remember clearly; we played tennis and baseball.

And later my grandchildren will be here to visit me.
All six are very special kids I hardly ever see.
My daughters said they'd all stop by to see me for a while.
It's been two years since I've seen them; it's like they're in exile.

My wife and I were just as close as green peas in a pod.
We only had ten years before she got called home to God.
On days like this I miss my wife; I miss her love for me.
Our years together we were close as any two can be.

I'll take a walk; it isn't far; I'll go down to the park.
I have to do it soon because I must be in by dark.
A walker isn't easy but it helps me get around.
I watch my step, for sometimes there are bumps upon the ground.
The park is kind of desolate; I sit here all alone.
A squirrel is running up the hill and climbing a large stone.
A dog is barking by a boy; both standing near the lake.
I see him throw some rocks and watch the ripples that they make.
The people walking by don't seem to know that I am here.
They're talking, eating lunch from bags and drinking their cold beer.
If only one would stop for just a moment, we could talk.
Like glass I seem transparent; they can't see me as they walk.

I speak to a young lady as she slowly saunters by.
"Good morning, Miss and how are you?" and that's all that I try.
She turns her head; a piercing look, the daggers penetrate.
I rise to leave, I've had enough; the hour is getting late.

It takes a while for me to get back home to where I live.
The nurse is waiting in my room; a shot she wants to give.
My daughters left a message that they can't come by today.
They're way too busy working and would not have time to stay.
The staff brings meals; they clean my room, for them the day will fly.
But no one talks, and no one cares, they wait for us to die.
Outside my window on a branch, I hear a robin sing.
I'd read except my glasses broke and I can't see a thing.

It's getting late; I wait and wait, I know my son will call.
The phone's around the corner where it hangs upon the wall!
I cannot eat my dinner; it just sits; it's getting cold.
Does no one care for those of us who've grown so very old?
For weeks I lived with just one thought, to last until today.
I've been alone, but every day I took some time to pray
that someone would remember, and today I'd get a call.
But no one; not a single soul remembered, after all.

The lights are out, it's still as sin, there's nothing I can see.
My daughters didn't stop by and my son did not call me.
I hear my heart; I feel my breath; I finally close each eye.
I've had my last hurrah and now it's time to say,"Goodbye".

I feel a peace, tranquility; I'm floating like a cloud.
I see my body on the bed; it's covered in a shroud.

My daughters weep, they seem so sad; they never did stop by.
Grandchildren stand there looking, and they do not even cry.
My son is angry with himself; he's pacing back and forth.

He's muttering a question, like how much a call is worth.
I see the tears stream down his face, how sad he seems to be.
If only yesterday he'd called, he could have talked with me.

REWARDS—A LOVE AFFAIR

To some, perhaps many, the void of romantic love in my life during my first seven decades may be difficult, even impossible to comprehend. Yet we know that we are each the product of the environment in which we are raised and live.

From my formative years through adulthood, I had no role models from whom I could learn about and understand "romantic love", particularly requited romantic love. In my world, love was a synonym for mutual respect among all family members. My parents, grandparents, siblings and extended family were all victims of the same Christian religious beliefs that placed the female spouse in a role subordinate to the male spouse. Roles were played, with the male assuming responsibility, as head of the household and family, for providing shelter, food and clothing while the female, in addition to attending to the needs of the male spouse, cared for the shelter, prepared the food for consumption, often made the clothes and trained (raised) the children. The relationships that existed between spouses seemed devoid of romance, of placing the needs and pleasure of one's partner before one's self and thereby deriving much of life's fulfillment from creating an environment of happiness for one's "significant other".

I married twice and raised four children to adulthood in a similar family setting. I became an educated, hard working and successful businessman, yet nothing; technical training, formal education, social network or work and home environment highlighted the absence of romantic love in my life. I was so consumed with parenting, spousal and business responsibilities that I was not even aware of the romantic vacuum in which I existed.

In the twilight of my business career, financial disaster, normally a huge stumbling block, suddenly became a stepping stone, a stairway to requited romantic love with my high school sweetheart from whom I had been separated for over fifty years. The embers of the love affair we shared as teenagers, that had been quiescent for so long, were rekindled the moment we met.

For almost seven years now she has inspired me to be my very best, giving me support when challenges are presented, understanding and counsel when I "under achieve" and caring, romantic love in our "personal" life together. I close my eyes and I see the beautiful, teenage sweetheart I dated in high school. I open my eyes and find a passionate, beautiful and sexual lady by my side. Our life and our love are like a multifaceted stone in a multidimensional setting. Excitement and contentment coexist in time, creating "rewards" that fulfill me beyond any of my hopes or dreams from my past. I have found my "Paradise on Earth".

From time to time I write a poem, especially for her, that she may better understand, from my perspective, the vastness of the life that she opened for me. Following is a sampling of such poems, each expressing the simple, everyday ways in which my life has been elevated into this beautiful world in which I now live.

SYMPTOMS OF A LOVE AFFAIR

Two eyes that flicker quietly, we're lying here in bed.
The touch of tiny fingers that I feel against my head!
Just like a morning breeze, her gentle breath against my cheek.
A simple, "Hello Darling"; all the words she needs to speak.

The symptoms of a love affair; it's little things like this,
that reinforce the love we share in our eternal bliss.

She wiggles over close to me, two bodies then embrace.
It's not a sexy motion, admiration on her face.
Small hands that search, two legs entwined, her fingers touching me.
My eyes may not be open, yet her beauty's all I see.

The symptoms of a love affair before we rise each day,
they reinforce our love; there's little more we need to say.

At breakfast we share stories from the paper that we read.
It's not an interruption; it's communion that we need.
Each sentence that she reads to me is manna for my soul.
To share in things, both large and small, has always been our goal.

The symptoms of a love affair as we "break bread" each morn,
it reinforces feelings as this day our love's re-born.

So many times each day I feel her presence; hear her voice.
With lots of things she could have done; she always makes the choice,
to let me know with every move; with every word and phrase,
our love's so strong we'll never have to bask in mutual praise.

The symptoms of a love affair in every thing we do,
show love, affection, caring words; this could one day be you.

WE'RE GETTING MARRIED TODAY

Every day's a special day when I'm with you, my Dear.
And each gets just a little better when I hold you near.
But near or far you'll always be so very close to me.
I close my eyes and you're the lovely lady that I see.
Yes, every day is special, but today outstrips the rest.
For me it's not just special, it's much better than the best.
Dear One, you're three score, ten plus three. Today you'll be my bride.
I barely touch the earth for I'm so filled with love and pride.

Your birthday and our wedding day, now who could ask for more?
But more there is, for on this date you opened a new door.
Today's our anniversary; your "Luv" fulfills my dream.
A simple word; a message strong, much more than it may seem.
Yes, on this date five years ago, you wrote a little note.
You didn't really know how much your message would connote.
But when I saw that word, three letters, "Luv" I felt new hope.
From Hell where I existed you had handed me a rope.

We shared a lot about our lives, those fifty years apart.
Each letter had a message, from our head and from our heart.
Some happiness, some tragedies; we wrote without restraint.
No matter what had happened, lives were shared without complaint.
I let you know that what you see's exactly what you get.
I knew my love for you was growing long before we met.
And my concern was only if you truly understood,
I carried lots of "baggage", most was bad, but some was good.

Dear, Happy Birthday; Happy Anniversary; and more,
Let's have a super Wedding Day; we know what's still in store.
Today I'm filled with love for you; I feel your love for me.
We know it can't get better, yet it's certain we agree,
in five short years our love has grown; it's greater than before,
and every day the two of us, each loves the other more.

CELEBRATING A BIRTHDAY AND ANNIVERSARY ON OUR WEDDING DAY

The sun may rise, strong winds may blow; dark clouds may shroud the earth,
no matter, for my world had changed the moment of your birth.
There was no way to know the loving person you would be.
That we'd become a couple, me for you and you for me!

You've given of yourself till there should be no more to give.
I know that you'll keep giving for as long as you may live.
And I'll try to return your love; a love that's just for you.
My love's so strong for you, Dear One, there's nothing I won't do.

We sit together on the porch. The planes fly overhead.
No matter where they fly, we'd rather be right here, instead.
Year's past I've flown around the globe, to lands so far away.
But now I'm here with you and here with you I wish to stay.
The patio out back beckons to us; "come sit a while";
a glass of wine, some peanuts; sharing small talk with a smile!
Enjoying the scene, the high school band across the street!
It doesn't take a lot to make our afternoon complete.

There always seems to be another anecdote to share.
A little story; an incident that shows how much we care!
Our love may be unspoken; fingers touch, your eyes meet mine.
The two of us are joined as one; that makes our life divine.

We rarely travel far, just to the store to buy our food.
Yet simply with you by my side, creates that special mood.
Euphoria, I can't explain; it happens all the time.
Your presence, just a word or touch; you make my life sublime.

So Happy Birthday, Darling, Happy Wedding Day and more!
The Anniversary of "Luv", my Bride, whom I adore!

WE'RE NOW LEGALLY ONE

A little movement, stretching, sunbeams dance across the bed!
There's no place on this earth that I would rather be, instead.
You lying here beside me, it's for me a dream come true.
It's more than that, a miracle that I am here with you.
And then I realize that you're the one that I just wed.
And lying on the pillow is the sweet sight of your head.
Your hair unkempt, it's beautiful, small waves of silvery gray.
Your curves beneath the blanket, as so quietly you lay.
I feel your tender touch; a little smile, your eyes meet mine.
And just like that the world becomes my Paradise; divine.

A gentle breeze outside, we hear the rustle of dry leaves.
The autumn colors vanished; now bare branches on the trees.
But here beside you as the day begins, it's cozy warm.
Together, you and I, My Love, can weather any storm.
The synergy of love so true creates great strength within.
Together we are one with God, devoid of any sin.
And more than that, together we each fill the other's need.
So hand in hand into our future we will now proceed.

We've now exchanged our wedding vows, so legally we're one.
Can it get any better? Life's exciting, filled with fun.
We'll love like this forever, Dear; on that we have agreed.
You make my life so rich each day, there's nothing more I need.
Can anything enhance the way we feel; the life we share?
As long as we're together, Love, I really do not care.
Five years of ecstasy and every day our love has grown.
You're mine; I'm yours; for life, My Dear, we'll never be alone.

THE DAY WE MET—A DAY TO REMEMBER

Today's a day of memories of that date five years ago.
I traveled day and night through blustery wind and driving snow
to see you standing on the porch, as lovely as can be.
I knew you'd be there Darling; open arms, waiting for me.
How can five years have passed since I first traveled here to you?
To be with you, Dear Love, there's not a thing I wouldn't do.
It's now been five long years and yet it seems like yesterday.
The time has passed so swiftly; yet there's so much more to say.

Each day our love renews and every night is more intense.
For seniors at our age, this love affair may not make sense.
It doesn't have to, Darling; every day I love you more.
Our love is so fulfilling, so intense we can't keep score.

We've built so many memories in this little span of time.
As every day comes to an end, our lives are more sublime.
You've filled the emptiness that followed me throughout my life.
And finally we are one; for I'm your husband, you're my wife.
I can't tell you how great if feels each time I realize,
that we're together now, forever, though time really flies.
We make the most of every day; we share in every way.
Yes, you're with me and I'm with you; that's how our lives will stay.

We celebrate by holding hands, a smile; a little kiss.
Or take a walk, admire the view; together life is bliss.
The feeling of euphoria consumes me day and night.
It's even greater, Dearest, when you hold me, oh so tight.
There's nothing in this world that ever felt so good to me.
And you're my world, my Darling; you're the only world I see.
So Happy Anniversary, tonight we'll celebrate.
And then again each night and day, before it gets too late.
I love you Patsy, more than I have ever loved before.
And every day we both know that we love each other more.

THE HOLIDAYS—A LIFE FILLED WITH LOVE

When I arrived five years ago, I loved you, totally.
The world around me disappeared; you're all that I could see.
Each day with you is filled with love, with happiness galore.
How could we know each passing day, we'd love each other more?
But that's the way it is for me, you are my "everything".
Today is so exciting; what more can tomorrow bring?
I feel your love for me, a love I've never felt before.
Each day and night's fulfilling, yes, so full we can't keep score.

This month begins the sixth year that we've lived together, Dear.
December the eleventh, we've begun a brand new year.
Yet I don't think of time in "years", it's minutes, every day.
Each minute with you, as we work; each minute as we play!
Five years ago I came to you, it started my new life.
You're birthday just a month ago! You then became my wife.
Sometimes I dream of how it might have been, so long ago.
No matter, life's so full right now; we'll never have to know.

We've weathered little storms, an aching joint; a little pain.
As geriatrics we will probably have them again.
A little more, a little less, we'll welcome what's our fate,
for we're a teenage boy and girl, each day is our first date.
It fascinates me more than I will ever understand;
the way I feel each time that we're together, hand in hand.
Each time I realize that it is you here next to me.
This feeling of euphoria consumes me totally.

Yes, holidays are special times; our home is filled with cheer.
Though I've not given you a "thing", just love forever, Dear.
And I'm inspired with gifts of love that I receive from you.
The world's a better place because our love's so pure and true.

So, Happy Holidays, my Dear, a small greeting I send!
I'm yours forever and beyond; I'm yours until the end.

CHRISTMAS WITH MY SOUL MATE

Each morning I awaken; you are lying by my side.
I pinch myself so I am sure I'm with you, I've not died.
For every day is Heaven, every night is Paradise.
Together life is perfect, Love; yes, we've each paid the price.
Yet every time I realize our lives have merged; we're one,
I feel I'm being rewarded now for good things I have done.
And God's forgiven all my sins; he's given me new life.
But most of all he gave me you, my dearest love, my wife.

At Christmas I reflect the many "gifts" you give to me.
Yes, we don't give each other "things"; on that we both agree.
The gifts that I receive from you are more than I can count.
Such gifts are not in shopping malls, no matter the amount.
Your gift of love is first, romantic love beyond compare.
I'd never felt a love like yours; I didn't even care.
Now I cannot imagine life without you, my Sweetheart.
Somehow we both could feel this love; could feel it from the start.

You fill my eyes with beauty every time I look at you.
It glows from deep within, yet it is on the surface, too.
That you're my wife fills me with pride, so much that I could burst.
I've never known "romantic love". You know that you're the first.
Each day is filled with little gifts, you may not even know.
They're natural as can be for you, yet they make my love grow.
A thoughtful word, a little kiss, you simply touch my hand.
You welcome, yet don't ask for help; there's never a demand.
You show appreciation for the little things I do.
"I love you." I feel special when you say, "I love you, too".
So Christmas, New Years, Easter, every day of every year,
My love for you is total, it's complete and it's sincere.

MERRY CHRISTMAS!

205

A VALENTINE'S DAY (NIGHT) DREAM

This night! It's perfect. It's that way each night when we retire.
Two minds, two souls, two bodies meld together; each on fire!
We could be full of energy or "pooped out", totally.
With bodies cuddled, we explore each possibility.
I barely have to move; I feel you lying next to me.
A lovely picture in my mind, your beauty's all I see.
I nuzzle up a little as I gently hold your hand
Tonight it's just a moment and I am off to slumber-land.

I know that I'm asleep, yet I can see you lying there.
The moon creates a halo; moonbeams sparkle through your hair.
Your skin so soft and smooth, a little twinkle in your eyes!
And even in this "dreamland" I respond. It's no surprise.
I see you slowly rise; the lovely curves beneath your gown.
You walk around the bed; you're then beside me, sitting down.
I touch your tiny waist; I feel your "buns" against my chest.
And then your lips touch mine; each part of you I love the best.
There's something new each day; it's an unending mystery;
Yes, we'll explore each other on into infinity.

You slip out of your gown like snow that's melting in the sun.
Moist lips form words, "Can we play now? Let's have a little fun!"
Your body, smooth and lovely, warmer than a summer breeze,
It resurrects the "man" in me; it's you I wish to please.
I hold you in my arms; we fit together, perfectly.
My fingers move like they have eyes; your every charm they see.
And you reciprocate in ways I've never known before.
What wonders lie before me? Loving deeds you have in store!
I think I'll burst as we embrace; such passion I've not known.
Inside my head I'm screaming as I feel your body "groan".
A stairway to the stars appears; we climb it, hand in hand.

There is music all around us, songs from God's own heav'nly band.
A wisp of breath against my face, the sun shines through the room,
I'm now awake. My bride lies here, beside her loving groom.

LITTLE THINGS ON MOTHER'S DAY

It's little things that make the difference; little things you do.
To honor you this Mother's Day, I think I'll name a few.
For we've not taken a long trip, we've not gone anywhere.
I simply wake up every morning; find you lying there.
Now, that's a little thing, but it's a perfect start each day.
We cuddle close and steal a kiss; and maybe sometimes "play".
And then before we rise, we know exactly what we'll do.
I'll do my daily exercise, yes, that's what you do, too.
I come up to the bathroom where you're doing your "toilette".
From exercising I breathe heavy, maybe even sweat.
You stop and hold my hand; I feel a tingle every time.
Another little "thoughtful habit", making life sublime!
Yes, it's these many little things that make me love you so.
A single gesture; a small word, they cause our love to grow.

A dozen times each day you let me know that you love me.
I may suggest some crazy thing; you'll do it happily.
You never balk or criticize; your love comes shining through.
It's like we're teenage lovers and each day we start anew.

I know the pain you feel each year when Mother's Day arrives.
Your husband and your daughter dead! Could God have spared their lives?
You wouldn't let the loss of loved ones ever be your bane.
For you picked up the pieces and became a "MOM" again.
Now that is not a "little thing"; you did it just the same.
You took responsibility, no time to cast the blame.
A son and both your grandchildren have grown to adulthood.
And on this Mother's Day they'll call; at least they know they should.
Then each of them, in their own way, will let you know, for sure.
That you're their special Mother, you're the Mother they adore.

And I adore you, Darling; love you more than I can say.
May happiness and joy abound for you on Mother's Day.

TOGETHER AS ONE

Together is a word that has become quite dear to me.
For when we are together you are all that I can see.
I love to be together, I don't care what others say.
I love to lie there next to you; we start another day.

With you I feel I am "the man", the man I want to be.
You've changed the way I think, my mind will only think of "we".
We share our love each day as though each day will be our last.
A year since we were married; God, this year has passed so fast.
Yet every day is filled with joy and happiness galore.
You fill my every want and need; I couldn't ask for more.

November second, thirty-two, so many years ago!
So many memories, life fulfilled; so much that you now know.
And yet with everything that's passed, there's so much more ahead.
We share the lives we've lived; each hangs on every word that's said.

November second is your day, the day that you were born.
November second is my day, restored from badly worn.
A year ago we legalized our love, as we were wed.
Six years ago your e-mail resurrected me from dead.
Your message wasn't special, little tidbits about life.
Yet one small word gave hope to me, you'd one day be my wife.
I guess I've always been in love with you, right from the start.
Love's embers burned quiescently, from deep within my heart.
One word unleashed a love in me that's stronger than desire.
Your "Luv" ignited flames that set my heart and soul on fire.

These past six years have been so full of happiness and hope.
There's nothing life can now present, with which I cannot cope.
I'm filled with love received from you; I'm filled with love I give.

You're everything to me; you fill the world in which I live.
I pray that you're fulfilled; that you are "happy as a clam".
When days and nights are good for you, you know how glad I am.

HAPPY BIRTHDAY—HAPPY ANNIVERSARY

DESIRE UNLEASHED

I have no needs. They've been fulfilled. You're everything to me.
Desire is quite another thing, for it grows constantly.
Your love makes me a better man. Our love expands each day.
I pray you feel my love for you in every word I say.

Desire for you consumes me; it has grown beyond all hope.
My mountain is desire for you; but I can scale the slope.

It starts when we awaken. We are lying side by side.
The warmth your body radiates, cool morning's air can't hide.
A little movement, then you cuddle; closer than before.
Your presence is enough for me; I cannot want for more.

I've had some dreams, but none have ever created desire,
that equals what you do to me; you've set my soul on fire.

So close we're one, relaxed, yet I'm excited to be here.
I hear you breathe and time stands still. Your body is so near.
I feel your love and I respond; each day so filled with fun.
Yes, truly we're two people living life as though we're one.

Back in my "other life" I'd never felt desire like this.
If you've not known romantic love, it's something you don't miss.
I had a lot of happy times with daughters who played sports.
And with my son who did the same with all of his cohorts.
I cheered them on to victory or I helped them through defeat.
They'd win or lose. They did their best. They always were upbeat.

My love for work, for friends and for my kids fulfilled my need.
I did not need romantic love in my life to succeed.

With you, Dear One, I'm born again. We two now share a dream.
Our love transcends mortality; forever we're a team.
Of faith, belief, of God and more, we need not comprehend.
We'll live our life in Heaven on Earth, until the very end.

I FEEL YOUR PAIN, MY DARLING

A pain so sharp she cannot rise; she crumbles to the ground.
An anguished sigh, a tiny moan, and that's the only sound.
I turn and see her crouched; her arms wrapped tightly at her side.
She doesn't want to startle me; the pain she tries to hide.
But it's too much. I see a tear; it moistens her soft cheek.
I feel her pain; I feel her hurt; a world turned dark and bleak.
She strains, a weakly smile, as tiny fingers touch my hand.
She can't rise to erect; the pain is more than she can stand.

I hold her close but carefully; I'm not sure what to do.
Is there someone to help? I look around; there's just we two.
I feel her gentle sobs against my chest; she holds me tight.
Soft words I whisper; stroke her hair; hope she will be all right.
She tries to move; a single step, a wobbly child I hold.
With gritted teeth she tries again; courageous, she is bold.
And then back to my arms she falls, the pain too great to bear.
I feel her pain; it fills my head; it's just downright unfair.

I stand beside her breathless, for I dare not move or breathe.
Her trembling body in my arms; I pray her pain will leave.
She moves a little; straightens up, I see a moistened eye.
No way to mitigate her pain, no matter how I try.

And then there's just the hint of a small smile across her face.
This lady's more than beautiful; her body's filled with grace.
Without complaint she puts the pain behind and starts to walk.
I take her hand; squeeze it a bit; there is no need to talk.
She's suffered more than I will ever know; yet she is strong.
She lets me know each day that it's with her that I belong.

We share our love together every way that we know how.
Our love grows stronger every day; it's all God will allow.

JUST THINKING OF YOU

I wrote a book about the love we share; it wasn't long.
I want the world to know about our love that's grown so strong.
Reflecting, though, you know, Dear Love, I wrote the book for you.
To reminisce our years apart and then how our love grew!
I realized the day we met, after those fifty years,
The love we share is so intense it allayed all my fears.
And I had many fears although I kept them well disguised.
I kept each person at "arms length"; a plan that I devised,
to keep from getting hurt by others when they "changed their mind",
I searched in vain for love; romantic love I'd never find.

The moment that we met I felt euphoric, even more.
I knew at once I loved you. Yes, it's you that I adore.
In place of each uncertainty that filled my life with doubt,
you let me know with tender touch, what love is all about.
I didn't know how shallow life had been before we met.
I simply thought that as I give, then so is how I get.
I didn't give my love to others, all throughout my life.
Not to my parents, siblings, children, and not to my wife.
How could I feel the love that others may have had for me?
When someone tried to get too close, I'd always turn and flee.
I guess that I'd been hurt too much in my first "love affair".
I'm sorry it was someone else, if only you'd been there.
But you were there, and I the fool, had turned my back on you.
Too young and filled with fear of God; so what else could I do?

These past six years in each poetic verse I wrote to you,
I've tried to make amends for what I did and didn't do.
To help you understand the kind of "guy" I was before.
And also share my dreams of what our life still has in store.

So every time you read a line, a page, perhaps a verse.
And think of how life could have been; mutter a silent curse.
Remember that I share each thought; each moment that we lost.
And yet rejoice because our lives are good; it's worth the cost.
We've filled our lives with love and we've made up for all the past.
We've said goodbye to yesterdays; our love will ever last.

ANOTHER DAY IN PARADISE

There's beauty in this world in which I live, beyond compare.
Especially when I feel your touch and know that you are there.
It starts with the first light of dawn; you're lying next to me.
My eyes are closed yet in my mind; your beauty's all I see.
A little movement, a small nudge, we're almost wide-awake.
Our first embrace; we cuddle close, each for the other's sake.
And silently I thank my God that you've become my wife.
You've given me new hope and more; you've given me new life.

As we begin each day you know that you're my heart's desire.
Your love consumes me totally; you've set my soul on fire.
There's no beginning and no end; I love you totally.
To please you is my daily goal, into eternity.
Dear, I find joy and happiness just being close to you.
For over five years I've approved of everything you do.
I know you can't be perfect, yet there's nothing I would change.
Our lifestyle is so great there's not a thing I'd rearrange.

When you are near the sun is always shining in the sky.
I laugh when you are happy; when you're sad I almost cry.
With empathy I feel your every thought, your every move.
And through it all there's not a single thing I don't approve.
I feel your love each time we take a walk or watch TV.
I have no other wish except to have you close to me.
In every way that's possible, I'll love you more each day.
It doesn't matter if you're by my side or far away.

Our life is full; together we're a team and so much more.
We "smell the roses" as we shop for groceries at the store.
We'll "hit" the Thrift Store and pick up some little thing we need.
Then shrubs from the Home Depot or a little garden seed!

At Kohl's you'll shop for "pants", a blouse that fits you perfectly.
I'll try the discount rack to find a "cheap" sweater for me.
In everything we do there's some adventure, always fun.
And we'll continue this "affair" until our life is done.

MY VALENTINE—FOREVER

It's only been a moment; it was yesterday; last year?
I drove through mountains, sleet and snow, before arriving here.
And found you waiting; open arms, my dream fulfilled, and more.
The two of us were one before we entered your front door.
Then I reflect a moment on the love that we now share.
How much your love has done for me, how much I know you care.
It seems that we have been together, always, you and I.
That's how it's always going be, till these two lovers die.

I waken to the rising sun; its beams across our bed.
Love's passion fills my body from my toes up to my head.
I think of water, crystal clear, pure as the falling snows.
Yet, love like ours is purer, as each day we know it grows.
No image is more beautiful, no feeling quite as strong,
as holding you so close to me, embraced, as we belong.
From just beyond the window is the chirping of a bird.
Each sound brings forth a memory of your every loving word.
The whisper of the morning breeze; your breath against my face!
I squeeze you; you respond and I am lost in your embrace.
I've visions of our life to come, no boundaries, anywhere!
No matter what may happen, for I know that you'll be there.
Together we can withstand any challenge on this earth.
My life is full; each need fulfilled; that's what your love is worth.

Oh Darling, do you understand what you have done for me.
The world is filled with beauty that you've taught me how to see.
Half blind, half deaf, sans taste or touch, a half a man at best.
Then your embrace; reborn, true love; and you know all the rest.
I walk with you, no matter where; I barely touch the ground.
You speak to me; the world stands still; I hear no other sound.
You touch my hand; a little squeeze, my poor heart skips a beat.
You warm my heart; you warm my soul; my whole being feels the heat.

This day that's set aside for lovers; lovers everywhere,
to us is just "another day", as long as we're both there.
Yes, just "another day" in Paradise, we sing our song.
Our melody is Heaven sent; together we belong.

REFLECTIONS FROM YOUR GOLFING LOVER

Each day in some small way I try to let you know I care.
Completing little tasks, I try to always do my share.
Yet Wednesdays when I hit the links with "senior golfing friends"
I feel you've gotten "the short stick" and I should make amends.
You stay at home and work, for dirty clothes are piled high.
I wouldn't blame you if you just refused and didn't try.
Yet every Wednesday I return to find your warm embrace.
If there's a problem it's well hidden; there is not a trace.

Yes, Darling, that's another reason that I love you so.
Your lover and your husband, yet I'll always be your beau!

If that were not enough, I do a practice round each week.
On Mondays I go looking for the perfect swing I seek.
Four hours, maybe a bit more, I'm gone and you're alone.
I have the fun; you do the work; so how can I atone?
Again, you're always there, a smile, a hug and a warm kiss.
You make my life so perfect that I'm in eternal bliss.
Somehow there has to be a way, some way for me to share,
with you the joy and love that fills my heart; show you I care.

You've never uttered a complaint, no not a single one.
You let me know you're happy because I am having fun.

And there's another aspect of this golfing game I play.
I take the car and leave you here at home, where you must stay.
But also, golfing costs us money, more than I can count.
You "keep the books" and "suffer through" for you know the amount.
Yet with a smile each week you give me money for my game.
I know we share our incomes but it doesn't "feel" the same.

You cut the corners; budget and you're careful what we buy.
And you accept my "waste on golf"; I wonder why you try.

So let me tell you, one more time, how much I love you, Dear.
My gratitude and love is stronger than it may appear.

SPECIAL MOTHER

You've been a mother twice, and then a mother twice again.
As mother/matriarch, you gave yourself to your domain.
Not just a loving mother of your daughter and your son,
but as your family's strength in battles lost, and wars you've won,
and as the "mother", grandmother when family needed you,
in every situation, you have known what you must do.

And your extended family, every one you've ever known,
should thank you every day; with you as friend, they're not alone.
You've shared your love and thoughtfulness with each of them, and
more,
Your caring love shows through with family, friend or visitor.

To share your love is natural; you don't even have to try.
If someone has a challenge, you are there; a fast ally.
Yet, I am sure you suffer pain when friends or family hurt.
But you don't give an inch against the pressures some exert.
Instinctively you seem to always know what's right; what's wrong.
You've sacrificed so you can always be where you belong.

I'm just your husband, just a guy who loves you more than life.
You made me whole, complete, the day that you became my wife.
We'd lived together five plus years, as close as two can be.
Our wedding brought us closer, me to you and you to me.
For me you've been a perfect mate; you've filled my every need.
It almost seems impossible; we've never disagreed.
It doesn't matter; we both know, whatever comes along,
We'll tackle it together, hand in hand as we belong.

You've set the bar up pretty high; there is no compromise.
You've shown as mother, grandmother, and friend, that you are wise.
But more than that, you've shared your love with all, unselfishly.
And that's okay, for you have shown there's plenty left for me.

Happy Mother's Day, Love!

WE

When I awaken every morn, you're lying next to me.
It isn't you, it isn't me; the beauty is the "WE".
We made each other whole; we simply melded into one.
The love we share creates the moods that fill our lives with fun.
We go to breakfast, hand in hand, two lovers, young at heart.
With every moment cherished, home together or apart.
I feel you in my heart, I close my eyes, and you are there.
It doesn't matter if you're home or you have gone somewhere.
Yes, in my mind you're here with me when you're out with a friend.
My love for you grows deeper every day, and there's no end.
And I can feel your love for me in every thing you do.
I'm more a man than ever, and it's all because of you.

Just you and I, our love affair, we two; it takes no more.
You've made me whole, a better man than I could be before.
And you've become more gorgeous, growing lovelier each day.
I hope that's been because of me, the things I do and say.
Yes, every hour of each day, we know our love will grow.
It's stronger, more pervasive than the mountain winds that blow.
And yet it's all so simple, it's not intricate or rare.
Each day in some small way, we let each other know we care.
There is no shouting; horns don't blow; the sun comes up and sets.
We never measure, judge, complain; about the "stuff" each gets.
There isn't any competition, maybe just a bit.
We may compete to share our love; on that we'll never quit.

Our two lives are fulfilled because they're shared so selflessly.
Two people so in love they don't know how to disagree.
We share a love that fills our hearts and permeates our souls.
To give the other happiness, is first among our goals.
Yes, it is you; because of you, I'm all that I can be.

Though I am I and you are you, there's so much more, you see!
For "WE", the two of us are one; in heart and soul, we're one.
And that's the way it's going to stay until our life is done!

LOVE'S SYNERGY

When one and one just won't add up, it's always more than two.
There's synergy that's working and it works in all we do.
I'm more than I have ever been because you are my wife.
It's there in every thing I do; you've given me new life.
And I believe that you are more than you have ever been.
Together we're a team in life. We're always going to win.
And that's what synergy will do when couples really care.
Results greater than all the parts, when synergy is there!
I exercise for health, but there are other reasons, too.
Good health alone is shallow if I can't share it with you.
And you work till your muscles ache and walk until you're "dead".
When you could sit and watch TV or work puzzles, instead.
And I appreciate that you are doing this for me.
Or should I say that, "it's for us", you're doing it for "we".

There's synergy in everything we do, our work, our play,
when we prepare a meal or, at night in bed we lay.
You give me energy that I have never known before.
You give your love unselfishly. I couldn't ask for more.
And I try to reciprocate. At times I might succeed.
A thoughtful word, a tender touch to satisfy a need!
The two of us are one and yet together we both know,
the love we shared so long ago will last, forever grow,
much deeper, more intense and with a passion that exceeds,
our wildest dreams, imagination, our desires and needs.

Yes, that's the synergy of love. It's in each heart, each head.
A love we've both shared every day, before and since we wed.
Together we will always be much more than "one and one".
Our love will grow forever, Dear, until this life is done.
Yes, our reward for what we've done; for every sacrifice,
is sharing life that's filled with love; we two in Paradise.

REWARDS—
OUR FAMILY BIRTHRIGHT

At some stage in our life we discover that we are, in large measure, the product of the family to which we became a member at birth. Family, particularly loving parents, most often serves as a "spring board" to elevate our own expectations and aid us in the achievement of our life's goals. From time to time rivalries develop within the nuclear or extended family that serve as obstacles to our development and excuses for our underachievement Children seem to have an innate tendency to be "exactly like" members of their family whom they admire. In contrast, they may have the same tendency to be exactly the opposite of those family members whom they dislike. As my circle of extended family, social, business and professional contacts expanded during my teen and post-teen years, these tendencies certainly played a role in the person, spouse and parent that I became as a maturing adult.

MOTHERHOOD

It's just a word, yet it creates a vision, fair and clear.
Throughout your life your mother's voice is music to your ear.
She gives you life then feeds you, as you suckle from her breast.
Then she keeps you from harms way as you pursue each great quest.
It could be any week, of any month, of any year.
She fills your heart with love and somehow allays every fear.
Each second of each minute of each hour of every day,
she gives her love unselfishly; your problems melt away.
Dear Mother, you don't have to be a relative of mine.
As Mother to your children, that's enough; you've done just fine.
With love that's unconditional, you love each child the same.
For you it's what your life's about, you are not seeking fame.
As surely as the oceans rise and fall with every tide,
a house is not a home unless a mother lives inside.
And love that you have known in life is truly incomplete,
until you feel her love inside your heart with every beat.

You love your spouse; your parents and you love your children, too.
For them there's nothing in this world you'd hesitate to do.
And, yet when thing's go wrong and there is nowhere you can turn.
You seek your mother's counsel, for from her you'll ever learn.
A son and daughter view their mother differently, for sure.
A daughter learns of motherhood and then learns much, much more.
Her son may be the "apple" of her eye, yet he's aware,
she loves each child with all her heart; her love is always fair.
So now that you're adult and you've been weaned from "Mother's Nest",
you understand her sacrifice so you could have the best.
It's AOK to call or write her; it will make her day.
Three words, "I love you"; that's enough; that's all you have to say.

MOTHER—THE CONSERVATIVE

The oldest of eleven, born in nineteen hundred nine,
to parents who were farmers, she's the first of a long line.
Eight brothers and two sisters; they're a Mormon family.
So having fairly liberal views is normal as can be.
They're independent, farmers and they're capitalistic.
They mostly go it all alone, for to their guns they stick.
They look out for themselves, maybe their siblings and their kids.
They're otherwise disorganized, utensils without lids.

I came along much later when my mom was twenty-two.
She separated from my dad, not knowing what to do.
Away from home and loved ones, she took work in a café.
To make it she was forced to work till nightfall every day.
Now, I was with my brother; we both stayed back on the farm.
My mother didn't want the rift to cause us any harm.
By working hard and saving, Mom was soon fully prepared,
to reunite the family; even Dad, for whom she cared.

Together as a family everything seemed good to me.
But what the future held was too distant for me to see.
Though quiet and conservative, and happy most the time,
inside her was a burn that to her family was a crime.
She willingly helped others; it was natural as can be.
She wished for independence for herself and family.
Co-ops were like a sin, a farmer's bane and weakness, too.
Yet farming was her heritage; that's all she knew to do.

While she was busy raising us, providing a clean home,
she washed our clothes and fixed our meals; our hair she'd always comb.
We had a mother, who worked hard and never did complain,
regardless of the views she held, of which she'd not explain.

I went to family meetings; every person aired their view.
The whole darned bunch was socialist, and many bigots, too.
It's like they thought they were on top, all others underneath.
I listened for a while, and then some more until I'd seethe.
We're equal at our time of birth; success requires work.
Some labor, dedication, too, it's not a freakish quirk.
Survival of the fittest may be harsh and ruthless, too.
A free market economy; it's what we all should do.

My uncles, aunts and cousins would all argue till they won.
To them, redistribution is the best for every one.
They couldn't understand we need incentives to be strong.
With wealth we do exactly what we wish; can that be wrong?
I'd argue, then I'd walk away; I didn't even care.
I never even noticed that my mother wasn't there,
for she had views that matched my own. My God, what a surprise!
But to avoid her family's wrath, she'd rather tell some lies.

It wasn't till I met with her when she was eighty-five.
We visited a while and then I took her for a drive.
We talked of family values, of her daughter and each son.
And family "get togethers" we enjoyed and all had fun.
That day my mother told me why she never talked that much.
She did the kitchen thing all-day and used it as a crutch.
She listened but she didn't speak; she never would argue.
She told me, "I believe in this and just as much as you".

A registered republican, she'd vote the party line.
To do it any other way she thought was asinine.
To her the democrats were wrong; she didn't need advice.
To be conservative is right; you don't need to think twice.
Her husband was a democrat, so to avoid a war,
she never talked of politics; she'd rather mop the floor.
But when she learned I shared her views, she cried with ecstasy.
"My son, we are the only two in this whole family."

MOTHER—FINAL CONFUSION—FINAL PRAYER
(I don't know who I am)

A silhouette at dusk! A fading shadow in the night!
Her memory wanes, it's disappeared. She's finally lost the fight.
No friends, there's only emptiness, with quiet all around.
There's nothing she can recognize; there's no familiar sound.
Not long ago I held her hand; we sat there, side by side.
My love for her was total, for she filled my heart with pride.
And now she can't remember. Nothing! Family, friend or me,
the laughter of her children as they played so happily.

I saw her yesterday; she can't remember that, somehow.
Her life, so full, and yet there's nothing she remembers now.
From childhood to the present, all those years lost in between.
She's not that old. Why can't her present life just be serene?
Her friends are strangers. There is not a single one she knows.
She tries. I feel her mind at work. Yet, her confusion grows.
She's been here for a while. She asks if this is a hotel.
It's going to be her final home; a fact I cannot tell.

She asks, "Where are the people that I knew throughout my life?"
I feel so sad; she was the greatest sibling, mother; wife!

With tearful eyes I hear her say, "I don't know who I am".
She says, "The folks around this place don't seem to give a damn".

She knows her life's behind her and there is nothing left ahead.
No family, friends or loved ones; she feels she's already dead.

"I'm all alone. There's no one, only you, Dear God and I.
Please take my soul to Heaven now, and let my body die."

I didn't see Mom after that. God answered her request.
She lives with Him in Heaven; now her soul can finally rest.

MY FATHER

I don't remember when we met; I think that I was five.
Before that age I don't recall; I must have been alive.
I went to school just down the street with kids I still don't know.
On Saturday my brother always took me to the show.
We rented a small house about two blocks from my first school.
I cut grass for the rabbits, everyday; that was your rule.
If sometimes I forgot and went to play with other boys,
you used a belt upon my legs and took away my toys.

Just hurting me was not enough, no sweat about my age.
There had to be some welts and blood to satisfy your rage.

I don't remember seeing you except at dinnertime.
The mood was stern without a word; did I commit a crime?
You went to work before we kids arose to start the day.
It didn't matter much; our chores left little time to play.
I had so much to say, but you did not take time to hear.
Your words and actions left no choice; I lived in mortal fear.

My brother got a job; he had some magazines to sell.
We tried with all the neighbors, but it didn't go too well.
We hiked a while to try our luck just seven miles away.
We knew the parents of some kids with whom we used to play.
We walked and walked, then found ourselves approaching Tank Farm Hill.
No problem, though it's steep, our goal gave each of us the will
to make the climb so we could sell the magazines we had.
A "black and white" pulled up. A cop approached and he looked mad.
The cop was not too happy with the distance we had gone.
He took us back to Mom in his patrol car, sirens on.
When you got home from work that day Mom told you what we did.
My brother sat there filled with fear; I wished that I had hid.

Down to the basement, that's the place we got our discipline.
You beat my brother bloody. Then I got it like a twin.
There wasn't anything that Mom could do, though she could hear
our sobs of desperation; resignation to our fear
She dressed our wounds; it didn't help the pain we felt inside.
For we were growing hateful of you; hate we didn't hide.

Our family moved to Covelo, a valley, very small.
It always was your dream to be a farmer, strong and tall.
I didn't go to school because they didn't have my grade.
Instead, most days I did my chores; helped Mom just like a maid.
You never said, "Good job my boy", or other words so kind.
But if I messed up just a bit, the belt hit my behind.
I never heard a word of praise; it didn't happen once.
I guess that in your mind I was a no good, worthless dunce.

The farm did not produce, so to the city you returned.
And that was fine with me for my behind no longer burned.
I simply didn't miss you, and I think that I know why.
I did my work and helped my mom, but now I didn't cry.

With Mom, my older brother, one that's younger, sister too,
we stayed to scratch for food in snow so deep it covered you.
We got snowed in for just about a full six weeks, I guess.
With beans and rice and milk, no more, our life was one big mess.
Spring thawed the snow; we loaded up to follow after you.
Our clothes were rags; we had no food; we were a motley crew.
We got down to the city and we found out where we'd live.
It wasn't much to look at and the roof leaked like a sieve.
But I was happy to be gone from piles of ice and snow.
The future that would face me, I thank God I didn't know.

With rabbits, chickens, geese and ducks, it's good there were no more.
I scrounged the food to feed them, not an item from the store.

There was a kindergarten class; I made it every day.
I met some kids; when work was done I was allowed to play.

But if I came in late from play and hadn't fed each pet.
I felt the belt upon my legs until my pants were wet.
I'm thankful for my brothers and my sister, siblings three.
For in your anger they would get the belt, along with me.
It didn't seem to matter who did what, who was to blame.
The belt came down on all our legs; we got it just the same.

I knew each day when you returned from that old factory.
The day was bad, your mood was grim and you would be angry.
I lived in fear; there was no love; I quaked when you were there.
I didn't know till I grew up that this was just not fair.

One day my mother told me she had bought a farm, again.
It had some pears, a tractor and a rooster with a hen.
Though you were not that happy, you did finally say, "Okay".
We'll have some cows along with pears, and maybe grow some hay.
If I thought you had worked before, it barely scratched the scratch.
You set your standards high; so high that no one else could match.
You worked all day and night times, too; I rarely saw your face.
Your absence didn't hurt at all; I never felt disgrace.

My mom left you and took us kids, my sister, brothers, too.
She gave us all the option; live with her or live with you.
My older brother, out of high school; went out on his own.
My sister, little brother and I went to our new home.
I missed the farm and schoolmates who had meant so much to me.
I tried, but I could not adapt to life in this city.
So after several months I left my mom to live with you.
Back with my friends and on the farm with lots of work to do.

Each day we walked our different paths; we barely talked at all.
Alone at home; I went to school; I played each kind of ball.

We worked together some; we had to milk the cows each day.
We sprayed the trees with pesticides; we harvested the hay.

At last we lived liked two adults; no fights, but still no praise.
Then sudden as a lightening strike, you started a new phase.
The "fear of God" became your guiding principle of life.
You read the bible night and day, as it replaced your wife.

In all those years I never once was held in your embrace.
You never said, "I love you, Son", at least not to my face.
Back then I didn't wonder, for each child was just the same.
It's like you were embarrassed; that we made you feel the shame.
In school I was a student; studied hard and got all "A's".
I played all sports; took drama, too, and starred in high school plays.
Not once in all those years did I see you attend a game.
To me it seemed your days were bad, with every day the same.

It went like that and nothing changed; life okay, but not grand.
One final time you beat me, and I didn't raise a hand.
A senior at the high school, I arrived with bloody face.
That I refused to press a charge became your saving grace.

When you became a "Witness" it was clear right from the start.
The family wouldn't make it and it further broke apart.
Because of you, for forty years, my brother disappeared.
I lost my sis for twenty; then she finally reappeared.
I wonder if you're proud of whom you were; what you became.
Wherever you have landed, are your actions still the same?

You said you'd be at God's right hand; you told me every day.
When my time comes I'll end up in another place, I pray.

I'm awfully disappointed, and some anger's still inside.
A kid's life shouldn't be that way; it was a bumpy ride.

And I felt sorrow for my mom until the day she died.
Such bitterness was not required, if only you had tried.

Our lives become the product of the things that we have learned.
We walk across a trestle and sometimes the bridge is burned.
And only if we do what's right, develop our worldview,
will love be spread throughout the world to more than just a few.
We live our lives the way we're taught by parents, teachers, too.
Thank God, I learned from many or I might have been like you.
My life became quite positive; the negatives were banned.
My father's gone; he lived his life the way that he had planned.

We're each alone before we're born, although there's lots of fuss.
And we're alone again when our Creator calls for us.
But in between we have some time; the choice we make is free.
I've walked the walk; I'm now exactly who I want to be.
I'm now a man of seventy; my kids are now adults.
I'm proud of each and love them; they get praise, never insults.
I tell them that I love them when we meet and when we part.
When distance comes between us, then I write them from my heart.

It's been my goal for years and it is what I want to be,
a role model to all my kids, with love that they can see.
So they will love their parents and their children, siblings, too.
And such a poem they'll never write to tell what fathers do.

FATHER AND EXTENDED FAMILY—
ANGER TO RAGE

My father treated anger in a very special way.
We kids would come home happy after we'd been out to play.
He'd seem to find some little thing that one of us did wrong.
Then with a belt on our bare legs he'd prove that he was strong.
For years we got the belt this way; what else can children do?
My brothers' and my sister's legs had scars, as mine did, too.
It happened much too frequently. We lived in constant fear.
Sometimes we'd simply try to hide when we knew he was near.

I know he lost his sanity when he was in a rage.
It didn't matter who he beat, a child of any age.
The welts would rise; the blood would flow; he didn't seem to care.
At times like this we children lived a horrible nightmare.
He'd lose complete control; his world would seem to fade from sight.
Yet there was no excuse, for beating children is not right.
We never got a chance to even try to understand.
Obscenities flowed from his mouth; the belt was in his hand.

Yet when the rage had passed, he was as normal as can be.
He never said, "I'm sorry" to my siblings or to me.
But that is no surprise at all; I never heard him say,
"I love you, Son" or maybe just, "let's go outside and play".

His anger dominated everything about his life.
I never saw him hug or kiss my mother, yes, his wife.
My siblings and I never heard a single word of praise.
Instead we shuddered when he went into an insane craze.
For years and years we lived this way, in fear of what would come.
For any little thing we did, or he might just feel bum.
He'd lose all sense of balance as his rage consumed his soul.
It's like he had to beat his kids so he'd achieve some goal.

My mother never intervened, though she would cry inside.
His hate and fury raged, while leather straps tore through our hide.
Until one day she'd had enough and left without a word,
and took us kids away with her, like a migrating bird.

And just like that my father changed; he studied night and day.
He learned to speak with God; for many hours each day he'd pray.
He'd saved himself and now it was his call to minister
to people whom he met and they did not need to concur.
It took the loss of family for my dad to realize,
his rage and fury cost him what had been life's greatest prize.
Estranged from all who should have loved him; living all alone,
he finally turned to God to help him heal his heart of stone.

When you react with anger it's not great, but it's okay.
It's natural; it's quite human when something has ruined your day.
Your anger is constructive if it's used the way it should.
With energy increased, you're now prepared to do some good.

When anger turns to rage it's not constructive, any way.
You're deaf and blind; don't listen to what other people say.
Adrenaline flows through your blood; you loose complete control.
The God within you fades away, as if you've lost your soul.
Destruction then results from every action that you take.
Without a sense of value, there's no telling what you'll break.
It may be something physical, emotional or worse.
Destruction of a soul mate's love; more bitter than a curse.

The damage done by rage is something you cannot repair.
To hurt another human being isn't ever fair.
It doesn't matter if you are forgiven or your not.
The ones who love you most will always be the most distraught.

It happens sometimes when we're young; we cry; then scream some more.
We kick a little, raise some hell and roll around the floor.

Our mommy and our daddy want to find out what is wrong.
They cater to these outbursts; we discover who is strong.
As time goes by we grow a bit; we've learned an awful lot.
Our memory's pretty good; we've won most skirmishes we've fought.
We scream a bit, then shout some more and kick what we can see.
It's worked for others down through time; it might just work for me.

Now anger won't do real harm until it turns to rage.
On Grandpa's farm I learned this at a very early age.
My Grandpa had a horse in which he took the greatest pride.
He was a jet-black stallion that he truly loved to ride.

A winter storm had left its mark with drifts of snow and mud.
Not fazed, Grandpa went out to ride his horse through all this crud.
Hoofs stuck, the stallion bolted; threw Grandpa into the mire.
His anger quickly turned to rage; my God was he on fire.
He stormed into the barn and there he found a length of chain.
Then into the corral he went to give that horse some pain.
He beat his horse; he beat him twice; he beat the horse some more.
He cursed; his blood was boiling as he evened up the score.
The horse tried to retaliate; his hoofs struck empty air.
My grandpa had a chain and so the battle wasn't fair.
The horse was bleeding from his neck and up across his head.
He lay there mixed in blood and mud; now Grandpa's horse was dead.

When Grandpa lost control someone was going to feel his wrath.
In rage he'd strike out mindlessly and damn the aftermath.
My brother felt his rage just once, and that was sad, indeed.
He had the scars for life, and these were scars he did not need.

Grandpa and Grandma had eleven kids throughout their life.
I learned that Grandma was more of a mother than a wife.
Five boys survived and every one grew up with Grandpa's rage.
I guess you'd say the boys were products of their parentage.
Yes, Grandpa's oldest son did just exactly what you'd think.

His anger turned to rage when he had alcohol to drink.
Then one spring morning after he'd been partying all night;
his hangover was no excuse; wild rage is never right.
He had a dog, a Shepherd that his wife and kids adored.
In contests, herding cattle, he'd soon won every award.
The Shepherd brought the cattle in for milking twice a day.
Instinctively he'd do his work; then with the kids he'd play.
Hung over with a headache, the whole world seemed angry, red.
My uncle didn't want to work; he'd rather be in bed.
His dog had brought the cattle in; his work was now all done.
He jumped and ran in circles; he was happy, having fun.
The Shepherd then approached my uncle, looking for a treat.
Sometimes when all his work was done, he'd get a piece of meat.
There, sitting on his hind legs, with his two front paws he'd beg.
Instead, my uncle threw a hammer, breaking his dog's leg.

It shattered and could not be set; his Shepherd was put down.
An incident like this was soon the talk of this small town.
It didn't faze my uncle; how destructive rage can be.
And so just like my folks, his wife then left him; set him free.

You'd think he might have learned to quell his temper and his rage.
Not so, his temper ruled him like a lion out of its cage.
He argued with his brother, who lived down a lane from him.
When anger turns to rage, then the results are always grim.
Their fists were not enough this time, a shovel and a gun.
Blood spewing from a gash so badly he could barely run.
Yet run he did, and luckily the shots all missed their mark.
Or otherwise my uncle, from this earth would disembark.

As an adult I've only once felt rage beyond control.
And I thank God for limits that he planted in my soul.
I'm probably a better man for what he did to me.
The benefits, when it occurred, were not that clear to see.

Back then a big executive, a man of corporate deeds,
integrity and honesty, the hallmarks that one heeds.
And I was as dependable as anyone could be.
For service to my fellow men was my priority.

He said he was a "friend" on that first day, when we two met.
"If you'll help me then I'll help you; you'll never have to fret."
I did my work and labored almost like a maniac.
And for that he, "my friend", then slipped a sharp knife in my back.
For he convinced the "powers to be" that he's the better man.
The corporate "dummies" listened for these "gods" don't give a damn.
I soon found I was all alone; a captain with no ship.
He'd promised me the world and then he'd given me the slip.

He'd pulled a rotten trick on me, entirely unfair.
I found a way to "square the score", though he'd not be aware,
that I had instigated what would now become his bane.
When I was through he thought he'd been run over by a train.
His staff was fired and so was he, all victims of his lust.
I hope he finally understands the value placed on trust.
It's something at the time I had to do; it wasn't fun.
So then I knelt and prayed that God forgive what I had done.

Now peace replaced the rage that had consumed me, totally.
Just like a miracle I shed the rage and I was free.
Now, anger, rage and fury are just words, gone from my soul.
I've substituted happiness, a worthy lifestyle goal.

I'm sad inside each time I see a parent strike a child.
I want to shout, "You're acting like an animal gone wild".
God gave us all the gift of life; it's there for every one.
It's in the soul of humans, round the world, under the sun.
Another gift from God is "self control", a gift, indeed.
It's like a governor controlling glut, excess and greed.

And it is there to neutralize your rage, right from the start,
replacing it with love that overflows within your heart.

Yes, hate and rage, revenge, retaliation, much the same.
It doesn't really matter who is right or who's to blame.
They're equally destructive; not a one does any good.
Replace each one with love; become the person that you should.

TOO YOUNG—TOO LATE

No second chance; I had just one.
The victim is my firstborn son.
His mother, only seventeen;
adulthood, nothing in between.
A child too soon, we didn't know
how much our love for him would grow.
What is responsibility?
Mom, Dad; new son; a family!
A diaper change, a little food,
his cries affect his mother's mood.
I work so I cannot be there,
to comfort him; to stroke his hair.
Now in our room, we sleep at night.
He's in his crib, out of our sight.
We hear so softly his small cries.
His needs we just don't realize.
His crying stops! We sleep some more.
No further sound beyond the door.
The morning silence wakens me.
At my son's bassinet I see
him lying there, two small legs spread.
His lifeless body in his bed!
"Crib death" the coroner would say.
My heart's been heavy since that day.
Would my son be alive if I
had answered his last pleading cry?

GOD'S GIFT—FOUR CHILDREN

It's taken almost all my life and uses all I've got,
to show my love for family, for my kids I love a lot.
I never hugged my father nor my mother or siblings.
I feel this loss; it's in my head and in my ears it rings.
I don't know why; I know they cared and love was in their heart.
We weren't demonstrative folks and not a one would start.
I wish I could have changed all that in my own family.
The habit held; it's stronger than the love that burns in me.

It doesn't do a lot to say to kids that are adult.
I wish I'd held you in my arms. It's now a damned insult.
We can't turn back the hands of time, no matter how we try.
The best I have are words for you, before more time goes by.

TO LAURA

No baby ever was as cute, all pink with long dark hair.
I wanted everyone to know that you were mine to share.
I gave you your first bath at home; you cried a little bit.
Into you mother's arms you went, you couldn't even sit.

It wasn't long until you wore your dresses with great grace.
With curled hair and sparkling eyes, a smile upon your face.
What greater joy could a dad have than feel his love for you?
Why didn't I give you some hugs like other fathers do?

You grew into a lady who is beautiful and bright.
And everything you tried to do, you did with all your might.
In high school you achieved each goal, the leader of the team.
The graduation speech you gave surpassed my every dream.

In college I was proud of you; your part-time work was great.
With three siblings behind to school, it helped us pay the freight.
No child was more responsible, deserving of my love.
Why couldn't I just hug you close, and thank God up above?

The years have passed and now you have a family of your own.
I thank the Lord you've learned to love your girls as they have grown.
You'll never have to look way back, with little thoughts of sin.
And wish you'd been more loving then, the way I'd rather been.

TO JANICE

How many ways might I explain how dear you are to me?
You've been a special daughter, for all time, eternity.
I've never told you how I felt when you were second born.
I held two jobs; I rarely slept; at times I was forlorn.

Aunt Emily came down to help; she fed you, washed your things.
Your mom and I, we both were gone to get what money brings.
Before I knew it you had grown, a teen so smart and strong.
I worked so hard we barely met, and that was very wrong.

I hardly know what happened, you're as bright as you can be.
The honor of my life was when you came to work for me.
You did the things that I had done, and then you did some more.
With all you did there was no need to ever keep the score.

I felt a pain clear through me when the car hit you that day.
For it was tough to realize all I could do was pray.
And then the crash with Heidi as you drove to visit friends.
I can't explain just how or why, for no one comprehends.

We haven't hugged like people do; it's not the way we are.
The time is gone; it's way behind and I live with that scar.
In spite of all that's gone before, and even going now,
I love you Jan and pray each day you feel that love, somehow.

TO PEGGY

We're both the third born, you and I, a special place to be.
When you arrived we had a home just like a family.
Aunt Emily was there for you to help, just like before.
How happy can a father be; a daughter, just one more?

It wasn't long before we knew you have a special gift.
You're happy and you laugh and you give everyone a lift.
You breezed though school; what need was there to study—crack the books?
With talent and with wisdom; with some humor and good looks.

You teamed up with your sister, Jan, and tennis you did play.
The other teams learned right away they'd ever rue that day.
You went right through the season and you didn't loose a set.
If I had known you were so good, a fortune I'd have bet.

I cannot mention college for you really got me there.
You didn't see the classrooms, but you lived with lots of flair.
As an adult with your three kids you have so much to give.
I often wonder how you cope; all that it takes to live.

I love you and respect you for who you've grown up to be.
I only wish you had received more love and help from me.
Now as we speak I hope you know, with every word I say.
How much I love and cherish you with every passing day.

TO BRADLEY

Son you were it, a real gift, a boy to call my own.
My father I had hoped would be my friend when I was grown.
So that's the way I wanted it, when you were very small.
Some day we'd play together, like some tennis or baseball.

The sixties kept me running while you grew; we'd barely meet.
How soon you were a bright young man, now ready to compete.
Some time was held to be with you; like dads and other gents.
I damn near burst, I was so proud you won all those events.

Your swimming and your tennis, wow, how laudably I'd blow.
And baseball, too, I loved the scene, more than you'll ever know.
For every dad I've ever known not only wants what's best.
But hopes his son will be the one that's better than the rest.

Your years in school, you made me proud; no problem anywhere!
With academics, sports and friends, you demonstrated flair.
Then suddenly you went away, the college of your choice.
No letters passed between us and I didn't hear your voice.

You're now a dad; you have a son and wife, so beautiful.
You've learned so well there is no chance you'll ever be the fool.
For I let time just pass me by. It drifts away from you.
I love you son; I hope you know, as only dads can do.

FIRST-BORN DAUGHTER

An evening in the fall, a Friday night so long ago!
Though winds and fog chilled every bone, at least there was no snow.
We thought we'd have a bite to eat and then take in a show.
But you did not agree; that's not where you wanted to go.

You moved around with energy, you'd not done that before.
There wasn't any question that you wanted out, for sure.
We went straight to the hospital and checked in, straight away.
The nurse that met us at the door said you were on your way.
It wasn't very long until that place was a beehive.
The nurse at the workstation said that you would soon arrive.
I sat there in the waiting room, a magazine in hand.
They said, "You have a daughter"; oh, that feeling was so grand.
And then I got to see you in the nursery bassinet.
Your skin was cherub pink; your hair was just a little wet.
Dark brown, your hair was thick and long; it covered both your ears.
That picture's in my memory; it's been there throughout the years.

There never was a "first born" who was half as cute as you.
You mitigated every fear of what we'd have to do
to raise you to adulthood, dealing with the aftermath.
In fact when you got home, I got to give you your first bath.

A generation, then another; then eight years have passed.
I pray that you'll be blessed and that your happiness will last.
For every time you've reached a goal, your dad's been happy, too.
Like every dad, I'll always want the very best for you.
Now in your middle age, you've done much more than I could hope.
You've conquered every challenge and you've shown that you can cope.
Two loving daughters and a super guy enhance your life.
I know that Jon agrees; you've been the perfect mom and wife.

I pray you find great happiness in every passing day.
And love transcends the distance when your family is away.
I pray that your companions are good health, prosperity.
And Jon's love warms your heart and you return it, totally.

A LITTLE BIRTHDAY TRIBUTE

Yes, you are something special from the moment you arrive.
A dad who'd lost his firstborn son; I prayed that you'd survive.
Survive you did and so much more, you filled a father's dream.
The child that you became sure helped to build my self-esteem.

My daughter you will always be, no matter what your age.
And it's my hope throughout our lives we're both on the "same page",
communicating often about interests that we share.
For I love you abundantly, I hope you are aware.

A daughter, "yes"! A sibling too! A leader without fear!
Your sisters and your brother; they are close to you, My Dear.
You carved a path as you broke trail; each sibling watched as you
built on a strong foundation, doing all that you could do.

Yes, then you found the "greatest guy" and he became your mate.
Your "plan"; it wasn't chance; luck of the draw, it wasn't fate.
And if you were the ideal daughter; sibling and much more,
you then became Jon's perfect wife; the gal he could adore.

If that were not enough, you carried on and soon you earned
the right to practice medicine; a nurse, how much you learned!
I've bragged so much I'm boring to my family and my friends.
But I'll keep bragging till my life here on this world ends.

And still the best is yet to come, two daughters of your own.
You sacrifice to raise them, up until they both are grown.
You always put your husband and your daughters first in line.
For you get your rewards from them. That does make life divine.

What things might I have done for you to help along the way?
It really doesn't matter now; what else is there to say?
I love you more than I can tell. I love your family, too.
And on through time I pray life brings the very best for you.

DAUGHTER'S FIRST HALF CENTURY

A child does not remain a child; each gains maturity.
Yet, to a parent, a child's a child; that's how they'll always be.
It doesn't matter what the age or how they may behave.
They'll be their parents' children till their parents go to their grave.
You may be fifty years of age; it happened, oh so fast.
I blinked and you were grown and gone; your childhood couldn't last.
You're off to college; on your own, it seems like yesterday.
I see you every day then just like "that" you've gone away.

Yes, that's the plan, the "western way", nuclear families spread.
It's right, yet it's a time in life that parents always dread.

Then out of college you've a beau; a warm, bright, gentle guy.
You want to marry right away; a dad does not ask, "Why?"
He knows you have a life to live. He wishes you the best.
So you'll find love and happiness in everything you quest.
Three thousand miles away you settle to begin your life.
Your dad and husband both are sure you'll be a perfect wife.
And that proves true, and more as you begin your family.
That you're a perfect mother, too, your husband will agree.

You bring your family to the west to visit every year.
Each speaks; we listen to what every parent wants to hear.
You're happy and your life's fulfilled; your family's happy, too.
Our granddaughters, we're proud of them, and also proud of you.

I pray that you'll be happy for as long as you may live.
That you'll receive God's blessings in abundance, as you give!

DAUGHTER ON MOTHER'S DAY

This father takes great pride in what his daughter has become.
It doesn't matter how she lives her life, he won't succumb
to anything that happens that would ever compromise,
his love, it's unconditional; there is on "otherwise".

And even more, he cherishes that she's a mother now.
The model for her children, she's the best God will allow.
Although her children are "adult" she loves them just the same.
No matter who does what to whom, she never casts the blame.
She helps them out in every way, yet lets them do "their thing".
By doing this, she wisely knows the happiness they bring.
So on this Mother's Day, my Dear, I pray your children know,
how much you've sacrificed for them before you let them go.
Show their appreciation for the love that they receive.
And thank you for your guidance toward the goals that they achieve.

May every day be filled with joy; may energy abound.
And pleasant memories fill your mind with each and every sound.
May love so fill your heart that there's no room for misery.
With caring love from all your friends so you'll live happily.
May every "problem" change its form into a worthwhile goal.
And may appreciation live and grow within your soul.

And finally from your father, from this distant place I live,
I pray you'll have requited love returned for love you give.
May friends and family let you know the love they have for you.
And they accept you as you are in everything you do.

HAPPY MOTHER'S DAY!

A FATHER'S REMORSE—AN UNINTENDED HURT

It can't get any worse for I'm as low as one can feel.
Remorse drops me to depths into a world that is surreal.
It doesn't matter what the cause or what I did or said.
It isn't realistic, but I wish that I were dead.

I can't remove the hurt I caused when I made that mistake.
There's nothing I can do; there's not an action I can take.
I can't unsay a word I've said; it cannot be undone.
I can't un-write a letter that I've sent to anyone.
I say I'm sorry and I am, but not a soul will care.
I swear I'll not do that again. It doesn't help to swear.
I feel remorse as it attacks my stomach, then my heart.
I know it's in my mind, but it is tearing me apart.

I want to share my feelings with another—anyone.
I know the hurt I caused is mine alone; it isn't fun.
I struggle, for I feel there must be something I can do.
She won't accept my letter and she won't talk to me, too.

I sit alone; all hope is gone; through tears I cannot see.
I've lost the love of someone who is very dear to me.
And worse perhaps, what I've held dear for all these many years.
With one dumb thoughtless act, a piece of me just disappears.
There is no pain as great as being hopelessly remorse.
Life seems to end, there is no path; I cannot chart a course.
The world as I remember it does not exist today.
This blackness envelops my mind. The pain is here to stay.

I know that there's a God above who watches over me.
I pray he knows what's in my heart; I pray that he'll agree.
And if that God is also there above the ones I hurt.

He'll let them know that what I wrote was just a thoughtless blurt.
I'll have the scars that this has caused until the day I die.
It will not matter what I do, or say, or how I try.
I'm left with just my hope that I can make it one more day.
And, over time that this remorse will somehow melt away!

BREAKING SILENCE

I'm taking a small liberty; I hope that you don't care.
I think of you each day and I do hope that you're aware,
I love you unconditionally, a love that's never quit.
This feeling's with me every day; it sometimes tests my grit.
So once more on your birthday I am going to break my word.
The silence that I promised; yet that promise was absurd!

I pray you've had a happy year with friends and family.
That you and Jon are healthy and enjoy prosperity!
And on this very special day your children call to say,
how much they love; appreciate you, every single day.

I know that I'm not perfect and I've disappointed you.
Yet should you ever need me, there is nothing I won't do,
to give what I can give, to make your life a bit more fun,
to make the dark clouds disappear, replacing them with sun.

Time passes and I miss you; miss the messages you sent.
Almost a year has passed; don't have a clue where the time went.
Yet every day I've missed you; hoped that I would hear from you.
I guess there's no forgiveness, and there's nothing I can do.

But I will live on hope that "time will heal"; the hurt will end.
The feelings separating us; that you'll somehow transcend!
That you'll again become my daughter, share your life with me.
And differences will not divide us, when we disagree.

So on this special day, I wish you every happiness.
May family, friends express their love; and may you never guess,
the value that I place on every thought I have of you.
I hope you're having a great life and a great birthday, too.

SECOND BORN

My daughter, Jan, was second born, a strong and healthy girl.
Her hair was short and thin and so there was no bow or curl.
She made a lot of noise to let me know she was okay.
Some how I knew at once she'd be a special girl, someday.

When Jan was born I worked two jobs; I didn't have much time.
As healthy as a horse, I was just entering my prime.
We barely got to meet till she was old enough for school.
It took half of my life to realize I'd been a fool.
Do fathers ever get to know their daughters when they're small?
Is work a good excuse they use to serve as a catchall?
For several years I barely realized that she was there.
She grew into a bright young girl before I was aware.

When Jan was just eleven we moved down the hill, a mile.
She liked the school where we had lived; she stayed there for a while.
We lived across the street from a small swim and racquet club.
For lots of kids on the swim team, our home became a hub.
The swim club was a special place where I'd participate.
At swim meets parents volunteered; some would officiate.
I went to school so I could learn to do it all just right.
I timed and judged and sometimes I provided oversight.
Jan practiced every stroke; she was the best in butterfly.
She beat the girls on other teams, no matter how they'd try.
In freestyle she swam with the best; the heats were always close.
I'd brag of her accomplishments. I'd even get verbose.

Through middle and then high school Jan competed with the best.
The challenge didn't matter; she was up for every test.
She took up tennis for one year to represent her school.
She partnered with her sister. It was like an April fool.

They played against each team and won; they didn't lose a set.
Jan didn't even feel she had to wear an amulet.
No person but the student knows just how much work it takes.
They study late into the night and then they need some breaks.
I certainly don't know how hard she worked to be the best.
She never asked for help with an assignment or a test.
Her grades were always at the top. Jan never did complain.
As almost a perfectionist, it had to be a strain.

Then walking in a crosswalk with her sister, she was hit.
The driver of the vehicle was something of a twit.
Thrown several feet into the air, she landed on her head.
As angry as I was, I thanked my God she was not dead.
She got a little settlement; enough to pay the bills
for hospitals and doctors and for the prescription pills.
There wasn't any left for all her suffering and pain.
The whole damned thing went down like I had mush inside my brain.

The summer after high school she agreed to work for me.
A student programmer was all that I asked her to be.
Before the summer ended her boss asked if she would stay.
He wanted her full time so she would be there every day.
She made her own decision for she didn't like the work.
Although a junior officer, she felt she was a clerk.
She quit; she didn't really like the work right from the start.
Just like a father, when she left, it almost broke my heart.

She played a lot of soccer and she was a runner, too.
And marathons were races that she seemed to like to do.
She entered lots of races that were held for charity.
They exercised her body and her generosity.
In soccer she was good; she always played the game to win.
A foul and muscles pulled; a tendon tore beneath the skin.
She had some surgery to fix the damage that was done.
Two years to heal with therapy; that's not a lot of fun.

She went to school at Cal State where she studied for a while.
She joined the Navy and her clothes were now a different style.
We met in Coronado at a Mexican Café,
then walked along the sidewalks near the San Diego bay.

To be a firefighter, she took training with the rest.
It wasn't hard for her, for she completed every test.
But fighting fires wasn't the career she had in mind.
She looked around at other jobs to see what she could find.
A lifestyle laced with friends, with work and playing soccer, too.
And as she grew mature, she left behind what she outgrew.
She worked in a facility that made and packaged yeast.
The shift work they required did not affect her in the least.

Then came a time I needed help in finance, once again.
It had to be a person that I wouldn't have to train.
Jan stepped right in and just like that, she had the job in hand.
She also served investors that I really couldn't stand.
It's hard to tell the joy I felt with Jan there by my side.
We had a lot of fun, but also shared a bumpy ride.
Each day when she came in to work, my being filled with pride,
without complaint, with no concern; she took it all in stride.

I've never worked with anyone who did a job so well.
She's bright beyond belief, and she can scrupulously spell.
Her math's above reproach and her vocabularies great!
In my eyes, she's the best. She's an employee, laureate.

Our business fell on hard times, and Jan felt that she should leave.
It's times like this, the cause be damned; that makes a father grieve.
Jan moved away up north to where her sister had a place.
To me it was like she'd just left the earth for outer space.
Just after that I lost my wealth. The business closed its doors.
Investors and the creditors stalked me like wanton whores.
I moved up north to get away and start a new career.
To locate near my daughters with a life that's less severe.

By now I'd lost the home my wife had counted on for life.
My world was shattered; nothing left; I even lost my wife.
For she could not forget the life we'd built through all those years.
And I'd lost everything, except a few small souvenirs.
Without her love, I'd now successfully lost her respect.
All feelings gone, I found that we had nothing to protect.
I'm bankrupt and have only dreams to move my life ahead.
And hope Jan will communicate sometime before I'm dead.

My life is rich because of hope and dreams that move me on.
But there's a gaping hole inside, through which my Jan has gone.
I don't know what to do but change this poem to a refrain,
repeating prayers that she'll return into my life again.

HAPPY BIRTHDAY

A birthday is a special time; it marks a great event.
We celebrate a special gift; a gift that God has sent.
We also celebrate the end; a year has come and gone.
Another will begin tomorrow, at the light of dawn.

A daughter is a precious gift and you're that gift for me.
I loved you as a little girl; I loved you totally.
And as you grew to womanhood, I loved you even more.
A father's love cannot be measured; there's no keeping score.

There's beauty in each memory and I have a ton to share.
Nostalgic moments here with Pat, she knows how much I care.
I've shared my hopes and dreams for you, prayers for your happiness.
There's nothing you can say or do to make me love you less.

Such love is unconditional; there is no compromise.
It endures life's vicissitudes, as we grow old and wise.
In fact it may just grow and deepen as the years go by.
It's inborn, it's innate, and its' so natural I don't try.

I pray that you enjoy each day, that you achieve success.
That you attain each goal you've set and never have to guess.
That you have a companion with whom you can share your life!
And happiness consumes your soul, eliminating strife.

I pray that as each year goes by, you have a loving mate,
a love that flows from her to you; that you reciprocate.
For love requited is a stairway to your Paradise.
It makes each day worth living, and each night so awfully nice.

So have a Happy Birthday—this "commercial's" from we two.
Yes, Pat and I wish all the best in every thing you do.

THIRD BORN

Four decades and a half now you've been here inside my heart.
You've met life's every challenge, and each win set you apart.
Time passes like a cyclone as the years go flying by.
These things I need to say to you sometime before I die.

The wind blows leaves along the street; they're graceful in the breeze.
Majestically the mighty oak stands tall among the trees.
And each in its own way brings pleasant memories of you, Dear.
For grace and strength exemplify your life, sans hate and fear.

The sun has shown on both of us; there's been a little rain.
Yet you have struggled through the dark and found the sun again.
A typhoon or a hurricane may soak you to the skin.
You lose it all; yet find the strength, to once again begin.

On days when I was lonelier than you may ever know.
Trapped there inside the things I'd done, with no place I could go.
You took the time you didn't have; you stayed there for a while.
I cherish every thought you shared, each frown and every smile.

You've given me grandchildren; I could never ask for more.
I hope I've helped you some influencing what they stand for.
And as they all become adults, each seeking life's rewards.
I pray their work and deeds make them proud of their own records.

The mountains and Great Plains may separate the lives we live.
You're always here inside my heart; it's filled with love I give.
Remember when life's bleak; you're into shit up to your butt.
Your father's love will stand the test of time, no matter what.

"OLD MAN" TO SON

How long ago; how many years; a lifetime, more or less?
I can't remember clearly; so much time; I'll have to guess.
Almost a half a century, my God, it's been so long.
Just "yesterday" a baby; he's a man now, proud and strong!

Right from the start he ran and played; excelled at what he did.
In school he got great grades; yes, he was always a smart kid.
Then he became competitive in different sports, galore.
He'd take the gauntlet; conquer it, and then he'd ask for more.
In every sport he undertook, how proud I was of him.
He took to water like a fish; I loved the way he'd swim.
In baseball and in basketball, a team player, through and through!
He helped his teammates look their best; he knew what he must do.
He never looked for glory, yet he gave it all he had.
I sat there in the audience, honored to be his dad.

I played a lot of tennis as a kid, then as a man.
Opponents got no "quarter", always played the best I can.
His freshman year in high school he decided he would play.
In one short year he's "number one", what else is there to say.
He "creamed" me every time we played; my best was not enough.
Yet it filled me with pride and joy; he really had the "stuff".

My son, he's now a father with a teenage son to raise.
He won't wait till he's old as me to give his son due praise.
Yes, he's the man and father every man would like to be.
And more than that, he's always been "the greatest" son for me.
I couldn't ask for more than he has been to this "old man".
Four decades and six years now and I'm still his greatest fan.
I pray that he find happiness, a little more each day.
So his life is as full as mine, when he is "old and gray".

HAPPY BIRTHDAY, BRAD!

MY NEW STEPSON

Each year you stop again to see the way that you should go.
It's on the anniversary of the date that you were born.
Though days fly by it seems to you, your progress is so slow.
Your mind is fresh, your spirit strong; your body is well worn.

You're forty-eight today, and count each day as it goes by,
still searching for the meaning, why the Lord has placed you here.
You want to know just who you are, the how—the where—the why.
You want to face each day anew, devoid of any fear.

At forty-eight you've passed the usual "mid-life" crisis age.
Yet there is much you wish to do while you're still young and strong.
You look back at the years and realize the World's a stage,
with you the only actor, whether you've been right or wrong.

While others live their lives, you interact from time to time.
Yet they are not important in the world in which you live.
They're simply "extras" passing through, a silent pantomime.
There's nothing you have asked of them, and nothing you must give.

You look into the mirror and see the face that's staring back.
The hair is graying, eyes are gaunt; deep pools within each eye.
This person staring back looks like he's ready to attack.
Is this the man that you've become? Yes, did you really try?

Relaxing for a moment, then you see a smile appear.
A handsome dude is there, with warmth and love projecting through.
You stand back and admire the face; you move up very near.
The mirror doesn't lie. This gorgeous guy is really you.

The way you feel each day is pretty much what you decide.
You take an attitude with you from when you wake each morn.
You may be single most your life or you may take a bride.
You'll grow the way that you decide, right from the day you're born.

So you can blame the world or other people that you meet,
for everything that happens that upsets the way you feel.
And you may never win or think that others always cheat.
It's your perception that makes this, your life, so very real.

In poker you receive the cards the dealer gives to you.
The deck is shuffled and he deals each one from off the top.
It doesn't matter what the game or who is playing, too.
For you decide if you will bet or if you want to stop.

So that's the way you live your life, just one deal at a time.
Sometimes you get a hand you'll bet; sometimes you throw it in.
When you are dealt a winning hand, it makes you feel sublime.
No matter how you bet the cards, you know you're going to win.

At other times it doesn't matter how you play the hand.
You've got to cut your losses and let others have a chance.
You throw your cards into the pot; you do not even stand.
That you would lose this hand is clear; it only takes a glance.

Today your life begins again; it's just like yesterday.
So what you do and how you feel is really up to you.
For you may wish to mix a lot of work with breaks for play.
Or redesign your goals and then begin your life anew.

You're just about the brightest guy that I have ever met;
with interests ranging broader than this earth on which we live.
You ask some searching questions, from occult to etiquette.
And many times you go beyond the answers I can give.

Yet every time we talk I learn a little more from you,
about a plumbing job you have, or book that you have read,
or something philosophical, or projects that you do.
You may discuss life's wonders, or what happens when you're dead.

For now I just want you to know how much this means to me.
To have you take the time to share the things that you hold dear.
Each broadens my perspective as a different world I see.
As you enhance this life I live with every passing year.

Son, all the best to you in everything you ever do.
Wherever you may find yourself within this world we share.
May happiness be friends with you; may love be present, too.
So you'll enjoy the life you live; your Mom and I do care.

PERNICIOUS PERSONALITY

Your anger's there most every day, we see it in your eyes.
An aura all around you; your demeanor never lies.
Yet every now and then, you wear a smile upon your face.
No sign of anger anywhere, there's simply not a trace.
You're volatile, a little more than unpredictable.
We don't know if your cup's half empty or if it's half full.
It's taken me a year or two to find out who you are.
I broke my pick. I really haven't done that well, so far.

When you were in your teens you were a member of a cult.
So young, how could you understand what might be the result?
You broke away, but not until the damage had been done.
The cult has followed you through life, no matter how you've run.
The cult is in your mind; it's in your memory and what's more,
you cannot seem to find the happiness you had before.
Experience is something we acquire, both good and bad.
For you this is a tragic thing. It really makes us sad.

While you were in the service, memories of the cult were there.
You lived each day with torment, yet no person was aware
that you lived in a Hell on Earth; it filled your every thought.
You couldn't shake it; it was there, no matter how you fought.

So then when you faced life, it was a compromise, for sure.
You'd fought your battles every day, yet knew you'd lost the war.
You worked at this and that and finally settled on a trade.
Without commitment it's a "job"; a bit like a charade.
You can't quite make a living, always coming home to Mom.
Sans self-esteem you're just about explosive as a bomb.
It's little wonder you are parsimonious with life.
No personal or business goals, you even lost your wife.

You meet a lot of people, yet you do not have a friend.
You're all alone much of the time; it's been a lifelong trend.
Yet when we talk I sense your loneliness, beyond compare.
At times I feel your struggle and perceive your deep despair.
As people come into your life, each for a little while.
Your anger seems to disappear; your face glows with a smile.
And this may last for several days, a week or maybe two.
It ends before a friend is made; there's nothing we can do.

We live together in this house, it's home for Pat and me.
We're happy that you live with us; you're welcome as can be.
When you come home you disappear into your room to hide.
Or you'll spend hours all alone, locked in your shed outside.
No matter how we try, we cannot seem to reach your mind.
Sometimes we get the feeling there is nothing there to find.
No love, no caring feelings, no concern for anyone.
Alone and in an empty world, a world where there's no fun.

Now lots of folks get trapped inside a job that they don't like.
They make the best of what they have, a finger in the dike
until they find an opportunity to make a change,
accepting life the way it comes; that's not so very strange.
You look into a lot of fields; you take a class or two.
Yet plumbing seems to draw you back; there's little you can do.
You work a job or two and then you're idle for a week.
Your present isn't really great; your future's pretty bleak.

Your life keeps dealing you a hand of cards you cannot play.
Each time you almost win, your winning hand gets thrown away.
And every time you feel that you've got life by the short hair.
It slips right through your fingers and is gone; now is that fair?
Yet, no one said that everything in life is always fair.
In fact, a life that's perfect is a life that's very rare.
But if you have an attitude that's positive and strong,
your world will be a better place, and that's where you belong.

It's not that weather's sometimes good or it is sometimes bad.
It shouldn't make us happy and it mustn't make us sad.
The weather's just the weather; it is there for all of us.
How we respond is up to us; it does no good to fuss.
And that's the way your life might be, if you can understand
that we want to assist you and give you a helping hand.
For how we give is how we shall receive, and that's a law!
You won't accept. We cannot give, and that's the real flaw.

I'd give the use of my right arm to get inside your head.
Removing all the "junk" so there's just happiness instead.
So you awaken every day with goals to be achieved.
To know your life is purposeful, we'd really be relieved.

So Son, your mother joins me in this hope, yet prayer, we say,
may life be filled with lots of joy and happiness each day!
We pray you free yourself from any baggage from your past.
And hope you find that special gal to share your life, at last.

TOUGH LOVE

Tough love—the kind of love we hoped we'd never have to use.
Tough love—we give tough love to halt another's crude abuse.
Tough love—is never called for till the end is close, indeed.
Tough love—is the last effort for a loved one to succeed.

You've never said a "thank you" for the things we've done for you.
You've taken all we've given and ignored all that we do.
You've squandered everything we gave, without a word of thanks.
You discard all our efforts like they're petty, worthless pranks.

Tough love—that is the only kind of love you'll ever know.
Tough love—negates ambivalence, so it might help you grow.
Tough love—is all you'll ever know; that's all we've left to give.
Tough love—won't flow right through your heart like it's an empty sieve.

You've never been responsible for more than just a while.
Antagonistic to a fault; you rarely ever smile.
You live with hate; you're all alone, there's no one left to care.
It may be a harsh truth, but to respond "in kind" is fair.

Tough love—it is the only love you share with anyone.
Tough love—that's all there is for you, beneath the moon and sun.
Tough love—it's really sad, tough love is all that's left for you.
Tough love—that's all you'll ever have, till you do something new.

It's clear that you have never known the meaning of a friend.
You do not seem to care how many people you offend.
The men and women that you meet, find you are not sincere.
As long as you remain this way, friendship will not adhere.

Tough love—will help you make a friend, if you will start to care.
Tough love—won't need to haunt you if you'll just learn to be fair.
Tough love—you know, sans love you've lost the only friends you've had.
Tough love—sans love, you're all alone and that is oh, so sad!

You isolate yourself from all our earnest prayers for you.
Beyond our prayers there's little that is left for us to do.
For you've rejected everything that we've done in the past.
We must assume your attitude toward us will always last.

Tough love—now is the only love that we can give to you.
Tough love—is all you'll find for now, there's nothing left to do.
Tough love—is all that people get who cannot give love back.
Tough love—engenders anger and gives very little slack.

You're all alone from early every morning, every day.
The people you encounter don't have much they want to say.
And when the day has ended, you are all alone at night.
To live your life alone like this is wrong; it is not right.

Tough love—may be the only love you'll ever share at night.
Tough love—creates the negatives that fill your life with blight.
Tough love—is not the kind of love a guy gives to a gal.
Tough love—won't help you make a start; tough love is not your pal.

You work a bit; you make a little money, not that much.
Excuses may appease you, but they're just a feeble crutch.
Somehow you won't take on a job that gives you steady work
If it takes conscientiousness, it's something that you shirk.

Tough love—it breaks bad habits so you'll never need to crawl.
Tough love—will lift you up and you will never again fall.
Tough love—will open up your mind and let the sunshine in.
Tough love—creates an attitude that helps you love your kin.

You won't communicate about the things that trouble you.
You walk away and stay away; we don't know what to do.
We barely see you here inside the home that we provide.
It's like you want to disappear, to find shelter outside.

Tough love—accept this love and it will help your self-esteem.
Tough love—stops useless floundering and lets you join our team.
Tough love—you'll feel more sociable, with every word and thought.
Tough love—will give more meaning to each battle you have fought.

If all the love the family has for you just doesn't count.
If you cannot accept our love, no matter the amount.
If you will not become a part of our small family,
and pull your weight, then something needs to change; you must agree.

Tough love—yes, it enhances love your family has for you.
Tough love—it's the alternative for all you wouldn't do.
Tough love—will do much more for you than you can comprehend.
Tough love—we'll give this love to you, until the very end.

We'd gladly give our lives if it would bring you happiness.
We've lived with pain for many years, while watching your distress.
We pray that we can get inside your head and in your heart.
And somehow let you know that it is not too late to start.

Tough love—can start right now and let your life begin anew.
Tough love—can be replaced with family love we feel for you.
Tough love—the last resort, will only work if you agree.
Tough love—we give this love to you, with hope it makes you free.

TO MY GRANDCHILDREN

You may have heard the stories about when I was a small kid.
Up out of bed at four o'clock, the chores we children did.
Three miles we walked through sun or rain to make it to our school.
A strap upon our butt if we did not follow each rule!
No dates for teens without a chaperone, then in by ten.
Just holding hands; kiss on the cheek; that's how it was back then.
Respect for self and friends and more respect for Mom and Dad.
The Ten Commandments—Golden Rule—that's how we lived—not bad!
No intimacies! Nothing 'till a man and woman wed.
And only then did men and women share the marriage bed.
Each pure, a virgin, body, mind and soul before their God.
I know it seems old fashioned now; back then it wasn't odd.

I'd like to be of help but there is little I can give.
No set of guiding principles or "rules by which to live".
You see I'm from another time. The world is not the same.
To shackle you from days gone by would be an awful shame.

Let's jump ahead and search to find some principles that work.
If yours are not like others, it is not some stupid quirk.
Society has changed; some folks will say that it has grown.
You choose the rules that work for you; and they become your own.
Your life's a matter of beliefs; not anyone's but yours.
It's just the same for everyone; for priests; schoolmasters; whores.
The principles by which you live belong to only you.
In every situation, you will then know what to do.

Make peace with your Creator then you'll know what's right and wrong.
Articulate beliefs you have; beliefs will make you strong.
Be rigid when you know you're right; don't compromise belief.

Your friends will stand beside you, not behind you like a thief.
There is no choice when you are sure what's right, what you believe.
You'll make decisions properly; you'll never need to grieve.

And one more thing before we end this little "guiding light"!
A doctrine that endures, a social law that's always right!
The principle of "giving" is prosperity's first law.
The more you give the more you get; occurs without a flaw.
It doesn't matter, love or money, give, you'll soon agree.
Your gifts create a vacuum; it's then filled abundantly.

FROM SURROGATE TO REALITY

I met you just three months ago. The meeting wasn't fate!
I'd come across four states to finally be with my "new mate".
My "new mate" was to you, Dear, a good friend and guardian, too.
It was your mother's mother, your grandmother, whom I knew.

I knew how you would look because of pictures I'd received.
Two poses, each one beautiful, and I was soon relieved
that you seemed to, implicitly, with no complaint or wail,
accept into your life this guy known only by e-mail.
I wasn't sure we'd hit it off. I knew it would take time
to bridge the generation gap between your life and mine.
A gulf of over fifty years is wide as hell to jump.
Yet I had hoped to do just that and never feel a bump.

I realized that I might be intruding in your space.
Sometimes we find we're all mixed up, competing in life's race.
But any thoughts I might have had were quickly all dispelled.
Your loveliness disarmed me, as my feelings for you swelled.
You're prettier by far than in the pictures I received.
Your long blond hair is full and fair; I felt I'd been deceived.
You stood there like a model, glowing beauty; full of grace.
Your eyes sent me a welcome, a warm smile upon your face.

You're very strong from growing up with pain and tragedy.
You lost your folks; your grandma now provides you family.
You don't seem callous, bitter or regretful of this fate.
For all the time I've been with you, your attitude is great.

Each day I kind of marvel! You're more gorgeous than Eve's sin.
Your presence I can feel, for it's a beauty from within.
It only takes a moment, just a glance from you to me.
To realize you're full of love that's fighting to be free.

You're now a high school senior and attend Pomona High.
You study; you have classes; then you work; how time must fly.
You're up at six; it's school today; a meal you may have missed.
And after school you go to work; you're a projectionist.
It wasn't long till I found out you work most every day.
Your schedule doesn't give you a whole lot of time to play.
You have good friends, more than a few, and some I get to meet.
The guys seem nice. I shake their hand; the girls are downright sweet.

You have some dreams; they represent your new reality.
A doctor you'll one day become; your field is surgery.
To start into this new career you'll go right on to school.
You know a lot about the grind, for you are not a fool.
For someone who is young as you and knows what she will be,
is like a little miracle, and it impresses me.
A little luck, a little work, perhaps a little dough;
you just may make it to your goal; you are that tough, I know.

You have some living habits; they're a gal's routine each day.
They make me feel so welcome that it's here I want to stay.
You know too clean a house will always create lots of stress.
You also know a home should feature lots of happiness.
I see as every day goes by, a person more mature.
You're wise beyond your years right now; of that fact I am sure.
I'm so damned proud to be with you, and maybe give a hand.
There is no doubt that if you fall, on your two feet you'll land.

It is my dream, in fact my prayer, that friends we both can be.
I learn from you, and by life's quirks, you may learn some from me.
As years go by I hope we find some things in common, too.
And maybe then sometime I'll be a "grandfather" to you.

A BEAUTIFUL PERSON

You're statuesque! You're beautiful! What else is there to say?
Just being in your presence for a moment, makes our day.
Your aura, like a diamond, casts its prisms all around.
Your presence creates music; it is such a joyous sound.
Your eyes communicate your thoughts, their message always clear.
They speak in silent phrases, all the words we love to hear.
With kindness, understanding and an inner joy to see,
a single glance from you and we're as happy as can be.

We know you've lots of guys who live their life under your spell.
To them you're like a goddess, but you know that very well.
They cling to you, each with the hope that he will win your hand.
That you will not commit to one, they do not understand.
It's great to see young men who gather round you day and night.
If ever you selected one; my God there'd be a fight.
But somehow you are able to be "friends" with every one.
And just by being as you are, with you each guy has fun.

A testimony to the inner beauty you possess,
is how you manage life sans any hint of harmful stress.
It doesn't' matter whether it is work or play or school,
you're just exactly who you are; there is no other rule.
With no pretense, you make it look so easy to be you.
You bring a flow of caring love to everything you do.
And everyone around you grows a little more each day.
Yet, most of us must reconcile, someday you'll go away.

Yes, we are your grandparents and we watch the way you grow.
We share in your "exploits" knowing the seeds you've yet to sow.
And every story you tell us says some more of whom you are.
When we write of our lives, you'll be the star in each memoir.

It's awfully clear you plan to live a life that is complete.
Seductive when it suits you; other times just being sweet.
In your priorities your work is first and then you play.
And in between you learn some more; add knowledge every day.
You're wise beyond your years, yet there's a world ahead for you.
So much you've never tasted yet; a lot you've not been through.
With all that lies ahead for you, we envy you a bit.
For you'll succeed beyond your dreams, we know you'll never quit.

If God grants us a single wish, we'll use that wish for you.
The two of us agree on this; it's what we want to do.
We'll wish your life be filled with joy and happiness, galore.
And love beyond your wildest dreams that lasts forever more.

DWY—DRIVING WHILE YOUNG

The day was cold with snow and sleet; the wind was blowing, too.
The sky was overcast with clouds; there wasn't any blue.
On dreary days like this sometimes the demons seem to play.
And things you thought were organized appear to go astray.

A Sunday morning just like this, three girls went for a ride.
They took Denise's Honda; seat belts strapped, the girls inside.
All three are senior students who attend Pomona High.
They study and they work, and on their word you can rely.
On residential streets they drove; they talked, as girls will do.
Good friends, they'd usually agree, the three did not argue.
They finished all their errands and soon started to return.
The mood was light for they'd enjoyed this short Sunday sojourn.

They drove along the parkway where the snowflakes fluttered by.
Relaxed and in control, inside the car they all stayed dry.
Then from a side street suddenly, a car came whizzing out.
It took their right-of-way; now what could this be all about?

The car then braked, it stopped right there; no warning did it give.
Denise must take some action if the girls are going to live.
A car is coming toward them on the parkway's other side.
A bank is to their right, so there is no place they can hide.
Then braking full, there is no choice; there's nowhere she can go.
Denise's car skids forward; hits the car a mighty blow.
It could have been much worse, but the three girls were all alert.
A little shaken, mussed a bit, but not one girl was hurt.

Arvada cops came to the scene to check the accident.
They wrote an accident report, for both the cars were bent.
And then with nothing more, for others were not interviewed.
They issued a citation to Denise; now that was rude.

For anyone who took the time to understand the scene,
could not have blamed the girls, although Denise is just a teen.
But being young and driving is a thing that gets you hung.
It's like there is a law against her driving while she's young.
The cop sat in his car; he didn't do a damn thing right.
The weather's cold but he stayed warm; he didn't seem that bright.
We didn't see a copy of the accident report.
Denise had a citation and a date with traffic court.

The judge reduced the charge when she appeared in court that day.
Denise then pled "not guilty"; that's the truth, the only way.
So now she had to meet with the city attorney, too.
And from this meeting she would learn her rights, what she can do.

She didn't have a lot to nullify the cop's report.
If witnesses did not respond, Denise would be in court.
The cop had said the accident was simple as can be.
Denise rear-ended a parked car, like she had hit a tree.
It's true the car was parked, but it had cut in front of them.
Denise had just a second to design a stratagem.
The right-of-way was clear; Denise did what she had to do.
She did it right and quickly, and she did it impromptu.

The cop made a mistake; the other driver did it wrong.
If he'd performed his job, he would have known it all along.
And then Denise would not have had to go through all the pain,
to go to court, and then once more, and then to court again.

In court it is a slam-dunk, for the witness statements show
Denise did what was right, and soon the whole damned world would know.
The judge did what good judges do whenever cops are wrong.
His words put this cop "in his place" where slothful cops belong.

And one good thing has come from this; that's there for all to see.
I've learned some more about Denise; she's learned a bit from me.
She's more mature than most and knows what's safe and what is not.
She drives just like a pro for she is not a "car hot shot".

SOUL MATE RELATIONSHIPS
(CHOICES—Getting PRIORITIES Right)

To Dave and Anna—with love—from Grandpa

Priorities affect our lives; they guide the things we do.
I choose to help myself, but then I may choose to help you.
You exercise priorities with every choice you make.
Like when to go to bed at night and when you will awake.
Priority is conflict, more to do than there is time.
You choose your course of action; it's okay; it is no crime.

Yet every choice you make defines the person that you are.
Your choices may put people off or make you popular.

So let me step back just a bit, to where it all began.
You don't learn this by magic. It's a predetermined plan.
It happens as you grow without a lot of conscious thought.
You learn from peers or relatives, or what your parents taught.

You learned the alphabet when you were just a little kid.
You learned to count from 1 to 10; at least I think you did.
So you learned what comes first and then what follows, that is good.
You learned about "PRIORITIES" exactly how you should.

You learned of love from parents, though it may not have been clear.
For sometimes things went south and you felt lonely, felt some fear.
You learned how to give love, to give your love without reserve.
And you learned to receive the love that you know you deserve.

Yet choosing the priorities for you and your soul mate,
still seems a little "iffy"; it's okay. It's not too late.

We all seek pleasure, happiness; life filled with love and joy.
We purchase things we think we need; sometimes it's just a toy.
And we expect our soul mate to be there when we have needs.
Our soul mate should take care of us, with loving words and deeds.

Look out for "NUMBER ONE" and everything will be all right.
For self-esteem, you've got to be the winner of each fight.
If there's a disagreement then your soul mate must give in.
For you to put your soul mate first—my God—a mortal sin.
"I need to rest. I want to play. There's shopping WE must do."
Somehow the "WE" gets lost as everything relates to "YOU".

NOW READ THESE WORDS I WRITE TO YOU—INTERNALIZE
EACH THOUGHT.
LET THEM AFFECT YOUR ACTIONS AND YOU'LL FIND THE
LOVE YOU'VE SOUGHT.
THEY'LL TURN YOU HALF AROUND AND YOU'LL FIND
MEANINGS THAT ARE NEW.
AND WITH EACH WORD YOU'LL REALIZE SMALL THINGS
THAT YOU CAN DO.

To make your life more perfect, add your love to every word.
The way your soul mate feels determines how your words are heard!
Express your love in caring ways; you'll see what this will bring.
For words unsaid do not exist, they cannot change a thing.
Your soul mate must be happy to send happiness your way.
You make your soul mate happy by the little things you say.

"Do you need help? What may I do? May I assist today?"
If you're in love these little phrases are not hard to say.
Express your love in every comment; show your mate you care.
And give your love with thoughtful words; be more than simply fair.

What you have done is demonstrate your soul mate's first in line.
Your soul mate's happiness precedes your own, and that is fine.

Then you'll be happier than you have ever been before.
A life that's filled with love and joy; with happiness, galore!
Just put your soul mate first and you'll receive more than you give.
You and your soul mate will enjoy the perfect life you live.
Get your reward from what your soul mate gives to you each day.
Reciprocating what you've done, the kind words that you say.

For as you give, you shall receive, that's God's first "law of life".
You'll be the perfect spouse, the perfect husband; perfect wife.
Enjoy the synergy that grows when lovers become "one".
You've earned the greatest gift on earth—beneath the moon and sun.
No greater happiness can you enjoy than "giving love"'.
Until you transcend earth and then reside with God above.

RENEWING RELATIONSHIPS—
MY BROTHERS AND SISTER

Perhaps we never were as close as siblings ought to be.
When young I guess I didn't care, no great big thing to me.
As children we had many friends, all just about our age.
And there were lots and lots of games in which we'd all engage.

We grew up in the city. There were lots of kids to play.
We went to school and did some sports, the good life everyday.
Then Mom and Dad decided to leave city life behind.
We gathered all the stuff we had, whatever we could find.
We moved to Potter Valley; it's a town remote and small.
A little farm we purchased with those pear trees, big and tall.
Our house had just a kitchen with a front room next to it,
and two small bedrooms on one side for all of us to fit.
We got our water from the pump outside the kitchen door.
The pump stood over holes we made right through the back porch floor.
The "pot" was just an old outhouse behind the chicken coop.
That's where you did your job when nature called for you to "poop".
We all worked hard and went to school, with little time to play.
And after school we worked some more, up to the end of day.
I guess it's right to say by now, without making amends.
We didn't take the time to talk, relax and become friends.

Then suddenly one Saturday a truck came driving up.
Great uncle Dee behind the wheel; his big hand held a cup.
Then mom told us that she and Dad were parting, right that day.
And she with Uncle Dee and truck, were going far away.

We had a choice to go with Mom, or stay behind with Dad.
It didn't seem to matter much; the whole damned thing was sad.
I know we each debated and we felt the mental strain.

We finally all went south with Mom to start life once again.
We moved to Santa Rosa where our mom had bought a house.
But leaving Dad behind made me feel awfully like a louse.
It wasn't long before I knew that somehow I'd been wronged.
I left you guys with Mom and went with Dad where I belonged.

We saw each other now and then, on every holiday.
Our lives took separate paths, we grew, and each moved far away.
Our sibling love was stretched too far; the distance was too great.
We each had families of our own; our love was left to fate.

Then Father died; it happened quickly; just a single day.
And later Mom departed, too; some gathered there to pray.
Now there are just the four of us; our families spread around.
Our children take most of our time, and that decision's sound.

What happens now to you and me? The world is getting small.
Should we just live life separately, not even talk at all?
Is it okay to move along, no words to show we care?
Some are; some aren't involved with God. Should I just say a prayer?
I'm probably the one that's worst, excuses all around.
Each day I wonder is this right or should I make a sound?
It doesn't matter much to me, if fault is yours or mine.
It makes no sense to sit around, like everything is fine.

If all of us are happy now, our lives are quite complete.
There isn't any reason to as much as move our feet.
If you feel good with what you know, each family in their "fence",
the cousins haven't even met; does that make any sense?
And second cousins all around, we don't know they exist.
Who cares, it's just our families; it is like a brewer's grist.
There is no value till it's ground; it sits in sacks alone.
We might as well be animals, or wood that's turned to stone.

It's only when you stir the pot you see what's down inside.
Should I keep stirring it some more; or maybe I should hide?

I have a plan, it isn't much, but it's a lot to me.
I'm sharing it with you today; limbs on the family tree.

We've lived our separate lives apart without a lot to say.
Our family's more extended every month; yet, every day.
It's okay we have lived this way, but now that we are old,
what story is it that we want our families to be told?
Is family less important just because it's far away?
Is it okay to just forget a wedding, a birthday?
Should time just pass right by our life like there's no family tree?
Can our lives really be complete without our family?

I'd like to start to make amends, begin a little game.
I'll write a letter once a month; each month I'll do the same.
And in the letter I will tell what all my kids have done
for this past month; a little news of work and maybe fun.
It may not be a masterpiece; I do not write that well.
But it will send a message only loving words can tell.
I'll send a copy in the mail to every one of you.
You'll then receive each letter in about a day or two.

I hope that you will share my words with all your family.
They may begin to see what friends their family can be.
Then, maybe once each month or so, you'll write a word or two.
And send it to your siblings; you may copy what I do.
It may not ever happen, but a few might say it could.
The cousins might communicate; they may feel this is good.
And if one member of our clan just makes a family friend,
for even if it's one of us, it may just start a trend.

In olden days the family was the center of the earth.
Respect your elders, love your kids, how much can this be worth?
Has so much changed that we don't need this bonding anymore?
As I grow old I can't accept this thought that I abhor.

Without ado I'll start my part before you even speak.
It doesn't take a lot to make each of our lives less bleak.
I'll take an hour; I'll spend a buck; that's what I'm going to do.
And then I'll hope you copy me and write a letter, too.

OLDER BROTHER—A ROLE MODEL

When I was just a little kid he let me "hang around"
with him and all his friends if I just didn't make a sound.
Some times they'd play some tennis or some baseball; maybe box.
Or make a sling shot from a twig and shoot some smooth round rocks.
Yet anytime that I could be with him, I felt just great.
We'd skate; play "kick the can" with friends until it was quite late.

My older brother always has been my role model, too.
I watched him more than he could guess, to know what I might do.
And when we got in trouble with behavior that was bad,
he always got the whipping first from Father, who was "mad".
And by the time I got the belt, my father's anger waned.
That we should not be beaten was a fact no one explained.

Throughout my youth he had a special place within my heart.
Then when our parents split, we ended up quite far apart.
He moved with Mom and helped make sure her life went on, okay.
I lived with Dad and stayed with friends; what more is there to say?
Then out of high school; I was lost; whatever should I do?
You guessed! He hired me, although there wasn't work for two.

I've never known a person who has not respected him.
For "friendship" and my older brother, that's a synonym.
Somehow he's never raised his voice in anger or despair.
And you can count on him to always do what's right, what's fair.
He seems to sense when you need help; he's always there for you.
No matter what your crisis, somehow he knows what to do.

Yes he's a man of seasons; he's a loving, caring man.
Throughout my youth and adult life, I've been his greatest fan.
His family knows he loves them, and they love him in return.

We all observe his actions for there's much for us to learn.
Yes, he's my older brother and I'll always cherish him.
He's been there to support me when my life's trials were most grim.

HAVE STRENGTH, MY OLDER BROTHER

Each day arrives; what will it bring,
a tear; a smile; perhaps something
to build the hope that wanes away
as Oosh faces another day.
The strength you've always had within,
fades just a bit; it's not a sin.
While you are healthy, full of life,
she's suffering, days filled with strife.
Must Oosh endure this awful pain,
this scourge that has returned again?
Is there something that you can do
beyond just saying, "I love you"?
A look, a word, a caring touch
may not seem like it's very much.
Yet, it's the stuff that lets her know
your love endures and it will grow.
We're each a part of our God's plan,
and we knew when this life began,
that God would call us back to him,
though when He does, it seems so grim.
That's when the faith we have in God
is tested; it may leave us awed.
For with strong faith we know each lives
forever, that's the life God gives.
Dear Brother, I would gladly give
some of my life that Oosh might live.
And trade God for a year or two
so she can stay right there with you.

YOUNGER BROTHER

I have a younger brother who is not small anymore.
But he's my "little" brother, just the way he was before.
He's never come to visit me since I became adult.
I doubt this was intended as a personal insult.

We both were raised as Mormon from the time that we were small.
Then he became a "Witness"; it did not take long at all.
And from that date we've been estranged; I really don't know why.
I'd like my brother back with me sometime before I die.

He wasn't born till thirty-five; that's four years after me.
Along with my big brother, Dad and Mom now bragged of three.
Depression babies all; there wasn't much for us to share.
Yet food was always plentiful; we had warm clothes to wear.
My little brother looked a lot like me when he was born.
Most gifts he got were "hand me downs"; the clothes that I had worn.
Yet we were happy little kids, for we had lots to do.
We did our chores around the house and helped in the yard too.

When he was barely two we went to live in Covelo.
With Indians and God who sent us drifts of freezing snow.
God sent another present in the winter of that year.
A little sister joined us, and we held her very dear.
We almost froze that winter, and there wasn't much to eat.
A glass of milk and fresh warm bread became a special treat.
We almost starved to death before we finally got away.
And settled in Pinole where we all hoped that we could stay.

The next six years zoomed by, a world in total disarray.
A war replaced depression, much to everyone's dismay.
My little brother never talked a lot about the war.

We lived our life about the way that we had lived before.
The war changed the economy, especially for our dad.
A buck a day became a buck an hour, and that's not bad.
It wasn't long till Mom and Dad had saved a little dough.
They added money every week, and watched their savings grow.

We kids were happy as can be; we went to school each day.
The school was on a hill; it wasn't very far away.
My little brother's classmates were the closest friends he had.
As siblings we were not that close, and that was kind of sad.

And then in forty-three, and much to all of our alarm,
our parents took their money and they bought a little farm.
We moved a hundred miles up to a place we'd never seen,
with mountains, rivers, brush and trees and not much in between.
At eight years old my brother made the move without chagrin.
Not so for me for I was lost; I thought I'd never win.
For all my friends were left behind. I tried hard not to grieve.
I said goodbye to every one before I had to leave.

Our house was old and small, without a washroom or a bath;
six people in two bedrooms; an outhouse down a short path.
Though we were close at night; we slept together in one room,
we parted with the dawn like a discordant bride and groom.
My brothers and I had some chores to do most every day.
And getting all the work done left us little time to play.
So rather than becoming close as brothers all should be,
we didn't talk a lot; my brothers rarely talked to me.

And then our folks went separate ways; our mother left our dad.
Mom wanted us to leave with her; that day was very sad.
I lived with Mom, my sister, and my little brother, too.
We moved to a big city where there wasn't much to do.

So I returned to Father to be with my many friends.
This really hurt my mother and I couldn't make amends.
I left my little sister and my little brother, too.
Back with my father and my friends, I started life anew.
I didn't see my brother very often any more.
Some years went by and I was called to train to fight a war.
My little brother finally left my mom to live with Dad.
I guess that's when it started; our relationship got bad.

When I returned my brother was a "Witness" to his God.
He now had all new values that to me seemed somewhat odd.
We didn't have a lot of things in common any more.
For he was an "Objector" while I'd gone to fight the war.
We didn't see each other though we were not far apart.
Without a past relationship, how could we make one start?
There was no common ground for us to share our separate lives.
Though both of us had children, and we knew each other's wives.

For thirty years it went this way, no problem, but no love.
We each believed in God. Mine was within. His was above.
Yet we did not communicate. Was anyone to blame?
Now looking back in retrospect, it seems an awful shame.

I can't be really sure of what went on inside his head,
when he declared that I, his older brother, Rod, was dead.
But from the day that he became a "Witness" to his God,
to him my life was done, like I'd been buried under sod.
His system of beliefs did not concern me, then or now.
I'd like to understand them, but I simply don't know how.
Yet, I accept his right to be the man he wants to be.
Whatever his beliefs they're his, they don't belong to me.

But I'm his older brother, which I've been for all his life.
To lose a sibling can create anxiety and strife.
I lost my sister for a while; then she returned one day.
Now she's been with me ever since, and with me she will stay.

I don't know why my brother cannot be the same as she.
And just accept me as I am; we don't have to agree.
I do not want to change him or endanger who he is.
And I fully support the fact that his beliefs are his.
He won't accept the letters I compose and send to him.
I'd hoped it wasn't permanent, a passing interim.
But we are getting older every day that passes by.
If there's a chance to reach him, then somehow I've got to try.

I really don't know who he is, and he knows less of me.
We've barely talked in fifty years; how can we disagree?
How many times can one forgive; are limits in God's plan?
God made forgiveness pervasive when he created man.

I don't know what I've done to drive this wedge between us two.
Without communication, how can I know what to do?
If he will give me just one chance, he may like what he hears.
Then his discovery, who I am, may allay all his fears.
If he'll accept this poem that lets him know the way I feel.
He may just understand the love these words try to reveal.
And maybe he will ask his God to let him talk to me.
And with God's blessing he will know it's not impiety.

I'll take him and his wife to lunch; we'll talk a little while.
And when they find out who I am, then all of us may smile.
Our hands may touch; we'll realize we care a little bit.
And on this day we may become good friends before we split.
I don't want any guarantees; I only want to try.
I want to do my best before my brother or I die,
to be the brother he would want if we could start again.
Exchanging caring phrases like a love song in refrain.

So little brother, here it is; the best that I can do.
Just words, but yet I hope it says how much I care for you.
If you'll just open up your heart and let my love come in.
Then we'll be brothers once again; that's surely not a sin.

GRANDMA'S CREAM CANDY

We went to Grandma's house on Christmas, the whole family.
Then, I was just a little kid and loved Grandma's candy.
My Mom and my aunt Melba helped my Grandma make the "stuff".
They'd make a lot of batches till they knew there was enough.
We filled the stove with wood until the fire made it "red-hot".
Then Grandma mixed the recipe in a huge metal pot.
My Mom and Melba stirred each batch the best part of an hour.
I watched and "licked my chops"; I knew some candy I'd devour.
When it was done they added nuts; spread it on a flat pan.
It always came out perfectly, exactly like their plan.
I got to help a little bit; I got to scrape the bowl.
I'd scrape till I ate every crumb; a clean bowl was my goal.

Yes, making candy was the highlight of each Christmas Eve.
We always took some home with us when it was time to leave
We only had that candy once a year, at Christmas time.
When Grandma died, the candy stopped, for me worse than a crime.
And then when Mom departed, and we'd lost Aunt Melba, too.
The recipe seemed lost and there was nothing I could do.
The years went by; Christmas arrived without Grandma's candy.
The whole process was so much fun; the memory haunted me.

And then one Christmas, in the mail, some Cream Candy arrived.
Somehow, without my knowledge, Grandma's recipe survived.
My little sister had it all the time, I didn't know.
A strong family tradition I did not want to outgrow.

So now I'm here with Pat and near the twilight of my life.
I've everything that I could want since she became my wife.
Yet it's an added plus to now have Grandma's recipe.
On Christmas we can honor her and make her Cream Candy.

And share a little bit with you, some candy, memories, too.
A tiny, small tradition from my Grandmother to you!
It's filled with love (and sugar, whoops) so just a little bit.
At least for me, the memories make this candy a big hit.

A VERY SPECIAL AUNT

You feel her warmth; it's like the morning sun upon your face.
The brightness of her smile projects into each tiny space.
Her presence can be felt before you know that she is there.
And when she hugs you, you can feel her aura everywhere.
The smile in every word she speaks will fill your day with joy.
It's there for you and me; each man or woman; girl or boy.
Eight decades; she's not counting; no two moments are the same.
If life deals her a bad hand, she holds no one else to blame.
She's been her person, no one else and she's spread loads of love.
She seems to have close contact with her God in heaven above.
Somehow she finds the good in every person in her life.
And through the years she's been a super mother, loving wife.
The matriarch, her family is now spread out far and wide.
Yet she's the "center piece" and she performs her role with pride.
Her pride is well deserved for she's a role model and more.
And she'll meet future challenges, no matter what's in store.

Yet there is something that my Aunt Lu doesn't really know.
She influenced my bank career; her comments helped me grow.
For every little step I made as I climbed to the top.
I'd hear her approbation and her feedback didn't stop.
She'd tell her coworkers and friends how proud she was of me.
Her words got back to me and like an eagle I was free.
Somehow I never thanked her for just being "my Aunt Lu".
She spoke of me with pride and that is all she had to do.
She added sunshine to my days, some moonlight to each night,
and sprinkled stars along the way to give my life more light.
Aunt Lu, it isn't much, but I do hope this poem will show,
how much I've always loved you, so forever you will know,
you've given more to me than you will ever realize.
Now Pat and I love our "Aunt Lu" and there's no compromise.

GLEN—VISIT FROM A TOUGH AND LOVING COUSIN

A plastic tube snakes through the room.
It seems to speak, portending doom.
Yet, through it flows a breath of air.
No hint that this does not seem fair.

There's strength in every step he takes.
No time for yesterday's mistakes.
A purpose to each word he speaks.
Is life measured in years or weeks?

We'll never know the future, yet,
be optimistic with your bet.
For none will ever know for sure,
tomorrow there may be a cure.

At breakfast he just eats a bit.
He won't give up; he'll never quit.
A strong resolve with every word,
communiqués we've never heard.

His heritage is clear to all.
Among his family he stands tall.
He gave life all he had, and more,
to wife and kids; grandkids, galore.

I'm proud to be his relative.
I hope these simple words I give,
will add some sunlight to his day,
so he'll enjoy his too brief stay.

FAMILY AT CHRISTMAS

Bright lights adorn the house outside; it's Christmas time, for sure.
With gifts under the Christmas tree, what else can be in store?
Three years and more of happiness, our love is rich and strong.
We're soul mates and we're both in love; at home's where we belong.

This weekend before Christmas, Dave and Anna are in town.
They traveled here from Granby, up the mountain and then down.
They'll talk to us a little, though they're really here to see
Denise, their sister, whom they love and don't see frequently!
The love they share is obvious; they all warmly embrace.
A sister and her brother, loving smiles glow on each face.
Though he may be a mountain man, he knows the city, too.
And for his little sister, there is nothing he won't do.

Denise is now a city gal, she knows her way around.
She works full time and then away to college she is bound.
Each busy with a life that overflows with things to do,
yet they take time at Christmas so their friendships can renew.

Another sister calls to say she'll be by with her beau.
On holidays like this we feel our love for family grow.
We're family, all together on this Christmas holiday.
We share God's most important gift, as silently we pray.

Love given is an absolute; it can't be taken back.
The love received fills up one's heart. There isn't any slack.
And in our home this evening, we can feel love, everywhere.
When family gets together, it's a wonderful affair.
The night wears on as Pat and I enjoy the interlude.
Kids interacting happily, none with an "attitude"!
Three generations strong and not a weak one in the crowd!
All animated, happy, as we hear them laugh out loud.

We're separated by two generations, plus some more.
Yet Christmas transcends ages with its gifts, its love and lore.
They say it's always better that you give more than receive.
The kids enjoy it all, for that's the way that they believe.

We're finally home alone; grandkids go to the movie show.
The three of us sit at the kitchen table, for we know,
son, Lee, will want to talk about his writing or a poem.
And that's the way we end a perfect Christmas Eve at home.

SEVENTY-FIFTH BIRTHDAY

Exciting life! I live each day with heart that's filled with hope.
Sometimes things get a little tough, but I've learned how to cope.
New dreams keep me alive as I pursue my plans each day.
I work though I'm retired; yes, being retired leaves time for play.

But, this day sadness permeates the world in which I live.
Too many "takers" as I age, each grabbing what I'll give.
Deep sadness comes more often as this day arrives each year.
My heart feels trepidation, though there's nothing I should fear.
Alone with empty memories of my friends and family!
Each took a piece of life from me, as they all went away.
Just flesh and bone remains as I await this fate once more.
"Old man, you're just about as useful as an aged whore".
Co-workers said, "Goodbye" when I retired; then they were gone.
For in life's corporate chess game, age transformed me to a pawn.
Bereft of all the corporate power executives enjoy.
Abandoned to my loneliness; aged child without a toy.

Where are my daughters? Where's my son? Each independent now!
I raised them so they'd be that way; young calves weaned from their cow.
They owe me nothing; they have lives and families to support.
In their adult lives I am now as useful as a wart.
So why do I expect to hear from them on this one day?
There's little left to tell them, and they don't care what I say.
This shroud of loneliness creates a feeling of despair.
I'd hoped it would be different, but I know life isn't fair.

The telephone! My oldest daughter! There's a call for me?
Call interrupt! My son! Through happy tears I cannot see.
Then grandchildren begin to call; I can't believe it's true.
And as each ends their call I hear, "Grandpa, I do love you".
Then two more daughters on the line; I've now heard from all four!
The best birthday I've never had; I couldn't ask for more.

SHOPPING—A PARODY

When I go out to get something, I do not shop at all.
I know exactly what I want; some tools or a golf ball.
Directly to the merchandise I march, with purpose, strong.
And when I've made the purchase I go home where I belong.
From time to time I need to buy a gift for someone dear.
I'm not exactly sure where I will find it, far or near.
On these occasions I may visit more than just one store.
As soon as I have found the gift, I don't look any more.

My wife goes shopping with her friends; they do it every day.
For me it would be work, but for the ladies this is play.
They even have a lookout who will scout each discount store.
And when new merchandise arrives, the ladies wage a war.
They have a calling chain that quickly lets each lady know
the store has lots of merchandise that it is going to show.
The first to get there has the broadest choice of clothes to buy.
Sometimes the clothes get mangled when the race ends in a tie.

I've talked to lots of guys about their wives' desire to shop.
We've even planned how we, as men, can get this thing to stop.
But we don't know what drives the wives to shop continually.
So mostly we just let it flow and sit by silently.

Then on a Sunday morning I'm as calm as I can be.
I've had my shower early; I'm relaxed and I feel free.
It's great to be alive with not a thing I have to do.
My wife is in the kitchen fixing breakfast—just for two.
With scrambled eggs and toast, a little coffee there to sip.
My mind relaxes as it drifts; it's on a pleasure trip.
I look up from the paper and I see her eyes on me.
There's something going on inside that pretty head, I see.

I know that someone has to shop to get our food and clothes.
I tell her women love to shop while men prefer repose?
Don't women garner energy from shopping all the sales?
And does it matter what they buy if they're not with their males?
A sunny day just right for lots of things I like to do.
I'd rather take a walk, play with the dog; hit golf balls, too.
We linger over coffee; I can tell she has a plan.
I want to hide beneath my chair like any other man.

She's got the paper organized; the sales are right on top.
There isn't any question that somebody's going to shop.
We've had our breakfast; I feel great; I'm ready for the day.
She has the cash and credit cards; a little golf I'll play.
She looks me in the eye, her finger pointed at my nose.
You're wearing rags; you're like a tramp; you've got to have new clothes.
"You know my size and what I like; just buy some clothes for me."
Her look communicates her thought; that's not how it will be.

It doesn't happen often, for I'm male, through and through.
And I prefer the golf course or the TV, just like you.
I say, "It takes an act of God" to get me to the store.
She says, "I've got a winch and chain to pull you out the door".

We get into the car and travel to the shopping mall.
She's cheerful as a cat with milk; I don't like this at all.
With fifty women to each man inside this giant store,
all grabbing clothes and pushing, the whole process I abhor.

We're in the women's section and I look around a bit.
Now she is checking lingerie; I find a chair and sit.
While she is trying dainty things, I simply sit and rest.
A gal is trying on a bra; it shows a lot of breast.
I perk up just a little as a lady passes by.
She's got a pair of "hot pants" that she says she's going to try.
Now this is getting pretty good; my eyes are open wide.
I guess a gal with "hot pants" thinks there isn't much to hide.

A lady in a two-piece suit walks right in front of me.
It doesn't have a lot of cloth; it's a string bikini.
I can't believe the flesh that shows as she strolls through the door.
I'm leaning as she passes till I almost hit the floor.
A gorgeous blonde walks by; she's got some outfits on her arm.
It doesn't matter how they look for I see she's got charm.
She comes back out and models a traditional sarong.
It opens and there's nothing where her pants and bra belong.
I see a lady modeling a two-piece evening gown.
It's causes men to smile and makes the ladies' faces frown.
I'm smiling just about enough to almost break my face.
For nothing covers her on top but dainty, see through lace.

This "shopping" isn't bad at all; I'm into it big time.
If this went on outside I'd be arrested for a crime.
I sit back and relax and wish I had a cigarette.
No smoking in these buildings. It's so easy to forget.

I barely catch my breath as a young lady slithers by.
She grazes both my legs, for she is not the least bit shy.
The skintight gown she wears reveals there's nothing underneath.
She wiggles down the isle; I give a big sigh of relief.
I haven't seen my wife; why do I feel so guilty now?
She dragged me here to shop; I didn't want it anyhow.
The lady in the skintight gown comes back and talks to me.
I can't help staring; I'm a man, and there's so much to see.

I'm so engrossed in "talking" I don't even see my wife.
She's staring daggers through me like she's going to take my life.
About a minute more and there will be a homicide.
She grabs my hand, and just that fast, we're on the other side.

She hasn't bought a thing for she's been watching me behave.
My freedom disappeared, and there's no doubt I'm now a slave.
We're in the men's department where I buy a thing or two.
There's not much conversation, and I don't know what to do.

We're home at last, the air is clear, a lovely day in spring.
My wife's now happy to take care of all of our shopping.
She says, "I know how bored you get, so I'll buy all your things.
The golf course is the place for you. I know the joy it brings".

This story may not be a panacea for all men.
And you may wish to join your wife, if she's a perfect "10".
For me it's with the guys, my friends, where beer's the drink of choice,
as we traverse the golf course; hearty laugh and boisterous voice.

REWARDS—
LASTING FRIENDSHIPS

In large measure, lasting friendships reflect the type of person we become as we travel life's journey. Enduring friendships are their own reward for being an honest, caring, loving, giving and appreciative person in all of our personal, social and business relationships. When young, what we have seems important. As we travel the uncertain paths of life, we become less interested in what we have and more focused on who we are becoming.

A CHRISTMAS GIFT

It's bitter cold outside, yet it is beautiful to see.
The sunshine smiles, reflecting from the snow upon the tree!
A freezing wind cuts through the air with fangs exposed to all.
For winter has arrived, pushing away the warmth of fall.
With open hearts we welcome bitter cold and freezing rain.
Old winter's just a visitor, spring will return again.
In spite of hail and rain, the ever blustering winds that blow.
Old Santa will somehow arrive, through drifts of blowing snow.

There's magic in this season as we find new ways to give.
For how we share with others helps define the way we live.
We may not have a lot to share, a smile; a helping hand.
Yet help that we impart returns warm feelings that are grand.
The Christmas Season, it's a time for friends and family,
exchanging cards and gifts with folks that we don't often see.
The Season brings out happiness in everything we do.
Hearts filled with love for everyone, we share with strangers, too.

How blessed we are to live our lives in this, a great country.
We all have opportunity; it's our democracy.
Sure, we know it's not perfect; that's what we try to achieve.
With faith and work it will improve; and that's what we believe.
The large majority of us have "excess" we can share.
To help someone less fortunate, whose cupboard may be bare.
There's not a feeling on this earth that ever felt so good,
as "giving from our substance", just the way we know we should.

We try, but we may never do the very best we can
to help each child and grownup, every woman, every man.
But just a single gesture, a warm smile, a word of hope,
may help someone less fortunate, in their effort to cope.

LIFETIME FRIENDS

The message says, "We're leaving Washington this afternoon.
And we'll arrive in Colorado very, very soon".

We stopped to see them months ago when we took our first trip.
A party, light refreshments and a very tasty dip!
And we broke bread together like the friends we've been for life.
The girls had lost their husbands and each guy divorced his wife.
The four of us were friends when we were students, long ago.
We didn't know as youngsters the directions lives would flow.
Yet, friendship did endure the ups and downs we faced each day,
as we pursued our lives in cities scattered far away.
And, they are friends. We've been good friends since all of us were young.
As students, they're the friends we always chose to be among,
for he was blond and tall, with laughing eyes and cheerful smile.
And everyone who met her wanted her to stay a while.

We all had tons of fun as we grew up in that small place.
It helped us all get ready to explore life's real "rat race".
Our lives took us to places we'd just read about before.
One started her career; the others went to fight a war.
But thankfully a "common" friend kept track of where we went.
And as the years passed by we got the messages she sent.
She organized reunions for the students, one and all.
Inviting every student she could possibly recall.

As years went by we'd meet each other, for a day or two.
We'd stick together for those hours like we'd used super glue.
Then back to where we lived, our lives like chaff against the wind.
We didn't keep in touch; our friendship was undisciplined.

Yet there's a chemistry of youth that's very, very strong.
We shared a lot of stuff about our lives, where we belong.

And, through it all, we had respect for what the others did.
No lies and no excuses, there was nothing that we hid.
A trust was built that transcended the separate paths we took.
We shared what life dished out to us, just like an open book.
It didn't matter that we'd made a bad mistake or two.
Whenever one spoke to the rest, we knew the words were true.

Four student friends that left the little valley that they knew.
Each went a separate way, with very little ballyhoo.
All found some work and married and all married once again.
I guess the challenge of each life created too much strain.
But life's a healing potion if you flow through every mess.
And do the best you can; accepting that there'll be some stress.
First husbands were divorced and then the second husbands died.
We guys divorced our wives; it didn't matter that we'd tried.
So after fifty years, we met again some months ago.
We guys looked just about our age; our hair resembled snow.
The girls were still attractive, just as though time had not passed.
Each wondered if the friendship we had known before would last.

If time can be reversed, then that's precisely what we did.
Instead of being oldsters, each behaved just like a kid.
For now together, we all knew our lives would be great fun.
if we renewed our friendship. That's exactly what we've done.
Like high school buddies we embraced; each knew that there was more.
It took some time, and conversation, to exact the score.
Not one of us knew how we could aspire now to our dream.
Yet, when the dust had settled, not one action was extreme.

Now over fifty years have passed, time simply won't stand still.
We're grandma and we're grandpa, but we're not "over the hill".
For when we are together, we're still filled with life and love,
and thankful for the health that's blessed on us by God above.
Two couples from the past are now together; not too soon
Each couple, so in love it's a continual honeymoon.

Now finally, bound together by a friendship "old as sin",
each day we start anew, for every day four lives begin.

We wouldn't do it over; not for any price you'd pay.
For finally we're together and together now we'll stay.
We understand that friendship doesn't waver over time.
And when old friendships come alive, then life becomes sublime.
We cherish every moment, every call that we receive.
Our friendship is the highest value that we can achieve.
And all of us enjoy the love that good friends share each day.
We love to share, so for a lifelong friendship we all pray.

FRIENDSHIP

How many roads we walk along as life goes passing by.
Sometimes we're happy as can be; sometimes we stop and cry.

We sell our home to travel and then travel far and wide.
Must we accept the loss of friends, and take this all in stride?
Where are the friends we had now that we've traveled far away?
Does work and family, closer friends, completely fill their day?
Do they forget that we exist because we're not next-door?
Or since we're gone, is it like we were just a visitor?
Is their life now so full of folks, they feel they have no choice?
Can they not take the time to call, to let me hear their voice?
Do they ignore the fun we had back when we shared our time?
Can it be right to make me feel like moving was a crime?

We both know how to telephone; our time's about the same.
I wonder if I'm thinking right. Should they take all the blame?
My e-mail works and I can write, and I know how to type.
Is friendship too far down my queue; is that what makes me gripe?
I look into my mirror now; my feet are on the ground.
Who is the one who changed his life? New people all around!
Did I take time to say goodbye, to meet with every friend?
Or was I just perfunctory, and did I just pretend?

If friendship has a meaning, and it does when you're alone.
Then nurture it and give it love; you'll see how it has grown.
A single friend can fill a void that haunts you, night and day.
So cherish all; make sure each one is in your life to stay.

To make a friend, just be a friend, let others get to know
exactly who you are and what you want and where you go.
You've got to give yourself to them; you cannot halt or swerve,

for as you give, you shall receive much more than you deserve.
It's simple to accept someone who's very much like you.
You're forthright, even candid; all your words are honest, too.

Accepting doesn't build a bridge; it's like an uncut gem.
You're only just acquaintances, till you approve of them.
Approval is an attitude; you know that someone cares.
It fills the gap, and lets you start your journey up the stairs.
You climb up to relationships that lead to friendships, new.
And from the top you see it all; you have a better view.
If everyone's behavior is for them alone to judge,
accept their acts; approve of them; and never hold a grudge.
As long as they're not harming you, their actions are okay.
If not your friends, they're simply folks just like you meet each day.

You won't be close or chummy, or be friends with all you meet.
It's okay just to smile and nod to those you wish to greet.
There is no obligation, and you do not have to be
a friend to all, that choice is yours; it's there for you and me.

So cherish all your friendships, and keep every one alive.
Communicate with each, and then proceed with all your drive.
Just give a little of yourself; don't measure the amount.
And you will truly be a friend to more than you can count.

A HOME SHARED WITH FRIENDS

If first impressions really are important, as they say,
we want to make a good one, for it helps us start each day.
How people feel inside our home occurs before they knock.
In our case, it's the house that's on the corner of the block.
It doesn't take much memory; it's as clear as it can be.
The first thing that I sighted was the Christmas shaped pine tree.
It's in the corner of the yard; for years that tree will stand.
It welcomes every visitor; it waves its branches, grand.

When first I turned onto the street and drove up to the curb.
The snowflakes seemed to say to me, "Please, please do not disturb".
They formed a pure white blanket, lying still beneath the trees.
The air was clear with just the hint, a whisper of a breeze.
The driveway's like a welcome mat; it's more than two cars wide.
There's extra room for visitors; cars fit on either side.
It's thoughtful and a little more; there's room for you to park.
It's even more convenient when arriving after dark.

The ivy nestles quietly between the walk and wall.
A juniper announces that it's there for one and all.
The entrance to our home is just about what you'd expect.
It welcomes you informally; its warmness you'll detect.
With planters in the window, and a cat that's big and black.
You quickly feel all warm inside; it's loose; there's lots of slack.
Three steps into the kitchen, it is bright and crystal clean.
You'll feel still better as you grasp the rail, on which you lean.

Five steps will find you in a room with fireplace and a flue.
It's organized for family, and for visitors like you.
The television doesn't blare; it's quiet as it can be.
The pictures placed around the room are mostly family.

An archway leads into a space, and further you will see.
An indoor laundry and half bath, convenient as can be.
Just one more step and through the door you find Denise's pad.
She let's her things rest leisurely; now that can't be all bad.

A door behind leads down the stairs to chambers just below.
A rumpus room where all can play! It's perfect when there's snow.
And through a door as you step off the very bottom stair,
another bedroom beckons, and its comfort fills the air.

We move up to the living room; in here there is no rule.
It's where Denise just drops her things when she returns from school.
You see your own reflection from the mirrors on the wall.
You even see the stairway that leads you up to the hall.

You cannot help but feel at home while music fills the air.
We like soft sounds; they fill each room with background, everywhere.
From where we live to where we sleep; three bedrooms on floor two.
On beds the pillows softly placed; they seem to beckon you.
With every step your mind can feel, as casually you roam.
That it took more than bricks and boards to make this house a home.
From out in front till you're inside, as softly as a dove.
You feel it from your head to toe; this home is filled with love.

For houses are on every block, they fill the city, wide.
They're big and small and in-between; some seem to exude pride.
It's not how houses came to be, or what they look like, too.
It's not how they were built that counts; it's how they feel to you.
No person ever rang our bell or knocked upon our door,
who's not potentially a friend, at times they may be more.
For it's the people in our life, some near, some far away.
It doesn't matter where they're from; our home's their place to stay.

The house is clean enough to be a healthy place to live.
The cleaning's done by all of us; our work's cooperative.

But you may find a few things placed at random on the floor.
That's comfort for our family and it doesn't mean much more.

We hope you know by now when you're in our home, you're the star.
Please feel that you are family since to us, that's what you are.
We tell you that our home is yours, with love and with a smile.
And all our lives will be enriched because you stayed a while.

LOST FRIEND—LONELINESS—
FRIENDSHIP FOUND

Can I be lonely with three friends? How much is friendship worth,
when one of them, without good-byes, departs from this good earth?
He's been a special friend, indeed; a friend "through thick and thin".
He's been my "brother"; helped me out of "fixes" I've been in.
We've shared in everything and we've been friends throughout our life.
Yes, he's the closest friend I've ever had, except my wife.

Just yesterday we played some golf, shared stories as we ate.
This morning without warning, he fell, victim to his fate.
Now three of us; for he is gone; sit quiet as a stone.
Although we're here together, we each feel we're all alone.
One friend lies still; he seems asleep; we don't know what to do.
He'll never be with us again; will he be lonely too?

No foursome now to play a round of golf on Saturday.
On Sunday three will go to church and there we each will pray.

From here we'll go our separate ways; the bond has disappeared.
Each all alone, each with his thoughts; it's just like we had feared.

I find myself with people; they are standing by my side.
Yet, as the ocean sweeps away the sand with every tide,
I feel alone, a faceless group, there's no one that I know.
Must I endure this loneliness? Is there nowhere to go?
A frown is fixed upon my face; I'm stern as I can be.
It's easy to feel lonely when my friend's not here for me.
How can I change this attitude and meet a person, new?
How can I ditch this loneliness when I am feeling blue?
Can any other person fill the gap? I feel alone.
Is just one friend all that I need, from youth until I'm grown?

Without my friend the world is bleak. It's dismal and it's dark.
Will someone come and talk with me while I walk through the park?

I'm all alone. I watch TV. I switch from show to show.
My eyes are fixed, just staring out; my mind's about to blow.
I'm here with no one else to share ideas, new and old.
I'm stuck. I cannot change my mood. My body's even cold.
Is loneliness a state of mind, just passing by today?
Or is it like a syndrome; like a plague that's here to stay.
I hurt inside; I feel the pain from feet up to my head.
It's hard to rise and face each day, how many things I dread.

Are people so important, like the ones that care and love?
Are they the very staff of life; are they sent from above?
As bread may fill my belly, do the people fill my heart?
Can I get rid of loneliness? Is this the day I start?
So many questions I have asked; these messages I send.
Can I find just one gal or guy, someone to be a friend?
Should he or she appear right now, I'll change without delay.
And drive away these feelings that torment me night and day.
Who really knows the meaning of this lump that's in my heart?
The emptiness; the dearth of goals; no hope that I can start
to change a bit and meet some folks. My life needs a new trend.
I've got to break away from this, somewhere find a new friend.

I finally realize that I'm in charge; that I control.
If "all the world's a stage" it doesn't matter what my role.
It's not what happens in my life that makes me who I am,
for I decide who I will be, or life is just a sham.
It takes but one decision for my attitude to change.
It's hiding there inside of me. It's well within my range.
For I alone can make it work, my personality,
with love and hope for others; that's the way I want to be.

Then "she" appears; an angel from my long forgotten past.
And just like that it's gone; the loneliness that I'd amassed.

Now hand in hand, I'm with my love; she's everything to me.
No longer am I lonely, like a limb without a tree.
We're two like one; together and our love is stronger still.
For us there is no loneliness, for that's our mutual will.
Our faces light the morning sky; we walk with vigor, too,
inside the giant shopping mall, out under skies of blue.
We greet each person like a friend we meet along the way.
With twinkling eyes and head held high, no loneliness today.

Now take a lesson from my book and read each page, complete.
Then study every word and phrase; assimilate each sheet.
This message calls for you to hear; it's clearer than a bell.
Make friends, make love and just be you, avoid that lonesome Hell.
Yes, I'm in charge of me the same as you're in charge of you.
It really doesn't matter what all other people do.
If you give words of kindness, with a smile and helping hand,
then music fills your soul; now you're the leader of your band.

For what you give is what you get, so give your friendship, strong.
Your friends will join the chorus as you sing life's sweetest song.
You'll never be alone again; your friends will seek you out.
And you will finally know that friendship's what life is about.

THE STROKE

We cannot comprehend. It goes beyond our every thought.
It isn't fair to anyone; this thing that God hath wrought.
For just as life was getting perfect for the two of you.
It hits without announcement, and there's nothing we can do.
Yes, we believe in God, and yes, we pray to God each day.
We pray that you'll regain your health; and then again we pray.
We pray that you will feel the strength of everyone who cares.
We pray that you'll fight back, knowing the pain that each friend shares.

My Dear, you're the most special person to the two of us.
You know why we're together for you were the impetus.
So much in love, we dwell here in our Paradise on Earth.
Like you and Dick, we're living life for all that it is worth.

We're filled with sorrow, yet relieved to know your family's there.
Your siblings, children, grandchildren; sit by with loving care.
Each worrying yet filled with hope that you'll come through, okay.
We know each prays you'll get a little better every day.
And yes, there is no limit to the love Dick has for you.
He'll be there all the way, no matter what you both go through,
a helping hand, a loving word, perhaps a little shove.
Each word and every action clearly demonstrates his love.

You know you've got a lot of reasons to regain your health.
Your family and your friends are testimony to your wealth.
So don't give up because the going gets a little tough.
Dig down a little deeper; prove again you've got the "stuff".

No matter what the future holds, you'll always be our friend.
And that will last forever, right up to the very end.
We've shared our lives this far; we'll share our lives some more and then.
When God says, "come back home", we'll get together in heaven.

CLIMBING BACK

There's no one on this earth that loves you more than Pat and I.
Except that guy who cares for you, there's nothing he won't try.
He gives his all to help you heal; he'll give you all he can,
so fight with all your might for him, climb back to Dick, your man.

It's comforting to know that you're a fighter, through and through.
And when you set your mind, there's not a thing you cannot do.
You won't believe the happiness we felt when we arrived
and understood, with love filled hearts, the trauma you'd survived.
Yet, in your eyes were words that spoke out loudly and quite clear.
We heard each thought you "said", for you're the friend we hold so dear.
With every touch we felt the words you formed with tearful eyes.
That we could feel your thoughts should surely come as no surprise.

We know that you can win, that you can overcome this thing.
That you will fight so you'll receive the blessings life can bring.
If ever there was anyone, who knows why she must fight,
It's you, for Dick deserves your best; and you know that's his right.
You've started a new life that's just been set in Paradise.
And you don't need this "poet" to administer advice.

You know my life with Pat's a living dream that God designed.
We've climbed the steps to Heaven, leaving everyone behind.
So now we want to grab your hands and help you climb each stair.
With Dick, come to our Heaven; live with us forever, there.

Yes, every family member and each friend you've ever made,
have all to their own Deities, with hope, sincerely prayed
for you to be the fighter that we all know you can be.
Fight one more round; you cannot lose; on that we all agree.
As surely as the sun will rise and clouds will fill the sky.

We'll pray for you with caring hearts; we'll pray that you just try.
For each of us is certain that with prayers from every one,
and work from you and love from us, your battle will be won.

If ever there's a moment when you have a little doubt.
Discouraged and with anger, to your Creator you shout,
"Why me, why me, oh God, why me, why now right at this time?
My life was nearly perfect with a true love that's sublime".
We hope you'll hear the answer as it comes into your head.
A lot of things could happen that are much, much worse, instead.
The challenge may be great, the mountain very high to climb,
but you can do it even if it takes a long, long time.
You're strong because of everything that's happened in your life.
You've gained a lot of strength, both as a mother and a wife.
So you are now prepared to meet these challenges, and more.
Just win a battle every day and soon you'll win the war.

We know that there's a future for "Dick's redhead" and "her guy".
With love that's so intense that you both fully qualify
to climb the steps to Heaven, to your Paradise on Earth.
With hearts that burst with joy as you share love for all you're worth.

BIG ED—BIG "C"

He came into my life because he has a girl and boy,
a daughter and a son who simply fill his life with joy.
They do the same for me; they even do a little more.
We fought some real battles; life became a metaphor.
His daughter, Vickie, worked part time in cosmetology.
And Mike, his son, tried lots of things, a little bit like me.
His son-in-law is Rich, for that's his name and attitude.
He's filled with love; has friends galore and he's got fortitude.

Then early in the 90's Rich was starting a new scheme.
He called me for he wanted us to share in the same dream.
We worked by day and night to make a business run okay.
No matter what we did the business tried to get away.

First Vickie came to work to help us out a little bit.
Then Mike joined in to demonstrate that he also has grit.
Big Ed first started working simply as a volunteer.
But soon we had him hooked, for with Big Ed all work is dear.
At first the business wasn't large, so Big Ed worked part time.
Like me Big Ed had grown "mature" and he was past his prime.
We got acquainted during breaks and over lunch one day.
We talked a lot of golf for that's a game we loved to play.

Big Ed was an investor for he shared in Rich's dream.
He wanted to be part of it; be on a winning team.
He couldn't know when he committed money, and then more,
the business would come tumbling down and go right through the floor.

Big Ed had driven truck for longer than he would admit.
He's one straight guy; he's honor bound; Big Ed will never quit.
He has a bigger heart than any man I've ever known.

I cannot tell you all the times the size of it has shown.
Big Ed knew every body shop; each towing service, too.
And every darned mechanic; Big Ed had a motley crew.
He managed all the cars that we got back from obligors.
He got them fixed to sell in either one of Rich's stores.

I never found a subject that Big Ed would not discuss.
But his vernacular was pure; I never heard him cuss.
And that's a lot to say about a man who deals in cars.
Four letter words are sprinkled from the earth up to the stars.
Our love of golf was evident most every time we met.
Big Ed would share a story of how his balls kept getting wet.
The record I recall was in a three-week span of time.
Some forty-two balls disappeared, just like they'd hit quicklime.

Discovery Bay was Big Ed's club; he played there quite a bit.
He tells it like it is each time; he is no hypocrite.
Big Ed invited me to play a round of golf one-day.
Would just a dozen balls be right to play Discovery Bay?
We joined up with two other guys who hit their ball a mile.
They can't affect our game; Big Ed and I are versatile.
Enough to say we played eighteen and still had something left.
The other guys were not impressed; we were not very deft.

When everything seemed lost and business wasn't very good.
Big Ed would come to visit, for he always understood.
He'd stop by every time he took his wife to town to work.
And each of us would share about this crazy car network.

I never heard Big Ed complain although he had the chance.
He lost his money, worked for free; there was no consonance.
And more than that he'd fought and won a battle with big "C".
To do what he did surely took a braver man than me.
You're never sure what life will bring; we parted years ago.
One thing for sure, he's just the same; the Big Ed that I know.

He's in that fight again with grit and prayers from every source.
And he will fight it just as well while playing his golf course.

Big Ed has many friends; his family's love is greater still.
But more than that Big Ed has bundled bushels full of will.
He knows each day is one more gift, and lives it to the hilt.
He'll live his life the best he can, without a sign of guilt.
Big Ed and I share memories, yet we each must live our life.
He shared his stories often, of the "golf dates" with his wife.

I love him more than I can tell, as much as I can say.
For his return to health; now that's exactly how I'll pray.

ROSEMARY

Silva, she is Portuguese.
She quickly makes you feel at ease.
Ethnicity, she doesn't care.
She's truthful, honest, always fair.

I met her just a while ago.
Like all new friends, we tell and show.
And as she speaks I feel inside,
this lady has nothing to hide.

We talk about our health and more.
It's not long till we know the score.
Some body parts don't work quite right,
but she is tough, with lots of fight.

We share a little story or two,
and then decide what we will do.
We'll take a trip to Estes Park,
have dinner there before it's dark.

The mountaintops are white with snow,
green grass sprouts from the floor below.
The lake is full; a crystal blue,
though clouds abound, there's sunshine, too.

Stanley Hotel, a lovely place,
then through town at a snail's pace.
Some shops are open; some are not.
The season starts when it gets hot.

For dinner all of us agree,
a small café with great coffee.
It costs a bit but it's okay,
for we don't do this every day.

Old friends or new, it's really great
to share these memories with your mate.
Renewing friendships from the past,
and building new ones that will last.

One afternoon is all we had
to share our stories, good and bad.
So now Rosemary's etched inside
my memory, there's no place to hide.

And as this day comes to an end,
Rosemary's more than just Pat's friend,
because we've met just this one time,
we'll each feel life is more sublime.

MARY

Good friends are precious treasures to hold dearly in one's heart.
And so it is with Mary; it was that way from the start.
It all began on Friday at the airport where we met.
Though Pat knew Mary many years, I had not seen her yet.
It only took a moment when she smiled and we embraced.
And any doubts I may have had were all quickly erased.
Her smile was in her voice and in her step and in her eyes.
That she is someone special should have come as no surprise.
For every friend of Pat's has been a joy for me to meet.
And making friends with Mary is for me, a unique treat.
For what you see is what you get, for her there's no pretense.
She speaks her mind with loving care; and that makes real sense.

I knew of Mary's age, three score and ten, a little more.
Some folks that age I've known seem to have "passed on" long before.
They only talk of illness or of dying or a pain.
No matter how you try, these subjects come right back again.
But Mary's quite alive and well; she still works at a bank.
She's healthy as can be; I guess she has herself to thank.
For she eats well, gets exercise; her attitude is great.
She knows exactly who she is and does not deviate.

She talks about her family with a very special pride.
You know her love for them originates deep down inside.
She speaks about her husband who passed on some years ago.
Adjusting to this loss is understandably quite slow.

We spend a quiet afternoon; we have a little wine.
We're sheltered on the patio away from the sunshine.
A rustle of the leaves, there is a breeze to keep us cool.
We hear the sound of students going home from the high school.

Soon we're relaxed as we can be; we talk of what we'll do.
We'll see some sites and eat good food; hang out a day or two.
And have a party every day; some wine with chips and dip.
To celebrate our friendship, then we'll plan another trip.
Up on this plateau there are many pretty sites to see.
For it's a year-round wonderland. On that we all agree.
Majestic mountains; lakes galore; deep canyons all around,
it's peaceful in the evening; there is barely any sound.

We make a trip to Evergreen, a quaint old mountain town.
Some homes are built around a lake; some up a slope, some down.
We find a quiet restaurant, an oriental fare.
We walk inside and quickly see there are no people there.
A "Taste of Colorado" is a large annual event.
And that's the destination where the restaurateurs went.
So we're alone in Evergreen, no crowd; the food is great.
Of course we're served quite fast because there isn't any wait.

We travel then to Blackhawk. Mary doesn't realize
that here there's open gambling, and that's a nice surprise.
I listen to the music while the girls each try their luck.
For me it is enough to by a coffee for a buck.
We don't stay very long for Mary wins in just a while.
To win, not lose is quite enough to make all of us smile.
So we depart from Blackhawk with a winner in the car.
And soon we are at home, for Blackhawk isn't very far.

Yes, we then have a party for we've had a perfect day.
We knew that we'd have fun; that we'd enjoy Mary's stay.
In just one day we've bonded and Pat's friendship is renewed.
With love for one another is how each is now imbued.

Together as good friends we know the next day will go well.
We drive to Estes Park to see the old Stanley Hotel.
The movie "Shining" features the hotel as "Overlook".

We meet a chef who talks and talks; he is an open book.
We walk around the quaint old town and shop a little bit.
An hour in these crowds and we are all ready to quit.
So in a sidewalk shop we stop to rest and have a drink.
We need a quiet repose for it will give us time to think.

At home again I realize the value of this day.
It isn't where we travel or that we have time to play.
The most important happening is being with a friend.
To know this friendship will endure until the very end.

Each day brings new adventures both for Mary and for us.
We eat our breakfast, really brunch, it takes no stimulus,
then off to see the city and the mall on Sixteenth Street.
We'll do a little shopping and some people we may meet.
The day is warm, the sun shines bright; there is a little breeze,
and at the mall folks rest on benches in among the trees.
A bus sails by and blows its horn; to take a ride it's free.
We walk along for there is much for all of us to see.
Then as we pass, a shop calls us to come and see their "stuff".
Now Pat and I don't need a thing; we've really got enough.
But Mary wants to buy some cards so we all look around.
While waiting I try on some wide brimmed hats that I have found.

We look for a café that has a sidewalk atmosphere,
to rest and have a drink; to watch the shoppers, far and near.
We finally stop at Starbucks and the ladies have iced tea.
I have a coffee regular; that's quite enough for me.
A quiet hour passes as we 'people watch' and talk.
And then we head back for the car; it's just a little walk.

At home it's cocktail hour for our party time is here.
While Mary has a wine, Pat has a Zima from Coors Beer.
Our party time is special for we share a lot of things.
We talk of what we did today and what tomorrow brings.

We're all relaxed and happy to be with each other here.
That Pat and Mary are good friends is also very clear.

Pat has some videos of when Denise was in the band.
I've seen them several times but always think that they are grand,
precision marching, color guard, with formations, galore.
One ends and there's another, for we want to see some more.
The evening ends with Lawrence Welk, well, really just his show.
We watch it for three hours, for we have no place to go.
The show is quite nostalgic for it "walks down memory lane".
For us it's like their shows of old, a musical refrain.
We check the Colorado lotto on the Internet,
for Mary has two tickets, though we've not been winners yet.
Yep, just as you would guess, she's got four numbers so she's won.
Although it will not make her rich, she's won and that is fun.

Another day has ended; it's as good as it can get.
We have a little rain but not enough to get too wet.
Tomorrow will arrive and we'll enjoy the time we share.
There isn't any plan for we may travel anywhere.

On Thursday it's to Golden, where the School of Mines we see.
We do a little shopping; just a little, happily.
And then we're off to Morrison; it's not that far away.
We'll see Red Rock Pavilion where the entertainers play.
The renovation is not done; we have to walk a bit.
Up flights of stairs, it takes a while; sometimes we stop and sit.
Arriving at the theater, it seems we've walked a mile.
The scene below and up above, makes all of this worthwhile.

We lunch in "Mexico" a place with Latin atmosphere.
We're hungry and eat tons, yet we are happy we are here.
A little shopping and we're on our way back home, once more.
We have no plan so we will see what this night has in store.

Yes, Mary is a special friend; in life we have too few.
For many years I didn't know how these close friendships grew.
For all of us are who we are; there isn't any more.
And Mary's just the same, like she is now and was before.
I think that Mary knows how much her friendship means to us.
That she accepts us as we are; there isn't any fuss.
And we're the same with her; she doesn't have to change a bit.
We're all "old shoes" with loving hearts; such friendships never quit.

MARY LOU

We haven't really visited for over fifty years.
We used to have some happy times and times when we'd shed tears.
Just kids in a small high school where we played and studied some.
Some things we did were lots of fun; some things were really dumb.
Then as adults we scattered searching for the lives we'd seek.
And some of us were full of hell and some of us were meek.
Then after many years apart, we all came home again,
with lots of things that happened in our lives that we'd explain.

So in the year 2000 we all met at Eddie's place.
Now some were kind of rowdy and the others filled with grace.
We got to talk a little; just enough to show we cared,
a prelude to her visit, so our lives could then be shared.

Now I'd known Mary as a child when she was very small.
In fact when she grew up, she still was not so very tall.
And Pat was Mary's friend for several years when they were young.
So she could still remember what they did, and songs they'd sung.
Long after the reunion we all tried to keep in touch.
We wrote a letter, made a call, it wasn't very much.
Then Mary Lou advised us she would visit for a while.
We welcomed her into our hearts again with a big smile.

We finally got together after fifty years apart.
Just like when we were young, we all thought we were pretty smart.
Each of us told the other how our life had been so great,
and how each one had somehow ended up without a mate.
Her hair is silver, wavy soft and full as it can be.
Her laugh is filled with energy, it happens frequently.
With each deep breath she coughs, for she's a lifetime smoker, too.
I'd like to help her kick the cigs; I don't know what to do.

A little over sixty she is active and alert.
Like women of her time, her preference is a mid length skirt.
She's motherly, attractive, like the grandmother she is.
She likes her booze with ice and mix; she doesn't need a fizz.
She gambles with great gusto; she has energy galore,
and pumps the coins into the slots until she has no more.
It's all for fun; she doesn't care if she should lose or win.
She'll laugh it off and ask the girl to bring another gin.

She has a balance in her life; exactly what she wants.
She's able to ignore what others say and people's taunts.
You're soon aware, with Mary Lou, she's happy as can be.
She "rides the horse" the way it goes, she gives love easily.

So we accept her as she is; that's how it's got to be.
But every time I hear her cough, it hurts a piece of me.
I can't be sure, but I would bet, there's poison in each lung.
For she sounds worse than any smokers I have been among.
Yes, Mary smokes, but she is trying to cut down a bit.
It was this afternoon before the second one she lit.
So one day she'll decide to stop, to quit this thing for good.
She'll throw away her last one for she always knew she could.
And on that day her friends will all rejoice; they'll sing a song.
They'll celebrate to Mary's health, for they know she is strong.
And they'll not hear her cough again, not once, not any more.
For Mary's in the game of life, and she now knows the score.

We wish her health and happiness, prosperity and love.
That she is blessed beyond belief with kindness from above.
That all her days on earth be filled with friends that she holds dear.
And love completely fills her life so there's no room for fear.

(Spring 2002)

Now months have passed and we have corresponded quite a bit.
We love to read her letters for they all present her wit.

And then in her last letter came the words we'd waited for.
She'd given up the cigarettes, no smoking anymore.
Unless you've been addicted and then tried stop this thing,
you'll never fully know the pain and anguish it will bring.
For minutes seem like hours; days seem endless with no smokes.
You watch TV; a comedy, you can't laugh at the jokes.
You go to sleep at night; the craving penetrates your soul.
Now everything that happens to you seems to take its toll.
You hope that one more day will make the longing go away.
You even close your eyes and to your deity you pray.

One day, then two, and then some more, and soon it's been a week.
You're feeling sanctimonious; a deeper breath you seek.
The hacking cough you used to have has almost disappeared.
You're even feeling better about all the things you feared.
And everyone who's ever smoked will testify, for sure.
The hunger for a cigarette is there, forever more.
But over-riding this desire to help you through each day,
will be your appetite for life, so here on earth you stay.

So Mary we are with you, every step along the way,
for Pat and I have smoked our share, but it was "yesterday".
We love the time you spent with us, a beautiful refrain.
We both look forward happily, to visiting again.

BOB & JOAN

For years they lived across the street, and raised a girl and boy.
Pat saw them out in front, and then would wave or just say "hi".
Sometimes she'd walk across the street; there wasn't any ploy.
And talk of gardens, children, food or weather, wet or dry.
She didn't take the time to get to know them very well.
She knew she had great neighbors though and really felt quite blessed.
When more than twenty years had passed, her home she had to sell.
Her family needed her elsewhere; she had to leave her "nest".

Nine years went by; she kept in touch with cards and pictures, too.
The things that happened in their lives they all survived, okay.
They raised their families and they did what parents have to do.
Success they celebrated; they met losses with dismay.

Then after all these years apart a letter we received,
for Bob and Joan were coming to this state where we now live.
We'd get together and we'd share the things we've each achieved.
Some subjects may be trivial and some provocative.
We called Joan just as soon as we had read the letter through.
For both of us are happy to see neighbors from the past.
We didn't know what Bob and Joan had planned or what they'd do,
or just how long their visit to their other friends would last.

We asked them to accept the offer of our home for them.
And make our house the place to stay while visiting their friends.
Then to our joy this fit their plans, a working stratagem.
We let them know we're just plain folk, and no one here pretends.
They came to DIA; our airport where the planes fly in.
A handshake and a hug told us that what we'd planned was right.
We met their happy faces with a welcome and a grin.
All afternoon we talked as we prepared for their first night.

When people are like Bob and Joan, so full of warmth and love.
They fit just like a glove into your life, no matter what.
It's like they come into your home with blessings from above.
And anything you do for them will never be for naught.
We didn't really have to plan a lot of things to do.
We'd simply hop into the car and take a little drive.
We talked and let it happen; it was handled impromptu.
The more we learned about these two, the more we felt alive.

We only had two days to visit with both Bob and Joan.
For they had other friends that they'd committed to call on.
The shortness of their visit is a fact that we had known.
Their stay was just a sprint; it never was a marathon.
We said goodbye to them as they checked into their hotel.
For two days and a little more we'd had a lot of fun.
A handshake and a hug; we felt the tears begin to swell.
We knew the real reason for their trip had just begun.

A wedding was the reason that they'd planned the trip at all.
For family is the rationale they used to congregate.
They went up to their rooms as we retired back to the mall.
We knew the balance of their trip was going to be just great.
Two casual friends from days gone by stopped for a day or two.
Because of who they are we're closer than we can explain.
It wasn't anything we said or things we planned to do.
It wasn't the nice weather gently sprinkled with some rain.

But Bob and Joan are people, simply people through and through.
The kind of folks you want to be around as you mature.
There isn't any pretense as they give themselves to you.
For what you see is what you get; and that's enough, for sure.
We're thankful for the time that Bob and Joan have shared with us.
We hope they feel the time with us was well invested, too.
Someday we'll meet again. There'll be no argument or fuss.
It doesn't matter what we talk about or what we do.

The two of us prepared these words especially for you two.
We want you to remember your short visit for a while.
To think kind thoughts of us when all the pictures you review.
And know when you return you'll find us waiting with a smile.

ANITA

I've now enjoyed your friendship, Dear, for over forty years.
We've shared moments of laughter and we both have shed some tears.
On nature's plan our children grew and went out on their own.
Except a special friend appeared, we might now be alone.

I still remember when we met; you bowled an evening league.
And even then your grace and beauty created intrigue.
A twang of southern drawl enhanced an aura around you.
That men were taken with your presence, I believe you knew.
Now there was no pretense about you, just a lovely gal.
A person every one around would like to call, "my pal".
Yet you had something special; yes, you let each person know
that you were just the audience and they starred in the show.

You cast a little light into my life each time we met.
Like making peace with God, your presence supplanted regret.
Your attitude so positive, no matter what life brought,
spread happiness throughout my soul; enhanced my every thought.

Yes, we have aged these forty years and both have lost our mate.
But little did we know that peace and love would be our fate.
It may have taken what we both have gone through all these years,
for us to shed our baggage, letting love replace old fears.
The sun will shine, it always does; it sparkles from your eyes.
The rain may fall from cloudy skies; for that's the way God cries.
The wind may cause a hurricane; a wild typhoon may blow.
As sure as time cannot stand still, your loveliness will grow.

A Tiffany casts crystals of its light across the room.
Yet, when compared to your bright smile, it's darker than a tomb.
The Venus may have awed the Romans; their Goddess of love.

Your loveliness still transcends hers. Yours comes from God above.
You've been a friend these many years; you've shared your happiness.
It is my fervent prayer that in return, your God will bless,
and bring to you the lasting joy and happiness I know
since Pat became my soul mate and unleashed my love to grow.

Your beauty comes from deep within; it grows with every day.
You've found the joy of love; you cast unhappiness away.
We're both the persons that we knew that we could always be.
You've made my world a better place; you're a true friend to me.

DOCTOR "ED"

I'm seventy-five years of age, so I have been around,
and Dr. Ed's the best M.D. that I have ever found.
Yes he's a Doctor, through and through, of medical science.
He's competent, he's friendly and he earns your confidence.

He worked and studied to become a "Man of Medicine".
It took a lot of sacrifice from him and from his kin.
He did it and he's now a member of the Kaiser staff.
His manner gives you comfort; he may even make you laugh.
Yet he will take the time to listen to your every "woe".
And fully tell you what to do before he lets you go.
He's thorough as he checks your history, digests every word.
There's nothing you can tell him that he's not already heard.
But you will never know, for he is focused, just on you.
With patience he will listen then suggest what you should do.
If you've a problem he can't solve he'll let you know, for sure.
He'll cover all your options. You could not ask him for more.
He may suggest a specialist or order a lab test.
You'll know when he is finished you've received the very best.

He doesn't work in "miracles" or "testimonials".
Or fall for advertisements that support a vendor's goals.
It takes good evidence with scientific tests; no ruse,
before prescribing medicine that's right for you to use.

No, even Dr. Ed can't solve your every ache and pain.
But follow his advice and you'll have everything to gain.
He'll never put you more at risk; you'll learn what you should know.
With Dr. Ed, each passing year, your confidence will grow.

I've just one wish, one last request to make of Dr. Ed.
That he stays here with Kaiser till I'm gone, until I'm dead!

THE BULLY

When I was just a little boy, as skinny as can be,
most people looked as large as sin and much too strong for me.
It didn't help when every time I messed up just a bit,
a belt was used across my butt until I couldn't sit.

I lived in a small town with lots of children all around.
We climbed the hills, played kick the can and wrestled on the ground.
Most everyone was playful, just young kids all having fun.
Sometimes we rang a doorbell then we'd turn and really run.

I lived this way till I was twelve and then I went away.
My family bought a little farm, with pears and cows and hay.
I went to school, the seventh grade, the place was new to me.
I'm growing tall, but still quite small, and thin as I can be.

With only three rooms in the school, the place was pretty small.
That's not a lot of kids to meet, so soon I knew them all.
I quickly knew that I had learned a lot more than my peers.
The school down in the city was ahead by some two years.
The classes were a snap for me; I knew the lessons well.
The other kids soon understood that I was no dumbbell.
So I felt really good, for in the classroom I would shine.
New friends, new school, no problems, I was really doing fine.

Then just like that one day at noon, right in the yard at school.
A guy I'd met but didn't know, taught me "the country rule".
Bean Miller was his name and he was big and very tall.
I got one in the gut, then on the chin that made me fall.

I'd never had to fight before; this thing was new to me.
And standing there above me he seemed larger than a tree.

Up on my knees I tried to stand; he threw me to the ground.
I guess he didn't like it that I hadn't made a sound.
The lunch hour finally ended; I was saved; we went inside.
I focused on just one thing now, how I could save my hide.
I knew I didn't do a thing provoking that attack.
Yet there I was, holding my gut and lying on my back.

When school was out I got my books and ran home to our farm.
I'd tried to stay away from him so he'd not do me harm.
Yet, he was sure that I'd return; I had to be at school.
I had no clue what I could do; it wasn't very cool.
He found me on the playground; it's exactly what I feared.
I'm dragged across the grassy field; my clothes are stained and smeared.
He hit me like a punching bag; I hurt from head to toe.
It finally ends; I'm on my feet, I run; away I go.

Can you believe I lived with this? It happened every week.
I got to hate the recesses, my life looked really bleak.
I greeted school vacation with great happiness and glee.
At last from this big bully I'd no longer have to flee.

I worked hard all that summer, milking cows and hauling hay.
Just like an athlete working out, twelve hours every day.
My muscles all got hard; in height I grew to six feet tall.
A fist into my gut was now like hitting a brick wall.

I met Bean Miller at the gate the day that school began.
We stood there eye to eye, for I felt every bit a man.
He made one move; I hit him in the gut then on the chin.
He staggered back; he knew at once, this fight he couldn't win.
I grabbed his arm and twisted it until it wouldn't bend.
The words came quickly from Bean's mouth; "I want to be your friend".
He laughed a little; struggled free and reached out for my hand.
I took it into mine; we shook. Now that felt really grand.

I guess I learned a bully doesn't bully any more,
as soon as he finds out that you can even up the score.
I went to school, yes every day, at recess we all played.
Old Bean and I were best of friends and friends we've always stayed.

BEAUTIFULLY UGLY

She's short and kind of square, she even waddled when she walked.
She moved her mouth, the words occurred with lisps each time she
talked.
Her lips were little lines around her teeth, as big as sin.
Her folks I'm sure were thankful that their daughter had no twin.
Her squatty little legs were fat; her ankles were fat, too.
Not pretty, but she's just as nice as anyone I knew.
I saw her by her house; it was the first time that we met.
We climbed the little hill to school; I saw how much she'd sweat.
Her eyes were small and squinted; they had freckles all around.
I looked to see her lashes, but two hairs were all I found.
Her eyebrows were as black as soot beneath a broad forehead.
Her bulging body said it all, how well that she was fed.
She wore a blouse in flower print, the neckline very high.
It wouldn't stay inside her skirt; she didn't even try.
Her shoes were boots with heavy soles, all scuffed and kind of brown.
Her wardrobe was about the worst I'd ever seen in town.

Her home was just across the street; she lived there with her folks.
We'd sometimes sit on her front lawn and drink some ice-cold cokes.
She helped me with my homework, for in school she knew it all.
We shared like friends and neighbors, for there was no protocol.
At night with other kids we'd play a game of "kick the can".
When she was "it" and I got caught, I knew how fast she ran.
She pulled her skirt right up around her waist with just one hand,
and moved her legs more quickly than the speed of a jazz band.
Her straight short hair would cling beside the roundness of her head.
Her chalky white complexion made her look like she was dead.
The fingers on her hands were short and stubby, slightly bent.
The fullness of her skirt concealed her hips, just like a tent.

There wasn't much to say to compliment the way she looked.
Her brain held data like the information had been booked.
It didn't take me long to learn that what she said was true.
With everything she saw or read her memory always grew.
We walked to school most every day; I held her hand in mine.
In classes we sat side by side, for she was my lifeline.
And after school we'd study with our books about the floor.
She'd ask a question; give a quiz till I could learn no more.
Each year we seemed to study more, and learn of worlds beyond.
We promised if we parted that we'd always correspond,
for though I learned so much from her, she also learned from me.
She wanted to be friends for life; with that I did agree.

We'd worked this way for seven years; she'd been my dearest friend.
We'd shared our lives and souls; was there yet more to comprehend?
Except for boys with whom I played, she was my closest chum.
I hadn't really looked to see just who she had become.

We're in the seventh grade; I see she looks just like a girl.
Her straight short hair is longer now and even has a curl.
She's just as tall as I and doesn't weigh a darned bit more.
What happened to this friend of mine? She's never been a bore.
She's tanned from head to toe from playing in the fields with me.
Her body is as slender as a newly planted tree.
She has a tiny waist with hips announcing that they're there.
I've been so busy being friends I didn't even care.

And now she has some soft round bumps protruding from her chest.
I look around and realize she's cuter than the rest.
Her legs are long and shapely with small ankles, tiny feet.
To hold her close has changed, for it is now a special treat.
I'd never noticed girls before; to me they were just kids,
like some of Mom's utensils with their loosely fitted lids.
They'd always been about the same; each had a job to do.
And kids were busier than bees; I'd been that busy, too.

She's full of fun; her attitude is stronger than can be.
What happened to that ugly little girl I used to see?
We'd been so busy being friends as each was dutiful,
that I forgot to see how she became so beautiful.

She always had this beauty; it was hidden in her head.
It sparkled and projected out with every word she said.
When you look in your mirror, don't believe what you may see.
For beauty lies there deep within your personality.

COPS

Some cops behave as we expect and some are hard to read.
Most cops exemplify their name; a few forget their creed.
It doesn't pay a lot of dough; their life is on the line.
They may be called a "pig"; at other times they're called a "swine".
Address them as "Peace Officer", for that is what they are,
although you may think otherwise if they should stop your car.
We drive so much and see them when they're cruising on patrol.
We may forget that traffic flow is not their only role.

For when you've a disturbance, and it's in your neighborhood,
across the street you hear a scream; it doesn't sound too good.
You call and just like that, a cop in uniform's in front.
The problem gets solved quickly; solving problems is their wont.
Your wife is in the family way; it's getting very close.
The baby's coming quickly; it's not hard to diagnose.
You call for help, before you get your wife into the car.
A cop arrives to escort you, although it isn't far.
Your kids are at the school where they are playing with their friends.
A student shows up with a gun; who knows what he intends?
A cell phone call and seconds pass; a cop quickly arrives.
Cops take control so no one's hurt and everyone survives.
If you have an emergency, you're bleeding from a cut.
And you call 911 while friends apply a tourniquet.
You'll look up and you'll see a car that's parked out in your drive.
It's black and white; yes it's a cop, the first car to arrive.

When you are with your friends they'll often talk of cops with you.
As frequently as not it's only what the bad ones do.
And if you let your kids hear this; the cops you don't defend.
They'll never understand a cop may just be their best friend.
Plain clothed or uniformed, whether a woman or a man.

If I'm in trouble I don't care, for I'm their greatest fan.
They risk their lives; they don't think twice; there isn't any time.
They rush right in and take control; they handle every crime.

I'm proud of and I'm thankful, too, for those willing to serve.
It's not an easy task; I know it takes a lot of nerve.
So hold them up as heroes, every one who serves with pride.
If you're a lawful person, they are always on your side.

OTHER COMPANIONS

The world's a happy place when you've a dog inside your heart.
Their love is unconditional; it's there right from the start.
They'll nuzzle up against you; raise their paw for you to shake.
And let you know they love you, for both your and for their sake.
It doesn't matter what the breed, the gender or the size.
Your dog will always know your needs; a dog just never lies.
A friendly bark when you arrive all tuckered out and tired.
Or share a walk around the block whenever you're inspired.
When you shout out with anger for your day has not gone well.
Or when you hurt inside and you need someone you can tell.
Your dog sits there beside you as tears well up in your eyes.
The comfort that he gives to you should come as no surprise.

Your day begins; your dog is there to let you know he cares.
It doesn't matter you're a mess with snarled, unruly hairs.
Your dog sits by the bathroom door as you do your toilette.
He's tireless as he waits for you; he never gets upset.
Your dog waits patiently as you get dressed and fix your hair.
With knowledge you'll be leaving, there is no hint of despair.
There's understanding in his eyes; a movement of his tail,
he demonstrates his love, a love for you that will not fail.
It doesn't take a lot, a gentle word, perhaps a smile.
Or maybe you take time to brush his coat for just a while.
The thanks that you receive from smiling eyes that look at you,
puts joy into your heart as you begin each day anew.

It doesn't matter where you live; a city, town or farm.
A dog's love never wanes a bit; there is no false alarm.
You'll never find another, who is loyal to the core,
accepting what you give, while he gives you a whole lot more.
Your dog does not complain, no matter how his day has been.

You may forget to feed him, but to him that's not a sin.
He'll tell you when he's hungry and as soon as he's been fed,
he'll wag his tail to let you know enough has now been said.
Your dog does not hold grudges; he does not retaliate.
He doesn't greet you angrily when you come home quite late,
for dogs are loyal friends who ask so little in return.
Yes, dogs could be our teachers and we'd have a lot to learn.

If you're alone at night for there's no one to share your house.
Your kids are grown and gone and you no longer have a spouse.
You get into your car to pass the time with a short ride.
With happy eyes and wagging tail, your dog is by your side.
Your dog will tell you when a stranger enters your domain.
Yet, let him know it's okay, and beside you he'll remain.
But let a stranger make a move to put you in harms way,
he'll come to your defense till the intruder shouts, "Mayday".
There's no one that's too large for him, too threatening or bold.
If they present a danger, whether they are young or old,
your dog, though just a little guy, will fight until the death
to see that you're protected, 'long as he can take a breath'.

When you got married and began to raise your family.
Perhaps a son and daughter, each starts as a small baby.
As soon as they arrive your dog becomes their closest friend.
And just like you, he'll protect them until the very end.
You have an understanding with your dog when you're away.
Your kids come home from school and go outside where they will play.
And if there's any danger your small dog will let you know.
He'll watch them every minute; he's "el jefe", "chief honcho".

My life's been long and happy, many things and tales to share.
I've even had some friends who let me know how much they care.
With love from friends and family for as long as I recall,
I should not need another thing, not anything at all.
Yes, I have lots of memories and they're almost all quite good.

Though I have made a few mistakes, I've done most things I should.
Yet, my life's been much happier because of canine friends.
And it will be that way for me till my life finally ends.

If you are ever lonely, if your life's filled with despair!
Though you have friends and family, there's not one who seems to care.
And loneliness fills every day. You don't know what to do.
Give love to a small dog and you'll feel love returned to you.

I've owned a lot of dogs that lived with me for many years.
We've shared a lot of happy times; we've even shed some tears.
And now though every dog I've owned is gone, we'll never part,
for they've been my companions and they're nestled in my heart.

MY FRIEND—HUGO, THE DOG

He's really not that old you see; a dog that's very small.
We met just after he was born, a warm day in the fall.
The year was eighty-seven and a gift he was to be.
I wanted him to love us all, and feel that he is free.
Four Winds is what he's called she said; his papers have a seal.
But "Hugo" is the name he knows and that's his name, for real.
He's bred a Shetland Sheep dog; he's just larger than a cat.
He let me know quite quickly, he can also be a brat.
We go for walks; he has a leash, a collar round his neck.
Though tiny, he has long brown hair; his white's more than a speck.
He needs to know that I'm the boss; I teach him what I know.
More than a pet, he's family. He is not a dog for show.

A Sheltie is so full of fun; he runs and runs around.
He scuffles and he barks and barks. There's always lots of sound.
One day when we went for a walk his leash was loosely fit.
A noise behind, a crash too loud, he thought that he'd been hit.
He bolted, left the collar behind, a leash without a dog,
and vanished through the brush, past trees, and over a big log.
He disappeared right from the earth; it almost broke my heart.
To find him I have no idea where I will need to start.
He's small, he's just a little guy; he's only three months old,
and I've got visions of him lost, afraid and in the cold.
Alone and freezing, whimpering, not knowing what to do,
just walking on forever with his body starving, too.
The vision's clear, it hits me hard, tears come into my eyes.
I drive all over, search and search, my body heaves with sighs.

I wonder, is it like this when your children run away?
I look and look, but finally all that I can do is pray.
Each place that harbors animals, and they're all over town,

his picture, name and number, too, they all have written down.
There's nothing more to do until I hear a phone that rings,
with just a word, encouragement, the feeling good news brings.

Then finally two days pass and I am sitting by my phone.
It rings, I jump, then answer it; I'm standing all alone.
The voice is music to my ears; sweet song, I listen hard.
A lady and her two sons have found Hugo in their yard.
The joy I feel, the happiness; he cuddles in my arm.
He made it through; he's okay now; there is no real harm.
A choker is his collar now; he'll never break away.
I won't allow what happened, not again to me, no way.

It's hard for me to let you know the joy that Hugo brings
into my life, from dawn to dark, his voice, familiar rings.
His eyes are dark. They seem to search each time he looks at me.
The love we share; we touch, and then it's his love I can see.
Each year we've grown together and each year we're closer still.
We walk the fields, across schoolyards, and up a little hill.
We laugh and play; we jump and run; life's good, it's never bleak.
We sleep together every night; so close we're cheek to cheek.

In doggie years much time has passed; he's getting kind of slow,
for Hugo's over ninety, he tries hard, but now I know,
as each day passes when we walk, he really wants to stroll.
He sways a bit and stumbles, too; we try to dodge each hole.

The saddest day that ever was, was when we had to part.
His eyes were moist and so were mine. My body wouldn't start.
Too old to change his residence, I left my friend behind.
I start the car; I'm searching for the life I need to find.
I think of Hugo often, like a child that's far away.
I know he's okay there at home, and that's where he must stay.

We met again a month ago for just a little while.
When our eyes met I felt the hurt, no hint of Hugo's smile.
He doesn't know why I'm not there to feed him every day,
to cuddle up, to brush his fur, and then go out and play.
He limps a little, walks slowly; his being seems to plead.
Can't we just share a little more and that will fill my need!
I hurry out; it's tougher than the loss of a close friend.
For Hugo doesn't understand our friendship had to end.
I only hope he has no pain, that days are never bad.
Each time I think of Hugo now, I once again feel sad.

SEASON'S GREETINGS TO FRIENDS
DECEMBER 2004

(Xeriscaping the Yard)
Our mighty oak stands five feet tall, adorning the front yard.
One juniper spread out so wide, like it is standing guard.
The strip has ornamental trees, grape holly in between.
And rock replaces lawn, three different colors to be seen.
A ramp of paving stone replaced the broken cement walk.
A front yard patio provides a summer place to talk.
Out back it's quite another thing; retaining walls galore.
New paving stones create a walk, a patio and more,
five decorative planters, ready for bright flowers to bloom.
A "Victory Garden" on the north side where there's lots of room.
And one last thing to make it perfect, you may thing it strange.
A pad with artificial turf for Rod's golf driving range!

(New Lifestyles)
We live alone, the two of us, the "kids" have moved away.
Son, Lee, now lives in Aspen with a new job, steady pay.
Denise turned twenty-one and she's mature beyond her years.
Employed and doing great in school, she's allayed any fears.
Yes, twenty-one; a trip to Vegas for this "big" birthday.
We know we've got to get accustomed to her being away.
And sure enough in August, near her work she found a place.
With seven bedrooms and five friends, each person's got their space.
Four guys another gal and that completes her household group.
She visits us each week so we are still here in her loop.
Denise's brother, Dave, still lives in Granby with his wife.
They both work and are happily enjoying their good life.

(Family and Friends)
We try to keep in touch with all our family and each friend.

The telephone, a letter or an e-mail we may send.
A little trip to visit with some friends in Washington!
In Oregon Rod's grandchildren, two daughters and his son!
We visited Pat's siblings and that made the trip complete.
And safely home together, life is always so upbeat.
We're happy for the healthy life that we enjoy so much.
We love it when you take a moment just to keep in touch.
Best wishes for a Holiday that's filled with happiness.
We feel the love you give and hope that you receive no less.

MUCH LOVE—BEST WISHES—HAPPY HOLIDAYS
DECEMBER 2005

A Merry Christmas—Happy New Year—All our best to you!
Politically it ain't correct; but we do what we do.
May happiness reign sovereign; for you and your family!
And may the warmth of love be yours; fill your heart, totally.

Our "dreaded" Christmas Letter filled with all the "stuff" we've done.
The challenges we've faced but mostly things that have been fun.
The biggest news of all we'll put up front; make sure it's read.
November second, Pat's birthday, the two of us were wed!
So now we're really "one", (but that's the way it's always been).
Our love so strong that even God declared it's not a sin.
We're happy as two teenagers; two kids on their first date.
So after fifty years apart, it still was not too late.

An update on the "kids"; there hasn't been a lot of change.
They're still out of "the nest"; I guess that's not so very strange.
Denise continues at "CU" and works at AMC.
Film studies are her quest; "Film Editor" one day she'll be.
Now Lee works in construction, does some "plumbing" on the side.
He works on poems he's written; works until he's satisfied.
We share poems when he visits; it is always loads of fun.
Denise we see each week when she has laundry to be done.
A word about our Grandson Dave and his wife, Anna, too!
This year they bought a home; it's "old"; for them the house is "new".
It's right "downtown" in Granby so their work's not far away.
They're settled; near their friends; Granby's their home where they will stay.

We're thankful for the health care we've "enjoyed" throughout the year.
On Rod the Doctor worked "up front"; on Pat it was "the rear".
A new lens in Rod's right eye, better golf he now can play.
Pat's surgery was tougher; Doctors fixed her vertebrae.

We both feel blessed to have so many friends and family.
Rod's son with wife and son stopped by en route to Tennessee.
Raleigh, their son, played chess at Nashville, where he did quite well.
Their visit was just loads of fun; too soon we said, "Farewell".
Surprise, surprise, the telephone! Sciborskis are in town.
We caught up on each other's lives from daylight till sundown.
Both John and Rod play golf so they'd arranged to play a round.
Their match gave way to thunderheads, a little too much sound.
Rod met Pat's friend Jan Cummings and her sister Wendy, too.
A luncheon at Red Robin, where we had our rendezvous!
It's so much fun to renew friendships; catch up on what's new.
For visiting with friends is something we both love to do.

Five long, short years have passed since this romance of ours began.
We're more than friends and lovers; we're each other's greatest fan.
We give thanks every day for all the blessings cast our way.
Yes, every day is special; every one's a holiday.
Great happiness and joy to all, and may you have good health.
A heart that's filled with love to share; for love's your greatest wealth!

DECEMBER 2006

A bit about our lives here in our "Earthly Paradise".
We maintain healthy lifestyles and for us it's worth the price.
For every morning exercise is our priority.
And healthy meals follow; that now happens naturally.
We walk to get our "bagel fix"; Paneras is the place.
It's just about three miles round trip. We set a taxing pace.
This year we ate the veggies from our garden in the back.
Some cabbage, beets, three kinds of squash, tomatoes by the sack!
Rod's on his practice range most days; hits golf balls at the net.
He hopes to "shoot his age" but hasn't quite got that done, yet.
The "mighty oak" we planted has now grown to eight feet tall.
In thirty years it'll be the most majestic tree of all.

Last Spring Lee started working as a chef; he's quite a cook.
Employed at Sombrero Ranch; still working on his book.
He rides the range with "trail hands"; prepares their every meal.
His poetry's been published now; for us that's a "big deal".
Denise is almost finished with her studies at C.U.
Her major is in film and that's the work she plans to do.
Her boyfriend, Tom, is in film studies, just the same as she.
They share so much and soon they'll share, each a Fine Arts Degree!
Way up in Granby, Dave and Anna care for Jim, Dave's dad.
They "shouldered" this responsibility, of course Jim's glad.
They both enjoy their work and Dave's advanced a bit this year.
That he's a master painter's now accepted, and quite clear.
Lisa, Charles, and both their dogs recently moved away.
They've settled down in Austin where it seems they're going to stay.
For Charles family lives in Texas; they enjoy the state.
Together they've found happiness; and we think that's just great.

Their busy lives constrain our contacts with Rod's family.
Yet every call and note tells us they're happy as can be.
We haven't traveled out of state to visit them this year.
We loved it when Granddaughter, Beth, came out to see us, here.
It may have been her boyfriend, Corey, whom she came to see.
But we don't care; we welcome every visit, happily.

We were so saddened by two Fowler Family deaths this year
A sister-in-law and a nephew, both of them so dear!
Pat's niece who lost her husband came to visit for a while.
A member of a Corvette Club, she drove here, every mile.
Another sister-in-law and her daughter let us know.
They're coming here to visit, soon as there's not too much snow.
We love it when we get to see our families now and then.
We hope to see a whole lot more when we "go west" again.

We both agreed; one page; and not a single sentence more.
What can we writers do? I guess some things we'll just ignore.
Now we will end by wishing all of you the very best.
May happiness and love prevail in your life's every quest.
The two of us are healthy; every moment is just great.
Our life's a bit euphoric, filled with love for our soul mate.
We're both so very thankful we're together, at long last.
We count our blessing every day as years fly by so fast.

FROM OUR FAMILY TO YOURS—MERRY CHRISTMAS &
HAPPY NEW YEAR

CHRISTMAS TRADITIONS

We've not been married long and yet "traditions" have begun.
Just little things we do each year increase our Christmas fun.
We write a plan; it isn't much; just things we need to do,
to celebrate the holiday with friends and family, too.
There's candy to be made and lots of baking to be done.
Then shopping for our Christmas "feast"; small errands to be run!
Some "goodie" platters for the neighbors and a special friend!
Enjoy the process, every moment, till the very end.

The tree is in the living room. No ornament or light.
It's waiting for Denise so it is decorated right.
Inside the house are little things that bring out Christmas cheer.
And Christmas songs are playing for the two of us to hear.

Icicle lights around the house, they're hanging from the roof.
The neighbors see we celebrate; our home provides the proof.
A Christmas wreath greets every one approaching our front door.
As we embrace the season's joy, there is no need for more.
The highlight of the season is with family all around.
We talk and sing; we laugh a lot, enjoying every sound.
The gifts are very modest for it's love that we exchange.
Yes, these are our traditions and there's not a one we'd change.

But best of all is having Jim and Peter for the day.
Two brothers, wildly different, yet they've each so much to say!
It may be "off the wall". Sometimes profound as it can be!
It's always lively whether we agree or disagree.
There's never been a time with them that we've not learned a bit.
It may be something they began, or something that they quit.
There's so much color in their past; such tragedy right now.
They make it through each day and yet we sometimes wonder how.

When Christmas day comes to an end and we say our "goodbyes",
I feel euphoric in my soul, yet sometimes my heart cries.
How long can these traditions fill our holidays with cheer?
I think of when the "kids" are gone; when they are not this near.
When we're alone, the two of us! No tree or gifts to share!
No sweat! I'll be a happy guy. My soul mate will be there.

REWARDS—
LOCATION AND LIFESTYLE

Where we choose to live, the type of career for which we prepare and the work we do, leisure time and the hobbies we pursue; all contribute to the quality of life we enjoy or endure. Sometimes seemingly small decisions have a dramatic affect on who we are and the values that define our lives.

MY COLORADO—EVENING IN GOD'S COUNTRY
(From the eastern slopes of the Rockies)

I live in Heaven, there's no Hell, God watches over me.
The sun spreads diamonds through the leaves that rustle in a tree.
There's laughter from the cotton clouds; the only sound one hears,
as thunderheads move toward the sun. The sun then disappears.
The mountains reach out in the west and seem to grasp God's hand.
Migrating geese honk melodies, as members of a band.

How can I paint this picture? There is beauty all around!
Now chirping birds; the caw of crows; then silence, not a sound!
Profoundly quiet, then the whisper of a gentle breeze.
A thundershower; the raindrops fall as nature bathes the trees.
A lightning bolt fractures the sky; the earth trembles below.
The twilight hovers overhead; skies open for God's show.

The squirrels now stop their feeding, not a single one around.
They've scampered to their lairs up in the trees above the ground.
A fox, its coat a rusty red, now leaps across the brush.
A rabbit in his path; there is a reason for his rush.
Bright beams of light across the sky; a colorful display!
The rain clouds dancing to and fro, like children as they play.
From purple to deep scarlet, as the sun and clouds compete;
they change their shades and tints, till Heaven's color is replete.

Wind from the west, clouds disappear, the air is fresh and clean.
The moon soon crests the mountains, moonbeams bright as I have seen.
Then evening says goodbye; the dark of night surrounds me now.
The giant oak protects me as I cling to its strong bough.
In quiet meditation, the whole world belongs to me.
I raise my arms to Heaven. Give God thanks, I'm here; I'm free.

FORMATIVE YEARS IN THE VALLEY

Just two miles wide it isn't big; six miles from north to south.
A river runs its length year round; it never has a drouth.
About five hundred souls with homes; most have a little farm;
there is no crime; it's peaceful and that gives the place its charm.
It's nestled in the rolling hills with mountains just behind.
A single road is access, so it's pretty hard to find.
Most visitors ask where they are, for they have lost their way.
The ones that look around a bit are just as apt to stay.

A road goes up the northern hill and down the other side.
It curves along the mountain; it's a kind of scary ride.
It takes you to a river that starts from a great big lake.
The canyon's fifty miles long, without a single break.
A lumber mill was built about the time the war began.
My uncle took a job there and became a lumberman.
Some families came from Oregon to build their life anew.
And kids worked there part time for they could use the money, too.
A great big dam was built to hold the water for a pond.
The fish swam up a ladder to the creeks that were beyond.
Below the dam were ripples where the fish would lay their eggs.
At night I'd try to catch the fish; they'd swim right through my legs.

The river came to idle where it formed a big round pool.
It's where we kids assembled for a swim right after school.
A soft sand beach was on one side; the other had a rock.
To leap from rock to water was a very worthy shock.
The people who lived on this side were mostly lumberjacks.
Their homes were simple structures; many may have called them shacks.
The children from the mill drove to the valley every day.
They went to school with me to do their studies and to play.

The valley is an oval, hills and mountains all around.
At night from any hilltop you see stars, but there's no sound.
Some lights will flicker here and there, a cricket you may hear.
And watch right close along the ridge and you may see a deer.
The town is kind of small with nothing special there to see.
You'll always find a "native" who will share some history.
A single road, a dozen homes, a church for Sunday school,
a wide spot in the river serves in summer as a pool.

Two aunts and uncles, cousins three live in the northern part.
They feed and milk their cows and tend to all the crops they start.
My mother found this place when she went up to see her kin.
One taste of rural life and Mom was there for thick or thin.
She bought a farm; it wasn't big, a house, a barn, pear trees.
There weren't any smudge pots so we hoped it wouldn't freeze.
Our family left the city life and moved to our new home.
We got a saddle horse with halter, and a currycomb.
A tractor and a shed were there; they came with what we bought.
I built a smokehouse to prepare for all the fish I caught.
A river separates our farm from neighbors on each side.
Some trees along the river are so old they're petrified.
A creek behind our house has fish that run in wintertime.
It's way down in a crevice with steep banks I have to climb.
An old wood bridge provides a way to go from front to back.
It looks like it was built by some impatient lumberjack.

Our farmhouse had just four rooms, with a porch in front and back.
Two bedrooms held the six of us, without a lot of slack.
I liked the kitchen best because it was the largest room.
It's where my mother worked to cook the food that we'd consume.
Our water came from a hand pump beyond the kitchen door.
Mom heated water on the stove to cook and mop the floor.
We didn't have a bathroom; nights we used a round white pan,
then emptied it into the yard before the day began.
There wasn't any power, so we used a coal oil lamp.

Our family life was sometimes just like living in a camp.
The pot was a "two holer" out behind the chicken coop.
That's where you went when nature made the call for you to poop.

Our farm was just a mile from town where farmers always met.
They sat around and smoked their pipes and no one got upset.
A general store, two bars and then the schools to teach us kids.
The valley folks were healthy and there were no invalids.
An U. S. Postal Office thrived; it put us on the map.
My mom worked there; when she began there was a little flap.
For jobs were hard to come by and some folks were not too kind,
until they got to know my mom, and then they didn't mind.

I quickly learned to love this place, with mountains all around,
to share with friends and schoolmates the discoveries that I found.
I fished in streams and rivers, catching salmon, perch and trout.
But hunting was the best, for with my gun I had real clout.
The deer from in the foothills were the entrée for each meal.
With salmon, duck or quail, getting food was no big deal.
The veggies from the garden supplemented fruit we raised.
And berries picked from bushes growing where the cattle grazed.
The dams along the river were to hold the soil back.
Each winter rain brought salmon up the river by the pack.
They'd try to jump each dam to get to creeks where they could spawn.
So there I was with hook in hand each morning right at dawn.
They jumped into the air and hit the water with a bang.
I sat there with my gaff hook on a concrete overhang.
They hit the water, paused and then began to swim again.
Prepared and with my gaff hook I was every salmon's bane.

I walked along the foothills up behind a little farm.
The season didn't matter for there wasn't any harm.
With shells inside my pocket and my rifle, I felt good.
I found a little knoll, and then on top of it I stood.
It never took a lot of time to find a deer or two.

The valley grass was green, and all the deer knew what to do.
As I walked up the mountain, they were coming down to feed.
I'd mostly take just one small deer; there was no call for greed.
Fresh venison was our main dish; some baked, some broiled, some fried.
But some was saved for jerky; it was stripped and smoked, then dried.
The smokehouse out across the creek worked every day and night.
While smoke provided flavor, it was dried by the sunlight.

The valley schools were small, but large enough for all of us.
The process was informal, so there wasn't any fuss.
I went to school like other kids, three classes to a room.
There were not many students for there'd been no baby boom.
Whenever I was needed on the farm to do some work,
I simply didn't go to school, and no one went berserk.
When all the work was done, I just returned right back to school.
That's just the way I did it, and I didn't break a rule.

The summers were a special time; I worked and played a lot.
I did some foolish things sometimes, but I was rarely caught.
There wasn't any special law that governed what I did.
I tried most everything there was, like any normal kid.
I drove at night to where the watermelons grew, galore.
I'd take a few and eat them; then I'd take a little more.
Sometimes the fish would run at night; I knew exactly where.
With points and hooks and flashlights, you can bet that I was there.
The wardens didn't bother much; they knew I fished for food.
It wasn't like I wasted fish like some "ole city dude".
On Halloween I'd play some pranks; just little stuff you know.
On July fourth I rode some cows there in the rodeo.

There was a festival each spring; it was a big affair.
It made a lot of money; the whole valley was aware.
But for us kids the festival was like a holiday.
With food and drink for everyone, and games that we could play.
The money from the first one went to build a tennis court.

When it was done school tennis then became an added sport.
We had some matches, then, there was a bigger tournament.
That I became the high school champ was not an accident.
For I'd played tennis long before I even started school.
To play against these first year kids was something short of cruel.
Although I liked a lot of sports, court tennis was my thing.
I did not realize the scholarship that it would bring.

This valley was my home till I was eighteen years of age.
I felt completely in control; the valley was my stage.
With just one general store I surely couldn't shop for much.
But when I needed something, neighbors helped me in the clutch.
Each neighbor was a friend who cared what happened, every day.
It didn't take a church for them to kneel to God and pray.
I made more friends in those few years than I will ever know.
With every passing day I knew that each friendship would grow.
They're special folks and handle every friend with loving care.
It doesn't matter if you're poor or you're a millionaire,
for they're all like a worn old shoe, just plain as each can be.
They're poor dirt farmers from my past, but they're the world to me.

When it came time to leave that place I was a full-grown man.
I went to be a "city dude" and lost my farmer's tan.
For years I didn't see my friends; our lives went separate ways.
Like herds of sheep without a fence, a few of us were strays.
But like a sheep that's lost and then returns back to the flock.
When I came back my friendships were as solid as a rock.
I shared the memories of my youth; I talked to valley friends.
With some I hadn't seen for years, I quickly made amends.

My life's now full of love and hope of dreams I will achieve.
I live each day to its extreme; I'll never need to grieve.
I'll not return to live again in this my early home,
for life's a labyrinth of chance; much like a honeycomb.
Our past is sweet; but it is gone; it won't return to us.

To try to live our youth again would be too perilous.
But I did find the girl I loved when she was sweet sixteen.
That our love lasted all this time could not have been foreseen.
When we were both in high school was when we began to court.
We fell in love. I quickly learned I was the naïve sort.
She had me on a pedestal, just like I was a king.
I had such fear instilled within; I did a foolish thing.

We parted though she never knew what caused the little rift.
Me tell her what I'd done? I let her think that I'd been miffed.
If there were any questions I'd just answer with a smirk.
I dated other girls and then I went away to work.
The years went by and each of us had families of our own.
Then fate brought us together when we each were all alone.
The teenage drama faded as the years went passing by.
At sixty-nine I told her; now I didn't have to lie.

So finally I am seventy; I've found my life long love.
A gorgeous valley lady and she fit me like a glove.
We're soul mates now and share a love that's more than you can see.
Our life is quite beyond our dreams; it's truly ecstasy.

THE VALLEY—REVISITED

It's been just over fifty years since we have been around,
to listen to the music of "The Valley's" rural sound.
And yet today when we arrive the music is so clear.
It fills our hearts with memories of the friends who are so dear.

"The Valley's" not the same, but then we're now three score and more.
And we were just young kids when both of us lived here before.
Yet some things never change; the rolling hills on either side.
Protect the many farms that make "The Valley" seem so wide.
We take a slow, long drive all up and down "The Valley" floor.
We hope that we will see the way "The Valley" was before.
Nostalgia in our hearts and age-old memories in each mind,
there's hope at every turn, anticipating what we'll find.

Pat's childhood home is here; it might have changed a little bit.
The memories flow; we park and there in front of it we sit,
remembering the times when we were dating, years ago.
We would have "coupled" then if we'd allowed our love to grow.
The home where I once lived is gone, yet I remember it.
To build a house like that, you could not now get a permit.
No water and no power and an outhouse down the lane.
I lived there, but that ancient house was a homemaker's bane.

Each road we travel leads us to another memory.
And each is so nostalgic, even sights we do not see.
The roads are just the same, maybe a little rough and worn.
And here and there an aged barn appears a bit forlorn.
We share our memories from the past, the fun we had back then.
The work we did, the friends we had, so many, way back when.
Then gradually we find that we have filled our memory banks.
Our fingers touch as to our God we give our heartfelt thanks.

Returning to the present we discover friends, galore.
Our classmates from the past, their spouses and a whole lot more.
Yes, we've returned to spend some time again with all our friends.
To laugh with those we loved so much; with some we make amends.
The people here are just as nice as when we two were young.
Each one we meet is friendly; they're so nice to be among.
There's not an ounce of pretense; they are real; there is no fuss.
And love flows from each heart as, one by one, they welcome us.
They come from everywhere, each with a different memory.
Yet some still live right here and they are happy as can be.
It doesn't seem to matter whether they stayed here or left.
"The Valley's" in their hearts and not a soul here seems bereft.

My cousins come from Arkansas; a fifth wheeler behind.
For several days they drive and you just know they do not mind.
They know when they arrive they'll see some friends and family.
And spend some time with everyone, and do it happily.
Another cousin's here although her husband died last year.
And then she lost her mother and an aunt who was so dear.
To top it off her brother who is here for all to love.
Is fighting for his life; he's in our prayers to God above.

A few are simply curious; their memories are not strong.
But they know that on this one day that here's where they belong.
For when you've lived here in "The Valley" for a little while,
each thought will be nostalgic, and will bring a heartfelt smile.

Two sisters whose dear father was the high school principal,
had gone just to the grade school; not to the high school at all.
They're just as warm and beautiful as when they went away.
The years have passed yet it seems like it was just yesterday.
My loving aunt attended from "the class of forty-two".
She's matriarch of her own clan that grew, and grew, and grew.
And every one she met gave her a hug and welcome kiss.
The love she has for this small place has filled her life with bliss.

A classmate that could not attend had suffered a bad stroke.
She'd lost the use of her right side caused by a clot that broke.
Yet when we were together just before this great affair,
her only wish was that she and her lover could be there.

"The Valley's" like a magnet that attracts from far and wide!
Just living here a little while seems to imbue great pride.
Not one who's ever lived here can forget the strong effect.
For all agree the years spent here were just about perfect.
Like Camelot, the sun is warm with blue sky up above.
It's like God cast a smile on us and filled our hearts with love.
The memories that we share are warming to our heart and soul.
Yet three short years that passed have clearly taken a large toll,
for there were only ten in my own "class of forty-nine".
Not one drank booze or smoked, so we should age like vintage wine.
Yet two are with their Maker. They were at the last affair.
We give their family and their friends our earnest, heartfelt prayer.

A classmate who was in a class two years ahead of me,
had hosted these reunions; she's a "Valley" devotee.
She lost her mate, yet there was a warm smile upon her face.
Though sadness filled her heart, we felt welcome in her embrace.
The Host who'd opened up his home so we could all enjoy.
Has lived here all his life; he truly is "a good old boy".
There's not a soul who loves "The Valley" any more than he.
He proves it every day, for here is where he'll always be.
The Hostess, his companion, to an informal degree,
with help from classmate friends, performed each task, painstakingly.
So all of us feel welcome and enjoy old friends and new.
We take some pictures; eat and drink; just what we want to do.
The afternoon is filled with joy; great happiness abounds.
A friend appears with every step we take around the grounds.
So many friends and family; there's not time for every one.
It's like each visit is to short and then we have to run.

It seems like only minutes pass and then the day is done.
It happens, oh so fast, but then we've had a lot of fun.
Each person who attended will remember this affair.
And when there is another one, you bet they'll all be there.
A last look at "The Valley" as we travel the west side;
we wave to other travelers, who wave right back with pride.
We try to capture in our soul what we have felt today.
It's in our hearts to stay as we now travel far away.

"The Valley" had more influence on us than anywhere.
It formed who we'd become beyond the years that we lived there.
Yes, we learned "right" and "wrong" and did a little of each one.
We learned to fish and how to shoot a rifle and a gun.
But most of all, "The Valley" imbues pride in where we live.
You harvest from the land and to your friends you learn to give.
All people here have values that enhance the human race.
There's love and pride that's shared by simply living in this place.

My Love and I return to Colorado; that's our home.
We love the place we live, yet we will let our memories roam.
And every now and then we'll sit and share bits from our past.
"The Valley's" in our hearts, it's there until we've breathed our last.

ARVADA, COLORADO

It's only been a month or two since I arrived in town.
I've seen a little, then some more; I've walked paths up and down.
I'm ready now to speak my piece and tell to all who care,
exactly how it makes me feel; there's so much I must share.

The air is thin; it's dry and cool; a breeze blows gently by.
The snow is melting from the ground; I look up to the sky.
White clouds there seem suspended, like they're hanging from a string.
The sun peeks through between them, for it's pre-announcing spring.
The mountains in the distance; a deep lavender they show.
Behind them even farther the white peaks brag of their snow.
I walk along a pathway with brown grass beneath my feet.
The snow along the sidewalk makes me move out to the street.
The ducks and geese surround the lake, for they have not gone south.
They search; they scratch; they find some food; it's tucked into their
mouth.
And then they squat and leave their mark, spread softly on the grounds.
I walk along with careful steps, avoiding squishy sounds.

Beyond me in the distance is a child wrapped up and warm.
She's playing in her front yard snow; she's pleased with last night's storm.
She slides and falls, then laughs with glee, snow covering her face.
Her actions speak far more than words, how much she loves this place.

Arvada is a mile high; the slopes will soon be green.
Across the gently rolling hills, small valleys in between,
the homes are warm and friendly; roads meander all about.
And in the lakes the youngsters will soon fish for summer trout.
But now they're walking on the ice; it covers all the lakes.
They walk, then run, then skid around; they don't have any brakes.
Because it's cold, they're bundled up; they're warm and plan to stay
here on this icy pond that's perfect for the kids to play.

I walk through parks. The trees are bare. Their branches stiff and long!
Then from my lips I hear the words; they form into a song.
For who can walk along these paths and not emit a sound.
To sing his thanks to God who made such beauty all around.

Upon a rise I pause to see what wonders lie beyond.
The sky so blue, the sun above reflecting from a pond!
The ice creates a mirror, sunrays dancing to and fro.
I change my pace, I barely move; I walk on, very slow.
How else can I appreciate this scene, so clear and bright?
It's beautiful beyond compare; it makes my whole world right.
I'm standing still, I breathe the air; a shiver down my spine.
The wonder of the world around; can all of this be mine?

It's there just for the asking as you open both your eyes.
You take a walk; go for a drive, your breath comes in deep sighs.
You too will feel the wonder and the beauty of this town,
in summer when the grass is green, in winter when it's brown.

It doesn't take a lot of time to learn to love this place.
With lots of homes and people yet, there's loads of open space.
There's so much here to see; it's an adventure every day.
Arvada's in my head and heart and here I plan to stay.

SPRINGTIME IN THE ROCKIES

The "Little Dry Creek", crystal clear, more pure than winter's snow!
The air around so clean I barely feel the winds that blow.
Pink blossoms blooming everywhere as nature's show begins.
The cloudless sky announces spring; sun melts last winter's sins.
A choir of robins singing breaks the silence of the day!
The mountains to the west seem just a step or two away.

Two squirrels approach; they beg for peanuts; somehow they survived
the winter's freezing cold and snow, till finally spring arrived.
I sense a presence in the air; I look up to the sky.
With wings extended, silently, a flock of geese flies by.
The parks around the lakes all beckon; "spring is here, come see".
Small buds announce the early growth of leaves on every tree.

In place of snow the ground is moist from rain each afternoon.
Wild grass and lawns turn green as though they're singing nature's tune.
The walkways filled with couples as they pass by, hand in hand.
There's laughter in their voices, yes, the whole wide world is grand.

The earth spreads open arms to us, to creatures everywhere.
Embracing life for all its worth; it's spring, God's love affair!
We've said goodbye to winter; we won't miss the melting snow.
Soft fragrance fills the morning air, as springtime flowers grow.

As we awake each morning there is music in our heart.
Sun beckons as we lie in bed, our day about to start.
And once again as we embrace with boundless love, galore,
we give our thanks to God for all our blessings, and much more.
Two lovers, living life as though each day will be our last,
yet thankful for our time together; time flies by so fast.
We love the seasons, every one; accept what seasons bring.
Two hearts are filled with love, especially in the early spring.

MY NEIGHBORHOOD

We're part of a society, no matter where we live.
If neighbors need a little help, we're always there to give.
We don't live on an island, though at times when crowds abound,
we'd like to find a peaceful place where there is not a sound.
Where you decide to settle is no life and death affair.
No one has ever died of it, at least that I'm aware.
And though it's not that crucial, yet the place you settle down,
should always feel just right to you, like it's the proper town.
Yes, proper places differ, whether you are young or old.
or whether you enjoy the heat or like it where it's cold.
How long is spring? Is summer hot? Will you enjoy the fall?
And in the winter does the snow get very deep at all?

You shop for houses; run around, check out the neighborhood.
You talk about how much to spend; you know how much you should.
A ranch style's nice; split level, too, perhaps three stories tall.
Since houses are so special then, should yours be large or small?
You find a place; it's perfect; it's exactly what you need.
The paper work is finally done and you receive the deed.
Then moving in is not much work; in fact it's kind of fun.
The neighbors mow their lawns and kids are playing in the sun.
You meet your neighbors right next door; they bring some food to you.
You sit around the floor with plastic plates, utensils, too.
It's almost like the farm where all your friends were just plain folks.
And everyone was welcome; ate some food and told some jokes.
The neighbor just across the street helps you install the wires
so your computer works okay and won't cause any fires.
You stop for coffee, meet their kids; this is a friendly place.
You thought you might feel homesick, but there's not even a trace.

You realize you don't know where your kids will go to school.
A stroke of luck for in this town the system's really cool.

Each neighborhood has its own schools; they're all close by for you.
You'll get to know the teachers and administrators, too.
Each way you walk, within a mile, you'll see a shop or store.
Some restaurants are right there, too; fast food and there is more.
A shopping center comes in view just two blocks down the street.
A golf course rests right in between; now that's a real treat.

You walk along the sidewalks, like a pathway through a park.
With trees and shrubs and lawns so green, some homes are light, some dark.
You feel the pride the neighbors have in how their places look.
It's almost like they copied from a home designer book.
You introduce yourself to neighbors up and down the street.
You feel a little more at home with every one you meet.
Some folks are white and some are brown and others have black skin.
It doesn't really matter for they all treat you like kin.

The neighborhood's a melting pot; that's what this country is.
It's not a dream, a fantasy; or story from show biz.
Deep down inside we're all the same, the same concerns and cares.
We love our spouse; we love our kids and help them with their prayers.

This place is great; the people nice, with service all around.
It's just about the same as every other place I've found.
For I discovered long ago, if I can ditch my pride,
it doesn't matter where I am; it's who I am, inside.
America is wonderful, just travel and compare.
Go visit every country; you won't find it, anywhere.
No matter where you choose to live in this, the greatest land,
you'll be a winner all your life and you'll feel simply grand.

I wave the flag; I'm proud as hell; I've fought for my belief.
I work each day; I do my part, for some may need relief.
And I'm a neighbor just like you; we're neighbors fast and true.
We'll stick together stronger than a bond with super glue.
For anyone is welcome and can move in next to me.

We may not all be brave, but every one of us is free.
I don't know what the future brings; I once again may roam.
My neighborhood will always be the place that I call home.

A TRIP TO ESTES PARK

The sky is blue; a cloud or two hangs lazily above.
I sit in back relaxing for the driver is "my love".
We're on our way to Estes Park, a place I've been before.
But every time I'm there, I want to see a little more.
There are not many cars for it's a holiday today.
Most people are not working; it's a time to rest or play.
The mountains to the west have rugged cliffs and gentle slopes.
The setting is majestic; it's the stuff that builds one's hopes.
We travel on through Boulder, slowing down a little bit.
I see a quiet college town back here from where I sit.
With shopping malls and restaurants on almost every block,
some people riding bicycles and some out for a walk.
A motorcycle cruises down the highway past our car.
We follow it through town; we haven't traveled very far.
We see some local firemen who are standing in the street.
They're holding "cash boots" in their hands; they wear boots on their feet.
We stop and give them money; they work for a worthy cause.
It doesn't take a lot of time for we just have to pause.
As we leave Boulder bicycles are everywhere we look.
A holiday, the students do not have to crack a book.
A lake out to the east is almost dry; the water's low.
The land's so dry that in the creek there is no water flow.
Instead of green the grass is brown; it's dry as it can be.
Although it's summer, leaves are turning yellow on a tree.

In Lyons we have breakfast; well it's actually a brunch.
It's too late for the morning meal and too early for lunch.
We're on our way again; the mountain road is getting steep.
The canyon to our left has rugged rocks and it is deep.
It's clear to me why this is named the Rocky Mountain Park.
Although some trees are growing, jutting boulders make it stark.

Then just like that the summit greets us like a friend we know.
The mountains show their rocks, for now there isn't any snow.
We see the lake below; it's crystal blue and smooth as glass.
The Stanley Hotel beckons; it's a place with real class.
As we descend the altitude makes all of our ears pop.
We want to take some pictures so we find a place to stop.

This little town is quaint; it's just the way it's always been.
To change a single thing to me would be a mortal sin.
Each shop shows us its merchandise; we all try to resist.
The clerks coax us a little bit and give our arms a twist.
We buy a frozen drink and buy two cups of coffee, too.
A summer/winter wonderland, there's so much we can do.
Pat wants to take the Tram to see the world that's far below.
It's way too high for me; I'll pass; let her view nature's show.

A perfect day has ended and we're home before it's dark.
We always have a perfect day when we're at Estes Park.
And even more, it's wonderful to share it with our friends,
so we can reminisce until our time together ends.

SEARCH FOR BAGELS

Some things in life are critical; they dominate one's mind.
There's just one type that satisfies; there is no other kind.
So we begin our search to find the "bagel fix" we need.
Across the plains and mountains, an exhaustive search, indeed.

We stop and have a bagel at "The Same Old Grind" one day.
An "onion and a garlic" taste the same, to our dismay.
We try a coffee shop that bakes its bagels and fresh bread.
The coffee is so weak we'd rather just drink tea, instead.
With desperation growing we then go into Einstein.
They're nationwide; you'd think that all their bagels would be fine.
It's only my opinion, but they have way too much crust.
We might as well just go outside and take a bite of dust.
The bakeries at the supermarkets bake fresh bagels, too.
We'll get a bag and take them home; yes, that's what we will do.
Then opening the bag we find these donut shaped "hard rocks".
It didn't help to smother them with cream cheese and fresh lox.

We're just about to panic when we take a ride "out west".
The quaint old town of Golden in the foothills is our quest.
With little parks to visit and small stores for us to shop,
the "School of Mines" white "M" displayed upon the mountaintop.
The "Table Rock" surrounds the city, like a mother's womb.
The flowers, lawns and shrubs around "Old Town" are neatly groomed.
The birds chirp in the trees; it is a welcome, pleasant sound.
And "Poor Boys Bagels" beckons us; it's yearning to be found.

It's kind of like an alcove, just a bit more than a nook.
Yet it reached out and grabbed us like it has a "shepherd's hook".
As though we'd both been drugged into a state of comatose,
we let our bodies follow the scent picked up by our nose.

The fragrance permeates the air around this little shop.
We breathed in deeply so we would not miss a single drop.
Then through the door we walked into this bagel Paradise.
We found the clerks and owner to be friendly, simply nice.
A décor that is rustic, with supplies stacked everywhere.
A tiny space for workers to prepare the daily fare,
with baskets full of bagels from the kitchen just out back.
They're freshly baked and there is not a thing these bagels lack.

At Poor Boys Bagels every bagel's fresh when it is sold.
Each day they donate extra bagels, so they won't get old.
And more than fresh, each bagel has a flavor of its own.
A texture that is perfect for each bagel is "home grown".
So here at Poor Boys Bagels we enjoy our "bagel fix";
so many flavors that it's hard to find the perfect mix.
For every bagel has a unique flavor it can boast,
to complement the service of the staff, our perfect host.
A breakfast bagel comes with all the trimmings you'd expect.
With ham or bacon, eggs or cheese, the flavor is perfect.
The crust then crunches with each bite, the way a bagel should.
The rest of it melts in your mouth; my God, but it is good.

Each day there is a special; it's the bagel of the day.
A unique flavor; every one; what more is there to say?
A basketful to sample; we decide what we will eat.
It really doesn't matter; every bagel is a treat.
It's easy to get hooked on just one flavor, maybe two.
For all are so delicious, what's a person going to do?
A single bagel's perfect for each bagel is quite big.
Yet most days I get two and sort of feel like I'm a pig.

If you like Cappuccino or a cup of hot and black.
The coffee comes in flavors; there is nothing Poor Boys lack.
Select a "Naked" health food drink; a smoothie, you can't lose.
Each drink will complement the perfect bagel that you choose.

Cream cheese in several flavors; spreads to meet each person's taste.
Each bagel's so delicious there is never any waste.
And if cost is a factor, Poor Boys is the place to go.
Your wallet won't believe it; Poor Boys prices are so low.

When we awake each morning we search for a rationale,
to get a bagel, although the decision's visceral.
We seem to find an errand that we've got to do today.
And Poor Boys Bagels never really is that far away.
Each Poor Boys Bagel has a flavor words cannot describe.
If they had home delivery, I'd be first there to subscribe.
I'd have a different Poor Boys Bagel every single day.
Then search for them in Heaven when I'm finally laid away.

I'll have a breakfast bagel, then another for my lunch.
I'll order one of every kind; I'll buy them by the bunch.
I'll share my Poor Boys Bagels with the angels up above.
A belly full of bagels and a heart that's filled with love!

COLORADO WEATHER REPORT—
FAIR AND BREEZY

We can't control the weather but there's something we can do.
The "Dopplers—Radar—Weathermen" and "Weather-Girls" too,
tell us how weather was today and how it is tonight.
They talk about tomorrow, too, but sometimes they're not right.
I kind of wish they'd go outside and look around a bit.
They'd see the sun shining above or know the rain has quit.
Or they might see some clouds forming along the eastern plains.
And with an eastern breeze they'd figure dark clouds portend rains.

Today they say the sun will shine; there'll be a little breeze.
The forecast for this evening, "calm" each Weatherman agrees.
We check them all before we start the picnic in the park.
With evening setting in, we'll be out there until it's dark.
With kids in tow and food galore we camp down by a tree.
We're in a public park and so the picnicking is free.
The tables set, the food is out; we sit and drink a beer.
The kids are playing ball on the small diamond that is near.

And just like that the winds begin; they're blowing from the west.
The shining sun has disappeared as though behind a crest.
An eerie feeling fills the air; the birds stop making sound;
and wordlessly we wait; a heavy feeling all around.

Wind from the west, a hurricane, some ninety miles strong.
It whistles through the mountains, every sound an eerie song.
A mighty oak uproots; debris is blowing everywhere.
It's like God turned his back on us and doesn't seem to care.
The picnic basket's gone; it disappears before our eyes.
The kids can't make it back to us, no matter how each tries.
As they stand up and try to walk, they're thrown back to the ground.
They crawl back to us on their knees, debris blown all around.

We make it to the car with what is left of our picnic.
It's probably illusion, but the air seems kind of thick.

We're in the car and driving home, the weather won today.
No, you don't make your plans based on what "Weather Persons" say.
Out here the weather changes faster than a new bride's mood.
Just picnic on your patio; there you'll enjoy the food.

Magicians cannot forecast weather patterns in this state.
Go with the flow; enjoy the day; accept your weather fate!

FIRST CAR—MY MODEL "A"

My sophomore year in high school; I was sixteen years of age.
And owning one's own vehicle had now become the rage.
But money was a problem, for my parents had just split.
I had to go to school full time; I didn't want to quit.
With no allowance, just small jobs, I didn't have much hope.
I had my bike and feet; it looked like I'd just have to cope.
A neighbor gave me work so I could earn some extra cash.
I guarded every dollar; every week I'd count my stash.

Then when I had a hundred bucks, Dad took me for a drive.
A Model "A" for sale, and it was only eighty-five.
I bought it on the spot and drove it home that very day,
about a hundred miles, although it seemed a long, long way.

The engine leaked some oil, and the doors would barely shut.
The springs protruded through the seat and scratched me on the butt.
A radiator filled with oil; that should have let me know.
To get my "A" to run okay could take all of my dough.
But nothing mattered for I knew that I could make it run.
And cruising with my friends was going to be a lot of fun.
So every day in shop I'd fix the things that had gone wrong.
At night with friends I'd drive around; we'd sing our high school song.

Its body was gunmetal gray; the running boards were wood.
Before I left for town each night I'd open up the hood.
The fenders rattled like a snake, all coiled and set to strike.
With nicks and dents most everywhere, they weren't at all alike.

The dollars that I earned were used to fix the things that broke;
gas leaking from the fuel pump or emitting too much smoke.
I somehow kept it running as I replaced every part.

Dead battery or broken crank, I'd get my car to start.
My Model "A" could climb the hills and traverse all terrain.
But when I tried to go too fast the engine would complain.
For forty-five was maximum, and not a mile more,
and even then the noise was something no one could ignore.

There wasn't any place I wouldn't take my Model "A".
To school, to fish or hunt, even to haul some bailed hay.
It took my friends and me to all the games in which we played.
If distances were far away, then overnight we stayed.

There wasn't anyone in town that didn't know my car.
No other car was like it; not a one was similar.
Some other kids had Model "A's" but none compared to mine,
for theirs had paint and windows, and the engines ran just fine.

My dad was right, for I stayed broke supporting that old car.
An empty wallet and no gas for me were shooting par.
Yet, every now and then I'd have some money I had saved.
I'd drive to town for apple pie, with ice cream that I craved.
My Model "A" took me to places close and far away,
from farms around the valley to the San Francisco Bay.
We'd travel down the highway going almost forty-five.
My friends and I all singing songs, my God were we alive.

We'd "borrow" watermelon from the farmers that we knew.
We'd fish with gaffs and sock downs knowing that's illegal, too.
And then one night my Model "A" just stalled and wouldn't run,
as we were being followed by a farmer with his gun.
The line up to the fuel pump broke and all the gas leaked out.
The dozen melons in the trunk I'd rather be without.
My friends threw melons back into the fields; they ran away.
I had no choice; my "A" was stalled; all I could do was pray.
My Model "A" and I were stranded; we were all alone.
The farmer with his gun approached; I let a silent groan.

"Good luck" he was the uncle of my friend who'd run away.
He'd seen us both together just a while before, that day.
He threatened he would take my car and never give it back.
His rifle pointed at my gut; no way I'd give him flak.
So scared I almost peed my pants; I couldn't even talk.
My body shook with violent force; my mouth was dry as chalk.

He saw he'd scared me more than he had hoped he ever could.
He turned and walked away and left me right there where I stood.
It could have been a whole lot worse; I didn't want to know.
That incident's still with me, though it happened long ago.

My Model "A" and I got home; I pushed it all the way.
I didn't know what problems would be present the next day.
For in a town this small there's nothing you can say or do,
that others don't know all about within a day or two.
To my surprise my buddies first apologized to me.
Then they aggrandized what I did like it was bravery.
And I became a hero to my other friends at school.
When all the time I'd felt that I had been a stupid fool.

I fixed my Model "A" so that the gas line wouldn't break.
Some brackets held it firm no matter how that car would shake.
I'd speed along at forty-five; that's all the "A" would do,
across the valley's rough dirt roads and on the highway, too.

One day I took the running boards off of my Model "A".
I planned to buy some new ones when I had my next payday.
That evening with two friends I took the Model "A" to town.
We saw a movie; cruised around till everything shut down.
Some fellows in another car pulled up along side us.
They sneered and heckled; called us names, we even heard them cuss.
They tried to force us off the road; we were not going fast.
I hit the brakes; my friend jumped out; their car went sailing past.

I hit a bump; a big one and I felt the back wheel jump,
like I had somehow left the road and run over a stump.
Then in my mirror I could see a body in the street.
I saw it move a bit and try to get up on its feet.
I stopped the Model "A" and went to see what I had done.
Now all at once this evening drive was not a lot of fun.
Behind my car I saw it was my friend that I had hit.
He got up to his knees then toppled back where he had lit.
It only took a single look to see what had occurred.
My friend began to speak but all his words were kind of slurred.
Without a running board when he had jumped out of the car.
He'd fallen underneath the wheels; he'd not jumped very far.
Across his chest was evidence; tread of my knobby tire.
I held my breath and prayed to God that he would not expire.
My "A" had run over his chest, the knobby print declared.
Not knowing what to do, my other friends just stood and stared.

A moment later he arose and dusted off his shirt.
He laughed as he discovered that it didn't even hurt.
My Model "A" was stripped down to the cab and not much more.
No extra weight inside the car or the exterior.
My friend told all the teachers and he told the students, too.
His story made it to all of the farmers that we knew.
They'd listen to the drama, some in awe and disbelief.
That he'd survived to tell his tale gave everyone relief.

I kept that Model "A" till I got out of school that year.
I cherished it as an old friend, a special souvenir.
Together we had gone where other cars could never go.
And we had shared a kind of love that most will never know.
I've owned a lot of cars as I have traveled through this life.
And some of them were fun to own and some caused lots of strife.
But none of them compare; there's little else that I can say.
I cherish every memory of that beat up Model "A".

REWARDS—
A SENIOR GOLFER

Like most male youths of my time, I was introduced to competitive sports, as is the case with both genders today. Baseball was the team game of choice, tennis the individual game. Then bowling followed, since through my uncle's employer, I had free access to a small bowling alley. All of these by age six. Later in high school the "sport seasons" dictated football in the fall, basketball in the winter, track and field in the early spring and baseball in the late spring and summer. Throughout life I remained active in sporting events, as an individual participant and later as an official for my four children's sporting competitions. Finally, age dictated some change. For me it was golf, a sport in which I witnessed players competing into their nineties. Shortly after I passed "mid-life" I was introduced to this amazing sport that has been a fulfilling experience ever since, both as a participant and spectator. I found that golf, indeed, is sometimes a "metaphor of life" and in this part of the anthology I share the many perspectives that have added unexpected, richly rewarding values and lasting relationships, enriching my life.

AVID GOLFER'S LOVE LETTER—A PARODY

I love you darling more than any lady I have seen.
A love just like I feel when my approach shot hits the green.
I love you when you're all dressed up; your beauty's all I see.
A love as great as when I'm set up, standing on the tee.
I love you, Dear; I love you in a very special way,
almost as much as when my drive lands on the first fairway.
I love you Darling, love you with my heart, and with my soul.
It's like the love of seeing my long putt roll in the hole.
I love you when you're sitting there and reading a good book.
Such love compares to when, around a tree, I hit a hook.
I love you Darling, for you're very sweet and oh, so nice.
It makes me feel the same as when I want, and hit a slice.
I love you when you're naked and I see you "in the raw".
It's like the beauty when I hit a drive, and it's a draw.
I love you when you're sitting there, relaxing in the shade.
You're beautiful, like when I need and hit a long, deep fade.
I love to take a walk with you and gently hold your hand.
It's soft and it reminds me of a great shot from the sand.
I love you and I also feel the love you have for me.
It feels so good, like when my wedge shot flies over a tree.
It's lonely when you're gone; I feel that we have lost our bond.
It feels the same as when I hit my ball into the pond.
I love you Darling, when we argue; when you're really tough.
It's like when I make a bad shot; my ball is in the rough.
I love you when you've had your shower; your hair is soaking wet.
Almost as much as when I win the match, collect my bet.

Yes, Darling, I love you in every way you'll ever know.
I've got to meet my foursome, so right now I have to go.

DESPERATE FICKLE LOVE

I started playing years ago, when I was forty-five.
I'd never heard of "putt" and "pitch" or "grip that club and drive".
For tennis was my favorite game, I loved the exercise.
It kept my body in great shape and I felt that was wise.
When singles matches got too hard, I changed to doubles play.
On weekends I had matches that would last almost all day.
But finally even tennis doubles took too much of me.
So golf became my game of choice; tennis was history.

I didn't play much golf while I was working for the bank.
That I play golf at all I know I have my boss to thank.
For he once asked me, "Rod, what is your life really about?
Is nothing more important than to have a lot of clout?
When you retire your coworkers will say you worked quite hard.
A dedicated guy who worked with total disregard
for everything in life that makes us each who we become.
You gave the bank your life; now don't you think that's kind of dumb?"

That wake up call was all it took for me to think it through.
For work had always been the very first thing I would do.
My family and my friends were always somewhere far behind.
It's like I couldn't see beyond my job, that I was blind.

I took a little time away from work so I could play.
It wasn't very often, once a month on Saturday.
I'd hit the practice range and then I'd putt and chip a while.
Out to the links with confidence; a warm and comely smile.
When I retired from banking I had just turned fifty-four.
We rarely realize exactly what life has in store.
I'd played a little golf, a dozen times or so a year.
It wasn't like the game of golf would be a new career.

I did a little marketing and financed autos, too.
It seemed that I was never without lots of things to do.
So golf remained a pastime that I didn't do too much.
Some practice and a little play; I never got "the touch".

And then a friend invited me to play a match with him.
We bet a buck on every hole; I had to sink or swim.
That day I hit them long and straight; each putt dropped in the hole.
I took his money; bought the drinks, for winning was my goal.

And just like that I fell in love; I had to play again.
The sun could shine; the wind could blow or it could even rain.
I had to have the power that I could feel with every drive.
And more than that, competing was a way for me to thrive.
We set a time to play again, a rematch with my friend.
It's like I had become the champ, and now had to defend.

We met on the first tee; I held my driver in my hand.
We checked golf balls so we were sure each played a different brand.
I felt a little sorry for my friend as we began.
He looked like a recruit against a seasoned veteran.
We tossed a coin to designate the order of our play.
He won and stepped up to the tee, while I just backed away.
His drive went down the fairway; it was straight and it was long.
How could he hit the ball so far? He's small and not that strong.
The confidence I had before I came to the first tee,
now disappeared to some deep place way down inside of me.
I shook it off and took my stance as I addressed my ball,
a perfect swing; a perfect shot; each there in my recall.
I waggled; took a practice swing and felt the stress decrease.
Just grip it and then rip it and be sure my wrists release.
I felt that sick vibration and I heard the awful "clank".
The driver head had missed the ball; I'd hit a dreaded shank.
I didn't need to look; the ball was only feet away.
That's not what I had planned to start a perfect golfing day.

I took an iron out of my bag; I needed confidence.
Without a practice swing, I hit the ball over the fence.
I dropped another ball; I'm lying three next to the tee.
My friend is laughing heartily; he's making fun of me.

With new resolve I step up to the ball that I have dropped.
It's like I'm on a speeding train, a train that can't be stopped.
I take a fairway metal from my bag and I'm all set.
I crunch that ball; it hits the lake; the damn things now all wet.
I drop a ball and hit it and I'm lying six; but worse,
my body shakes; my mind is blank; it's like an awful curse.
And then my friend makes his approach; it's two feet from the hole,
ten feet inside the ball I hit, pain fills my heart and soul.

What happened to the swing I had when we played yesterday?
I had it then, I lost it all; the loss was not halfway.
A putting stroke; a rolling ball, a hole that's way too small!
It finally stops about a foot outside of my friend's ball.
A snowman; that's an eight and it's exactly two times par.
I want the pain to end right now so it won't leave a scar.
My friend is happy as can be; he laughs and kids with me.
I know I've got to focus and erase this memory.

I've got a mental checklist of the things I need to do.
So one by one I check them, a cerebral overview.
He's down the fairway once again; he's hit it long and straight.
I form a picture in my mind, a shot that's really great.
My fairway metal in my hand; the driver feels all wrong.
I need to hit the fairway, though I won't be quite as long.
So I address the ball and take a practice swing or two.
I'm going to hit the ball so hard there'll be no residue.
I feel the tension building as I now address the ball.
I grip the club with all my might; I stand there very tall.
My swing is like a rusty gate; I cannot follow through.
The ball slides through the grass like it's held down with super glue.

Enough to say it's not my day; each club's my enemy.
The worst is yet to come and it's a real tragedy.
I poke and hack the ball around the course, with no finesse.
The score I shoot is sickening; my game's an ugly mess.
My friend has won each hole as we approach the final tee.
He's feeling pretty good by now; he's tired of taunting me.
With all the generosity of Scrooge on Christmas Eve,
he says, "I'll let you press it all; your money you'll retrieve".

By now I've almost given up; I want this thing to end.
This game is just too much for me; I simply can't pretend.
The day has been so futile that I don't care any more.
I take the bet and just like that, I'm ready to wage war.

His drive is pretty good but it's a long par five, uphill.
I set up for my drive and I'm relaxed; the world is still.
My knees are flexed, my left arm straight; I take a mighty swing.
I feel the tension as I turn, releasing like a spring.
The click is music to my ears; I hit the sweet spot, true.
I see it flying long and straight; I hold my follow-through.
I reach the green in two, a ten-foot eagle putt to make.
My friend's ball hit a bunker when deflected by a rake.
He's on the green in four; I'm there with two great shots I made.
The bragging rights transcend all of the bets that I've been paid.

I cannot wait until I have another match to play.
A round of golf is one great way to have a perfect day.

COLORADO WINTER GOLF—FIRST VISIT TO A GOLF COURSE

No one has a greater love, for chasing that white ball,
down fairways long, into the sand or rough that's wet and tall.
To fully understand this game you need to play a round,
in winter at my golf course when there's snow still on the ground.

I'm somewhat shocked as I observe some men and women, too,
out on the course, fairways are brown; the sky is azure blue.
What do you call the putting greens when they're not green at all?
They're all dark brown; yet they seem willing to receive the ball.
I go up to the driving range; the snow is shoved away.
A white frame forms around the mat, a winter holiday!
Yet on the practice tees are two; they swing with all their might.
The frozen balls make funny sounds; it doesn't help their flight.

I see my breath; I clap my hands; there's hardly any sound.
The parking lot is full of cars with golfers all around.
With frozen nose and ears so cold I don't think I can hear.
I walk up to a golfer who is drinking a cold beer.

The starter's busy scheduling the foursomes for the day.
I see that there are fivesomes and they also plan to play.
I guess it's not the speed of play that's on the golfers' minds,
but just surviving in this cold, as round the course each winds.
I stare at golfers bundled up so they can barely move.
Knit hats on heads, gloves on both hands, a swing they cannot groove.
Yet each seems happy he or she is on the course today.
For work is their alternative, I guess they'd rather play.

It's just about at freezing; that is normal, but it's cold.
The golfers playing on this course, I've got to say are bold.

For though we're at a mile high and golf balls here should fly.
The frozen ball clicks like a rock, no matter how you try.

I walk up to the teeing box; there's white stuff on the ground.
The golfer here is ready so I do not make a sound.
He takes a practice swing or two; he looks straight down the line.
And then he swings for real, with a tempo smooth as mine.
In freezing cold, with muscles taught; a small breeze in his face,
I wonder in amazement that the ball goes any place.
It takes off straight; it gains its height; it's fading just a bit.
Two hundred fifty yards away, the fairway it has hit.
It bounces high and then it rolls; I can't believe my eyes,
three hundred yards from where I stand; my God how that ball flies.
I know I'm in the mountains, a plateau that's near the sky.
The air is thin; it's cool and crisp; I'm a full mile high.

The other members of the group, each tees his ball and swings.
And like the first, I stand in awe; it's like the balls have wings.
They walk right down the fairway like it's any summer day.
I guess they just don't realize it's way too cold to play.

I wait here for the next group that will play hole number one.
The wind picks up; it's colder still; what happened to the sun?
They've got to really love this game, in summer, spring and fall,
to play it in the winter with stiff shaft and frozen ball.
I find a man who's with his wife; they're ready to begin.
They look somewhat like polar bears, their coats up to their chin.
They're laughing, telling stories just as though they're warm and fine.
They're having so much fun I hope they're future friends of mine.
I ask them why they're out today, in wind and freezing cold.
Is it because they have their youth and maybe I'm too old?
With laughing voice, good-natured smile, a single voice I hear.
"There's not a crowd; it's perfect to play golf this time of year."

For years I've lived the city life, a long ways from the farm.
Now if I'm out too long in this, the cold will do me harm.
Yet as I stand among these groups, negotiating bets,
with envy I turn green as I am freezing in my sweats.

The pro approaches me to see if I would like to play.
My feet and hands are frozen; there is little I can say.
The lake here may be water but today it's solid ice.
I'll go home to my fire where it is cozy, warm and nice.
I'll wait a little while to golf, till spring comes breaking through.
With short-sleeved shirt I'll play this game out under skies of blue.
The water in the lake will shimmer as a small breeze blows.
Some clouds may float up in the sky to shade a sun that glows.

Yes, I will wait until the ladies dress like ladies should.
And guys dressed up in shorts and shirts even look pretty good.
When fairways look like my front lawn, not dry and chocolate brown!
And greens are green; this course is then the best-damned place in town.

HOME GOLF COURSE

It's nestled in a grove of homes and condominiums.
The water in the lake is a golf ball aquarium.
It isn't awfully long, yet there are challenges, galore.
You hit the golf ball straight or add some strokes onto your score.
The water on the 1st hole is in play for a long drive.
A little fade, a slice, the lake will eat your ball alive.
On number 2 a little hook and you can say, "Goodbye".
Your ball has left the golf course and it doesn't help to cry.

The trees are right in front of you when you're on number 3.
They stare you in the face as you get set up at the tee.
A draw and you will shout with joy; a fade goes the wrong way.
A slice and you're out in the rough; you're not in the fairway.
A par 3 can't be very tough; you're up to number 4.
A golf pervert designed this hole to add strokes to your score.
You draw the ball and there it goes, over the fence, O. B.
A fade will bounce right off the green and end up near a tree.

You're warmed up now and ready at address on number 5.
You fade the ball and there are lots of trees to catch your drive.
A little hook, O.B.; another ball has gone astray.
You hit it straight on number 5 and it will make your day.
The 6th hole is a bit uphill; it isn't long at all.
The homes along the right side represent an O.B. wall.
Again just hit it straight and par or birdie is your score.
A hook or slice will make you pay; you'll add a stroke or more.

The 7th hole is short for a par 4, a dogleg right.
The homes here block your view so you can't see your ball in flight.
A power fade is perfect or just hit one long and straight.
No matter how you drive your ball, the lake here lies in wait.

The bunker on the eighth hole is a magnet to golf balls
A little fade, that's all it takes, and in the sand it falls.
Or play a little draw; the lake is on the other side.
So hit the damn ball straight, and to the green you'll watch it glide.

You're almost at the corner as you tee up number 9.
A drive that's straight; a little draw, both shots will work just fine.
So grip the club and rip it, hit the cover off the ball.
A slice or too much fade and you won't find your ball at all.

The front 9 is the easiest; or that's what they told me.
I've played both 9's a lot of times; I'm not sure I agree.
A little rest, a hotdog and a "cold one", maybe two,
you're ready to attack the back; the match will start anew.

The fairway opens on the 10th, it almost looks too wide.
Then why do golf balls find the trees along the left-hand side?
Or with a little fade or push, apartments catch your ball.
To hit it down the fairway should not be that hard at all.

A lay up gets your ball to where you can attack the pin.
It's vital to consider the position you are in.
There's water that protects the green and trees on either side.
The bunker's incidental, swing and give your ball a ride.
If ever there's a birdie hole, you've found that hole at last.
Eleven has no trouble and a fairway that runs fast.
A par 5 you can reach with a good drive and fairway wood.
A putt for eagle, just stay cool; make birdie like you should.

On 12 you're elevated as you set up to your ball.
Trees to the right and left and now a few of them are tall.
A driving iron or fairway wood will be all that you need.
An errant drive on 12 will make you pay up for your greed.
The 13th hole's a short par 3; a place that you can score.
It measures just one hundred yards, maybe little more.

Two bunkers here protect the green so take an extra club.
And swing it smooth with follow through; avoid another flub.

You're coming down the stretch as you approach the 14th tee.
The green's around the corner; it's not there for you to see.
A long, high fade with lots of roll; the perfect shot to make!
A few yards left or right and you will pay for your mistake.
The 15th hole's as easy as a short par three can be.
Imbued with confidence you place your ball upon the tee.
A little hook, you're out of bounds; your ball's in a backyard.
You hit it straight, my friend, or you will find this course is hard.

You're finally at a hole where a long drive will help you score.
So drive two hundred fifty yards, straight down the corridor.
A little less you'll land on one of "Dolly Parton's" breasts.
A sexy metaphor, it's one each golfer here detests.
The 17th is short, so short it's got you feeling good.
A driving iron will do or maybe just a fairway wood.
You keep it in the fairway; a short iron, you're on the green.
A sadist shaped the slant and slope and he was downright mean.

The final hole, my God, you can't believe the way you've played.
You do this to relax yet every nerve is torn and frayed.
You'll hit your dream shot of the day, forgetting all the rest.
This once you'll set up properly and do your very best.
A hook, oh shit, you've pulled it way out over the left fence.
You push the next one out of bounds; this game does not make sense.
You finally hit it straight and watch it bounce into the sand.
It's up against the bunker's edge; there's no place you can stand.

You squat; one foot is in the sand, the other's on the grass.
You take a mighty swing and "whoops", you land upon your ass.
It isn't golf you're playing, you are now performing tricks.
Across the green and in the hole, my God, you've made a six.

Yes, my home course is easy; or that's what some golfers say.
You hit them long and straight and it's an easy course to play.
When you decide to play a round of golf on my "short course",
hit drives straight down the fairway or expect to feel remorse.

NATURAL BEAUTY

There's not a place on earth that is more beautiful to me,
than early in the morning with the sun on the first tee.
My partner is my lover and we both adore this game.
It doesn't matter what occurs, there's never any blame.

The dew sits there like crystals; little diamonds all around.
A chirping bird, a rustling leaf and that's the only sound.
Long shadows from the trees define the fairway and the green.
It's just like heaven on this earth, with nothing in between.
The sky is blue beyond belief; a billowing white cloud.
We look into each other's eyes; I couldn't be more proud.
It's taken over fifty years but we're together now.
We're drinking from the cup of life, all that God will allow.

Another couple joins us; they're young and full of life.
With welcome smile he tells us that this lady is his wife.
We're ready to begin; the starter calls us to the tee.
When we are done we know we'll have enhanced humility.
We make a bet; it isn't much; a dollar for each hole.
For bragging rights, not money, we will play with heart and soul.
A little breeze behind us, it's exactly what we need.
With trusty driver in my hand, my Titleist is teed.

The lake's two hundred yards away, a little to the right.
I see its natural beauty for it's clearly in my sight.
The sun reflects the images of trees along its banks.
The leaves wave gently in the breeze as if they're saying thanks.

The ladies take their places at the tees that they will use.
Each knows that when the match is done, they'll win or maybe lose.
It doesn't really matter for each lady is aware,

this game, like life itself, is full of wonders they will share.
I see my soul mate take her stance; her muscles do not move.
Then smooth as glass she starts a swing; her club is in the groove.
There's beauty as she moves her club, fluidity and grace.
Her stroke will launch that little ball to any given place.
She's standing on the tee from which the ladies plan to play.
A second practice swing and then she hits her ball away.
It rises toward the clouds as though a magnet pulls it there.
It drops; the fairway holds it like a teenage love affair.
Our lady-playing partner takes her place upon the tee.
She doesn't need a practice swing; she's loose as she can be.
Her take-away and turn would make a touring pro turn green.
She hits about as good a drive as I have ever seen.

I set up for my drive; I stand relaxed and straight and tall.
My mind is filled with confidence; I strike the small white ball.
A thing of beauty to behold, it rises from the tee,
then bounces and it rolls and rolls, three hundred yards from me.
My playing partner duplicates the perfect shot I made.
We saunter down the fairway, an undisciplined brigade.
The mountains to the west create a picture window view.
Like steps leading to Heaven that's beyond the sky of blue.

Each breath of air exhilarates my body and my mind.
The feeling of euphoria cannot be far behind.
Four golf balls in the fairway on the first hole that we play!
It doesn't take a whole lot more to start a perfect day.

The green's a silky turf that's manicured with loving care.
The flag stands tall within the cup; we know the hole is there.
And in the fairway each of us prepares to strike our ball.
A shot that's perfect in our minds is what we each recall.
Unerring tempo, fluid swings, four balls land near the hole.
A little cheer, high fives around; we've each achieved our goal.
With loving care the ball marks are repaired so we restore

the natural beauty of the green, just like it was before.
A putt or two and just like that, some pars, a birdie, too.
With velvet touch on fresh soft turf, there's not much else to do.

Two couples move from green to tee to play another hole,
while words of praise flow lovingly, as fodder for the soul.
To us this is a flawless way to start a perfect day.
It could have been quite different although, that's the way we play.
The game of golf is fickle, yet its beauty reigns supreme.
We tolerate the setbacks as we each pursue our dream.

There's beauty everywhere we look as we follow our ball.
The bunkers filled with sand just like a beach, not bad at all.
The grass a little longer when our ball flies left or right,
sometimes it digs down deep and is completely out of sight.
Our ball may fly out on a street or lodge up in a tree.
Then in the fairway we lie one, or maybe we lie three.
Although our score's important, it's dwarfed in every way
with beauty in our heart, for that's the reason that we play.

It doesn't really matter where we choose to play our game.
The beauty that surrounds us will be different, not the same.
We may be in the desert where there's cactus all around.
Or on a mountain course, alone, where there is not a sound.
We'll find a natural beauty on each golf course that we play.
It doesn't matter who is in our foursome on that day.
Each course design is different; they are not alike at all.
Relaxed, we love the beauty as we strike that little ball.

FIRST WINTER GOLF—FIRST FREEZE

It's twelve o'clock, we're all checked in, we start at twelve-fifteen.
The sun is out, a little breeze; the chill keeps the air clean,
The temperature broke thirty-two; a mid-winter heat wave!
To even be outside a guy has got to be quite brave.
Since autumn came two months ago and snow began to fall.
It's been so cold we only play a very soft golf ball.
The fairways stretch before us, colors changing, kind of queer.
On days like this we've got to love this game to be out here.
Two pairs of pants, five shirts and vests; a wool cap on my head,
I'm here to golf; I look more like a polar bear, instead.
A golf-glove on my left hand and a lined glove on my right,
Some stretching and I'm now prepared to swing with all my might.

I lean to place the tee into the ground for my first drive.
The creak of frozen bones lets the whole world know I'm alive.
The tee won't break the ground; it's frozen solid as block ice.
I turn to my three partners asking them for their advice.
They laugh and one throws me a rubber tee tied to a string.
I place my ball upon the tee, cold body quivering.
What other "winter secrets" are these guys keeping from me?
I'm ready; "grip and rip it"; soon enough I guess I'll see.
The lake's two hundred fifty yards, a little to the right!
My drives won't go that distance if I hit with all my might.
I take a warm up practice swing; it's short but tempo's good.
A miracle I swing and hit the drive the way I should.

The ball fades to the right and then it hits the frozen ground.
It bounces fifty yards, rolls to the lake without a sound.
It isn't lost; it's out there, sitting on a film of ice.
I guess my "power fade" somehow became the "dreaded slice".

With fairways hard as asphalt, that white ball rolls on and on.
You hit a little left or right and your golf ball is gone.

I learned a bit and damn near froze; but I had fun today.
For nothing matters when you love this game; you simply play!

A MATCH—A LITTLE BET

The Rules of Golf say it's okay to make a little bet.
Just so you can afford it and it isn't too much sweat.
For most it is the principle, it's for the bragging right.
You win a bit or lose a bit; but never get "up tight".
Still, when there's money on the line, the juices flow a bit.
You concentrate a little more and plan before you hit.
A bet may help you strike the ball a little sweeter, or,
it may "work on your head" and then play havoc with your score.

STRATEGY

You notice how competitors come limping to the tee.
And say how much they hurt, how difficult this round will be.
Their handicap is way too low; their game's a shambles, too.
But they'll accede, yes, they'll accept a little bet with you.
They look so crippled; struggle when they walk; and even more,
their "pain" helps them get strokes from you to "even up the score".
You know their GHIN and they should give a stroke or two to you.
But they are so persuasive; on each side you give them two.

THE PLAY

Shake hands; the bets are made; five bucks a nine and dollar skins.
It's just enough to make you think; to care a bit who wins.
You watch as he "sets up"; he looks like he can barely swing.
You "see the money", knowing all the bucks this match will bring.
He takes a warm up swing and then he sets up to the ball.
What happened? He's now standing straight and he is six feet tall.
You hear the "crack" and see his ball, three hundred yards away.
Now where is that "old crippled guy" that you're about to play?
Oh, miracle of miracles, he hits them all that true.
He turns around and smiles; he knows he "got one" and it's you.
You might as well have paid the bets right there on the first hole.
He knows he found a "sucker" and it's you who'll play that role.

RESULT

You played your best; you tied six holes and even won on three.
He plays to scratch; bogey's your best; all golfers will agree,
that sixteen bucks was not too much for what you learned that day.
Now you're the "crippled guy" when bets are made before you play!

MATCH PLAY BETS WITH A DUFFER

I'm not a touring golf pro; no, I'm not a pro at all.
I'm barely just an amateur; that's how I hit the ball.
A handicap that's in the teens is one I'll never see.
But when I play I'm honest; there's no fudging scores for me.
I know the rules; that's probably the best part of my game.
No matter where I hit the ball, it never causes shame.
I'd make the USGA proud with rulings that I make.
All from the book or score card, for a rule I'll never break.

I warm up like I know the game; my practice swing is great.
Each ball flies from the mat and tee out on the range, so straight.
With confidence I make my bets; I get strokes I can flaunt.
It's not the money that's the thing; it's bragging rights I want.

The King, himself, and Nicklaus are the people I would play.
For just two strokes on every hole, all bets would come my way.
The match is mine before we start; it's on tee number one.
I get exactly what I need; it's then I know I've won.
We play the round to just confirm the proper money flow.
There's fellowship, a few good jokes; I feel my wallet grow.
For on each hole I get a stroke; on every hole I par.
It's tough for you to understand; you hit the ball so far.

It's not how well you play the game, your drives or chips or putts.
It's how you make the bets with me; when betting, I've got guts.
My drives don't travel very far; my chips may not be sweet.
But with the added strokes I get, I'm very hard to beat.
Some day you'll learn before we play what I have done to you.
The handicap that's on my card, are all those numbers true?
You know I never fudge a score out on the course we play.
But how my index got this high, just ask USGA.
I've never understood the way they take what I report.

Then add, compute and print a card or something of the sort.
The old scores seem to disappear; the new ones take their place.
I just accept what I receive; I do this filled with grace.

Now when I'm on the course alone, no other golfer near,
I practice every club I have; I don't have any fear.
I strike the ball; I swing clear through; I feel the impact, strong.
I hold the swing with balance; that's the way that I belong.
I watch the ball; it flies up high; it sails so straight and true.
It's comforting to see my ball fly out through skies of blue.
Then other times I try too hard; my tempo isn't good.
The ball just goes to where it wants and not to where it should.

Sometimes I wish that I could play like Irwin or the King.
Like Tiger Woods would be okay, what joy that swing would bring.
I'd challenge every one I play, big bucks on every bet.
I'd win by strokes at every hole, their money I would get.
Then soon by shooting sub-par rounds, competitors would know.
I can't be beat; I'm just too good and soon no one would show.
Nobody here at tee time for they spread the word so wide,
the only thing that I'd have left is just my hollow pride.

So playing like I do I guess, is going to work for me.
There's not another golfer who I really want to be.
I'm me; I play; I love the game, yes, each and every day.
So when I see the sun shine, I am going out to play.
And when you see me on the course, I'm with a group of friends.
We kid each other; all tell jokes, we talk of business trends.

And then we meet at hole "nineteen" when finished with the round.
The social part rewards me with the new friends I have found.

The game of golf may mean a lot, a metaphor of life,
or just a friendly outing for a husband and his wife.
For me it fills the gap when I stopped working for those banks.
To play a round of golf with friends; I'll ever give my thanks.

SPRING GOLF IN THE ROCKIES

It sparkles like the facets of a diamond on the plains.
The brilliant sun denies the weather forecast of spring rains.
With golf clubs on my back, I wear my shorts, shirt and straw hat.
A round of golf in warm spring sun; forgot where I am at.
Some warm-up putts with seniors on the practice putting green.
A little breeze; a bright blue sky; the clearest day I've seen.
Old timers at the range; our bones creak loudly with each swing.
With hope inside our hearts, not knowing what this day will bring.

The starter calls our foursome as we meet on the first tee.
Negotiate the bets until we four players agree.
Big bucks are on the line and even more if there's a press.
Two dollars risked on each nine holes; now that creates some stress.
We're ready to begin; four drives sail down the first fairway.
Step lively as we seek our balls for that's the way we play.
The rounds begun, we're happy as school kids out on spring break.
With second shots up on the green, no balls land in the lake.

Before we reach the second tee the winds at forty knots.
It's hard to walk against the wind, much less make our golf shots.
The clouds are forming overhead. It's dismal, dark and gray.
Ignoring changing elements, teed up we hit away.
What happened to the sun? There's not a speck of blue above.
To make headway against this wind I'm going to need a shove.
And now the bosom of each cloud opens to let us know,
There's rain inside and then they'll likely drop a bit of snow.

Wet clothes, we're cold and miserable; straw hat, shorts and tee shirt.
Each swing creates vibrations that go up our arms and hurt.
We all agree to "pack it in", go back and have a beer.
And just like that the sun breaks through; rain stops; God this is queer.

It's springtime in the Rockies, wet and dry then hot and cold.
Golf's not a game for sissies here; a guy's got to be bold.
So wear your shorts but bring long pants, umbrella and rain suit.
Expect the weather that you get. A great round you can shoot.

"OLD GEEZER" TOURNAMENTS

The staff stands ready; always there to help improve our game.
But we old "geezers" keep on playing just about the same.
That never dampens how they try to help us with our play.
They "talk the talk" and "walk the walk"; they're pro's in every way.
Against the drought the greens keeper has challenges galore.
He waters by the city rules, but can't use any more.
Some turf builder—a water saver—lots of loving care!
And most of us appreciate the fact that he is there.

Yes, lots of us complain when we approach our perfect shot,
and find it in a hole; our tempers get a little hot.
Sometimes we may forget the law of gravity prevails.
"Rub of the Green" is there no matter how one "rants and rails".
We've got to blame someone for all those bogeys on our card.
We'd rather blame the staff than to admit this game is hard.
Oh well, the staff can't hear the comments made out on the course.
So yell your heart out, all you get is just a voice that's hoarse.

We like to blame the weatherman on "golf day" when there's rain,
or when the lightning strikes and we suspend our play, again.
We've blamed our clubs and golf balls; we have sometimes blamed our
bag.
And when our chip shot doesn't' drop, we'll even blame the flag.
It's sometimes very difficult to know why we're out here,
until we hit the clubhouse with a pitcher full of beer.
It's then you hear of all the shots struck straight with perfect role,
and putts from thirty feet that hit the center of the hole.

It takes one perfect drive or an approach that hits the green.
And suddenly this golf course is the best course we have seen.
A round below our index; we're as proud as we can be.

We want our golf scores posted so that everyone can see.
Just win a "skin" or take low gross or even second net.
Or flash the dollar bills around as we collect a bet.
And golf becomes the game of choice, the greatest sport of all.
A round that wins "the bragging rights", and we stand very tall.

LADY GOLFERS

Each Monday and each Thursday you'll see ladies on the tee.
They're animated, talking to each other, happily.
For they enjoy the game of golf as much as any man.
And most can play this game as well as male golfers can.
It's something like a fashion show around the putting green.
Shorts skirts with halters, some long pants, and all that's in between.
Most ladies dress for comfort; some may dress to "show a bit".
Old "geezers" round the clubhouse stare at them 'til they can't quit.

I've had the opportunity to play golf with a few.
Most play the game for exercise and fun, the way I do.
I shouldn't be surprised when they out drive me from the tee.
Their bodies seem to fit the game; they swing so naturally.
And when we're all around the green to chip and putt the ball.
My ball goes sailing by the hole as I watch their ball fall.
For ladies seem to have a touch that's light as chiffon cake.
As smooth as glass they stroke that ball; most every putt they'll make.

If you're misled and think these ladies don't compete to win.
Just place some money on your match, a buck, perhaps a fin.
The chatter turns to silence as she sets up for her shot.
She'll play each stroke deliberately; much better than you thought.
And soon you'll have to press to have a chance to win the bet.
The pressure strains your natural swing; your brow becomes all wet.
She's gracious in the end and happily buys you a beer.
A sheepish smile and you accept; the worst fate you could fear.

Yes, ladies play this game like men; no, it's not quite the same.
Their pace of play is brisk and they add color to the game.
They do not make excuses for the scores that they record.
With great appreciation they know golf's its own reward.

THE "EASY" 7ᵀᴴ HOLE

It starts the final third of the front nine, an easy hole.
To get away with par is mostly every golfer's goal.
For though it's short it helps a lot if I can work the ball,
from left to right, around the fence that stands there, straight and tall.
Three hundred fifty yards, my God, it can't be difficult.
To even take a bogey on this hole is an insult.
With any kind of drive at all, a wedge into the green,
this hole's among the easiest that I have ever seen.

The drive is blind from either tee; the fairway disappears.
I'll be okay if I control the space between my ears.
A little fade around the trees and fence and I am there.
My ball sits in the fairway; there is no need to despair.
But hit it straight and long and I am out-of-bounds for sure.
A simple hole but I'll be adding two strokes to my score.
Or maybe I'll just cut the corner, up over the fence.
I hit it low; it bounces back; does that make any sense?
Or a high fade that slices and I'm in a neighbor's yard.
Another way to add some strokes; it really isn't hard.
A draw and I now face a second shot that's really long.
If my ball's on the left side, I know I've done something wrong.

Okay, let's say I drive it well, two hundred fifty yards.
I'll hit a wedge up to the green, a birdie's in the cards.
I try to focus on the ball; forget the lake in front.
The club comes through; I hit it thin; it trickles like a bunt.
A wasted stroke but that's not bad, I still can make my par.
My ball is fifty feet ahead; the hole's not very far.
Just stroke a sand wedge; follow through, my ball will find the pin.
My club slides under; up it goes; that's water I am in.

I find a phrase describing just exactly how I feel.
If this were not a game of honor, I'd just cheat and steal.
Another stroke is added to the score I'd hoped to make.
My ball is finally on the green; it's been one big mistake.

Above the hole but on the green, it may just take one stroke.
A twenty footer snaking right to left, I go for broke.
I hit firmly, watch it roll, and roll, and roll and roll.
It's like the green is made of glass, without that little hole.
It's hard to make a par when I am lying six or more.
The rules do not allow me to subtract strokes from my score.
But three putt on this little green! It's not that hard, you see.
That's why the course has eighteen holes; forget this hole bit me.

I'm optimistic every time I'm on the seventh tee.
I set up for a little fade and swing my club freely.
It doesn't seem to matter how I swing or how I feel.
What happens next is fantasy; it makes this game surreal.
I find a hard spot on the fairway or I'm near a tree.
I always have to play it short and hope I'm on in three.
The only time I've parred this hole is when I've had one putt.
I try to just accept it, for I'm deeply in this rut.

Yet one day I am going to hit my drive around the curve.
I'll simply hit my "power fade" and watch that white ball swerve.
A wedge onto the green that stops just inches from the hole!
I'll score a birdie; from now on that's going to be my goal.

10TH HOLE—"NEW BEGINNINGS" ON THE BACK NINE

It's straightaway, the driving range borders the left hand side.
A hazard to the left, behind the trees, it tries to hide.
In front of the large sloping green, a water hazard lies.
It's like a magnet catching balls, no matter how one tries.
The fairway's wide on either side, the short rough's wider still.
No fairway bunkers, lots of space for that drive you can kill!
The condos on the right are set well back and far away.
You'd have to hit a screaming slice to lose your ball that way.

We're on the tee, we've finished nine; we're happy as can be.
This fairway seems to open up as far as we can see.
I've shot three over par and here is where I get one back.
I'll set that ball upon the tee and give it a huge whack.
My partners are not really sure; they haven't done that well.
I've asked the Marker for their scores; he doesn't want to tell.
It really doesn't matter; we've got nine more holes to play.
And any score that's close to par will really make our day.

We had a little rest when we completed number nine.
A cold one at the turn and now we're all feeling quite fine.
I've got a swagger in my walk as I approach the tee.
This little ball will rise and run farther than I can see.
A short par five, the hole's less than five hundred yards away.
With all this room an idiot could keep his drive in play.
A long drive and you're home in two; two putts; the ball is in!
A little less, you lay it up; then knock it to the pin.

The trees along the left-hand side protect a water slough.
You hit your ball inside of this; there's not much you can do.
A drop, a stroke, your looking at a score of five or six!

An ugly slice, you're O.B. right and really in a fix.
If confidence is what I need, I've really got a ton.
My front nine score was great; it is the best I've ever done.
I'm swinging like a touring pro; I swing with all my might.
I want that ball straight out in front, not to the left or right.

I feel the contact as I let the club swing through the ball.
My arms extend straight down the line; I'm standing firm and tall.
Without a glance I bend to pick my tee up from the ground.
The drive is perfect, long and straight; I know it from the sound.
"You'd better hit another;" that's my playing partner's voice.
He says, "It's O.B. to the right," there isn't any choice.
Another says, "A bad, bad bounce, it went over the fence".
I thought my drive was straight and long; this game does not make sense.

Then three great drives my partners make; I've got to drive again.
The confidence I had is gone; it's like that now and then.
I tee my ball up high and setup for my second drive.
I'll hit it straight and long and with a bogey I'll survive.
A little draw with lots of roll; I'll make the green in two.
I might yet even par the hole; I'll show them "who is who".
Relaxed, I let it rip; I give this drive all that I've got.
I feel the ball compress; it leaves the club head, super hot.

I watch it climb and draw a bit and then it hooks like hell.
It hits a branch and jumps the fence; I can't tell where it fell.
And then I see the splash as that damned ball goes for a swim.
Three happy faces grin at me; I've never been so grim.
No choice, I'm lying four, three hundred yards yet to the green.
My friends "help" saying, that's the worst drive they have ever seen.
A lay up and I'm just a wedge away from that damned pin.
What happened to the game I had? Did I commit a sin?

A double bogey's not that bad, I'm only lying five.
A great wedge shot; a one putt green; I'll just forget my drive.

I skull the wedge; good God above, it's in the water, too.
I drop another ball, but now I don't know what to do.
I put away the wedge and pull my nine-iron from the bag.
It doesn't matter what I hit; this is no time to brag.
Relax and hit it smooth and it will fly up to the green.
I swing and give a heavy sigh; I finally picked it clean.

Ten yards above the hole, the putt is slicker than wet snot.
To stop it near the hole will take the best putt that I've got.
My putter's like a sledgehammer; it feels like twenty pounds.
My friends are in and standing by; it's quiet, not any sounds.
I barely touch the ball and it starts rolling toward the hole.
It travels fifty feet, like it is going for a stroll.
Two putts back up the green and I have finally got it in.
A "perfect ten", in golf that's not the way you play to win.

I know this is an easy course; at least that's what "they" say.
"They" need to play hole Number 10 the way I did today.
Play safe and maybe make a par, now that's a proper goal.
Your score is not supposed to be the number of the hole.

SENIOR GOLFER TOURNAMENTS

My God! It's Wednesday! Got to play the senior tournament!
Old geezers congregate like a religious sacrament.
These mornings come too early since I've passed my middle age.
The stiffness of my legs and arms are now my best health gauge.
And like the engine of my car, when cold and snow abounds,
I warm up kind of slowly as I hear the morning sounds.
A cup of coffee, cereal, I'm ready to begin.
My body screams as joints creak; this is a mortal sin.
Yet I can hear the calling of each fairway and each green.
I picture perfect shots, much better than I've ever seen.
My golf bag and my clubs are in the back seat of my car.
I'm off to play the tournament; a mile, it isn't far.

A few old timers waddle round the well-kept practice green.
They putt their balls while making conversation in between.
And those who have the energy are on the driving range.
Each has a dream that for today he'll see his golf swing change.
A foursome on the tee, the tournament is under way.
Old timers using power carts or pull carts when they play.
Brave souls like me will walk and carry as they play their round.
Each hole we play makes our golf bag increase about a pound.
Eight eyes are on the ball as it is placed upon the tee.
A well-hit ball will fly beyond the distance we can see.
The line of flight as it comes off the club head tells us where,
the small white ball may come to rest, so we can find it there.

Four hours later, tired souls, drag bodies from eighteen.
Some brag about the shots they made; the best they've ever seen.
And others slowly cross the parking lot to find their car.
They're finished; not a single shot they've hit has gone "that" far.
Then most will congregate at the Club House to reminisce.

Some curling putts were made, some three-foot putts they couldn't miss.
The highlights of each round replayed for all that care to hear.
Some laughter, lots of talking; "Bring another glass of beer".

MEMORABLE GOLF SCENES

A golf course can intimidate an amateur like me,
when everything is manicured; each fairway, green and tee.
But when the staff says, "welcome" and they greet me with a smile,
I feel that I can sink each putt and drive the ball a mile.

The beauty of the lake is there for everyone to see.
It sparkles in the brilliant sun as I approach the tee.
Two hundred fifty yards away, green grass around its edge.
I hit my drive in front of it and then I hit a wedge.
A little breeze brings cool relief from the warm sun above.
Its soft caress refreshes me; a feeling that I love.
Tree leaves wave little gestures as I walk beneath each bough.
A waft of wind removes the perspiration from my brow.

There's not a real forest; just some trees placed here and there.
They're nestled close together like they're having an affair.
The trees add beauty to the course, each stands there straight and tall.
Their charm wanes just a bit when back of one I find my ball.

The lake is small and narrow; it's attractive to the eye.
A duck or two glide overhead; gaggles of geese fly by.
It borders fairways one and eight; protects the green at ten.
That lake is always hungry, eating golf balls now and then.
The lake feeds water to a pond that glistens in the sun.
The pond protects the seventh green; adds challenge to my fun,
a dogleg right; a perfect drive; an eight iron to the green.
Less than a perfect drive, there's all that water in between.

The view is great on number three; an elevated tee,
the fairway doglegs left; a little draw around the tree.
I visualize that shot each time I set up to my ball.
A perfect picture in my mind, no trouble here at all.

My fade's a thing of beauty as it rides the gentle breeze.
A little spin, the fade's a slice; my ball drops in the trees.
Or worse the ball keeps fading 'til it nestles in the rough.
It's hitting shots like this that helps make senior golfers tough.

Yet in between each golf shot, whether bad, or good, or great.
Or whether you must hurry, or you stand around and wait.
Breathtaking scenes surround you from the mountains to the west.
And, friendly playing partners make this game of golf the best.

A TASTE OF HUMILITY

Like footprints in the sand, the beads of dew upon the grass
record each step I make as by the practice green I pass.
It's Wednesday morning; that's a very special golfing day,
for that's when seniors congregate before they start their play.
The "Pro's" are ready in the clubhouse with our starting time.
I pay the green fee, just three bucks; so little it's a crime.

Some guys are warming up out on the range with practice balls.
They interrupt their practice as they hear the starter's calls.
A foursome on the tee, another standing by "on deck"!
Will this be a "smooth sailing" day or more like a "shipwreck"?
The first hole's always special; sometimes nerves come into play.
A long straight drive, a "center cut" and it can make your day.
More often the ball travels near the cart path by the trees.
Or maybe toward the lake as it is carried by the breeze.

A par or birdie on the first hole and I feel just great.
I brag a bit; I've hit my first drive long and high and straight.
It doesn't take a lot to put me on a "golfing high".
It's simple when I just relax and do not really try.
Yet, golf involves an incongruity, at least some say,
"The harder that I try the 'worser' golf I seem to play".
I may be old but I'm a man, I want to show my strength.
How better than to hit a drive that demonstrates my length?

So at the second hole I flex my muscles on the tee.
A five par, just stand back so there'll be lots of room for me.
I'll hit the cover off this ball; you'll really see it fly,
two hundred fifty yards or maybe more if I just try.
You guessed it; I try harder than I've ever tried before.
With muscles taught, swing like a stick, my partners all shout "fore".
I hit the green but it's the first hole, fifty feet away.
Golf gives us all humility; what else is there to say?

RUB OF THE GREEN

You win some and you lose some, or that's what "they" say you do.
I don't know who "they" are my friend, or how it is for you.
But 60 seniors start at every Wednesday tournament,
and six to eight are winners; that's some "average" argument.
If "averages" applied to golf I'd be a touring pro.
I'd never have those 9's or 10's that make my golf score grow.
A par, a bogey or a birdie scored on every hole.
Scratch golfer, zero handicap! That's fodder for my soul!

A par three and I hit an iron; the ball is in the air.
I know the shot is perfect long before the ball gets there.
It's flying high right toward the pin; it's going to be just great.
Perhaps a hole in one; I stand there breathless as I wait.
I can't believe my eyes; it hits the pin while on the fly.
And ricochets into the sand; I think I'm going to cry.
That swing and shot was just about the best I've ever seen.
And now the ball is in the sand; that's the "Rub of the Green".

I hit a drive; it's in the air; it's long and straight and true.
I feel the impact on the sweet spot as I follow through.
This one will have my "signature", the best drive of the day.
I'd golf each afternoon if I could always swing this way.
The ball comes down but doesn't roll; it's hit a sprinkler head.
It bounces back a hundred yards and sits there like it's dead.
I bite my tongue for if I speak I'll say something obscene.
A chuckle from my partner as he says, "Rub of the Green".

Your golf ball comes to rest under a tree—Rub of the Green.
Your ball's against the bunker lip—again—Rub of the Green.
Your drive rests in a divot—yep—it's just—Rub of the Green.
Your putt goes in the hole and bounces out—Rub of the Green.

We play this game for fun, and bragging rights if we might win.
"Rub of the Green" permits complaints; complaining is no sin.
Yes, golf's a game, a game between the golf course, God and me.
You can't control "Rub of the Green" so play golf happily.

FOURSOME

I learned to play the game of golf like many I suppose.
A friend, a borrowed set of clubs, the feeling quickly grows.
I set aside a little time each week, a half a day.
My friend would meet me at the club; a round of golf we'd play.
We'd wait and join two other guys, a couple or two gals.
Four people, not a FOURSOME, just two sets of golfing pals!
Each match was fun as we became acquainted with new friends.
But then after the eighteen holes of golf, the friendship ends.

I heard that I could book a starting time for my golf day.
Then I would know exactly when to show up for my play.
I'd never have to wait again to join some other folks.
A starting time for less than four! I learned one of golf's jokes.

I tried to book a "starting time"; they asked, "Do you have four?"
I answered, "I've got two"; they said, "You've got to have two more."
"It takes a FOURSOME or you cannot book a starting time."
I felt rejected like I'd just committed a golf crime.

The "starter" didn't know that day, the favor he'd done me.
I found that when it's "rules of golf" you don't have to agree.
The starter's the club master and you play at his behest.
I vowed I'd form a FOURSOME and that goal became my quest.
It only took a week to find some friends who "love to play".
I found an alternate to play in case one was away.
I have my FOURSOME; now I'll book a starting time each week.
We all agree on how we'll bet on our "match play" technique.
Yes, golf's a game of matches and you've got to bet a bit.
It focuses attention on the shot you're going to hit.
It doesn't matter if it's just a quarter or a buck.
A bet will help you make the shot and add some to you "luck".

So now we meet each Friday afternoon at 1:00 P.M.
For six long days I wait, knowing that soon I'll be with them.
I guess they're nothing special; they're just golfing friends of mine.
Yet every week when we're together everything is fine.
Most times on the first tee you'll hear some comments that may sting.
These "friends" will move about and argue while you take your swing.
You're going to be the butt of golfing jokes they tell on you.
It takes some concentration; that's one thing you've got to do.

This friendly banter sets the mood; it's manna for the soul.
Relaxed and happy we're now ready to achieve our goal.

Beyond the first tee we get tough and play golf by the rules.
We know the etiquette of play; we're gentlemen, not fools.
We'll make each golf swing count, for there is money on the line.
The winner buys refreshments when we finish the back nine.
Of course it costs more than I win to treat my golfing friends.
Yet being "host's" important, for the message that it sends!
The winner has the bragging rights as we review our play.
We reminisce about our scores till there's no more to say.

I've learned the treasure of a golfing FOURSOME, that's for sure.
A set of clubs, a golf ball and a FOURSOME! Who needs more?
Make no mistake the friendship that we share runs very deep.
So never lose your FOURSOME, that's one thing you need to keep.

ANOTHER LOUSY ROUND

The fairway grass is way too long; there isn't any roll.
The greens are hard; you cannot hold the ball close to the hole.
The rough's so long you lose your ball embedded deep in it.
This golf course is so lousy that I think I'm going to quit.

The fairway grass is short; my ball rolls straight through to the rough.
The fringe and green are soft so my ball just won't bounce enough.
The rough's so short it isn't there, like fairway all around.
Without some rough there's hardly any challenge to be found.

It's cold; it's hot; it's windy or it's going to rain today.
How come they plant the trees right in the path I always to play?
Who put the lake in front of the seventh, and the tenth green?
How come the wind is in your face on that long hole, sixteen?
And who designed the green on number four that slants that way?
The ball won't hold; it's off the green no matter how I play.
Do bunkers have to be in front of most of the par threes?
How come we seniors cannot play the course from the red tees?

Who made my swing so smooth and sweet when on the practice tee?
What happens to my tempo when the fairway faces me?
It cannot be the balls I play, they cost five bucks apiece.
And every time I buy some more the price seems to increase.
I chip on to the practice green right next to every pin,
and skull them on the course so badly that I never win.
I know that I should not complain; the price is pretty good.
But I'm not getting pars and birdies like I know I should.

And then one day I hit them sweet; the fairways seem so wide.
My putts role smoothly to the hole and always drop inside.
There is no rough, no bunkers and no trees or out of bounds.

439

There's just that "swish" and click of every shot, golf's sweetest sounds.
I play so well; my score's so low; it's karma; it is fate.
I've got to tell my friends about this golf course; it is great.
The fairways and the greens are manicured to perfect length.
I'll play this course forever if God just gives me the strength.

IT'S THE EQUIPMENT

Today I couldn't putt, like there's a cover on the hole.
I three putt seven greens; I just can't get that ball to roll.
I buy a putter guaranteed to roll it "straight and true".
No guessing about speed or break; it knows what it must do.

I'm ready for another round, with confidence galore.
Can't wait to try my putter, shave those strokes off of my score.
I had just twenty-seven putts; the best I've ever done.
Except I couldn't hit a drive, this round would have been fun.
No sweat, I bought a driver that will hit it straight and long.
I'll hit the fairway every time; now nothing will go wrong.

I'm ready for the Wednesday Senior Tournament, okay.
New putter and new driver; oh, my God how I will play!

What's wrong with me, I cannot hit long irons up to the green.
I scuff 'em, top 'em, shank 'em and there's nothing in between.
Long drives, great putts don't make it when long irons don't work at all.
It's like I'm hitting rocks instead of "that small dimpled ball".
Dejected when the round is done, I read the Golf Digest.
Just change long irons to Hybrids and I'll outscore all the rest.
And now four brand new Hybrids replace irons I used before.
New putter, driver, Hybrids; God, I'll really shoot a score.

When Wednesday comes, I'm ready; boy will I surprise those guys.
I'll hit 'em sweet, no matter, even from those ugly lies.
I've got the tools and confidence; the "Golf Gods" smile on me.
I feel like Palmer, Nicklaus, Woods, as I approach the tee.

I drag my sorry ass around the course again today.
Drives scatter rough to rough; it's like I don't know how to play.

I scuff and top the Hybrids; even two-foot putts won't drop.
My pitches fly the green and I can't get my chips to stop.
My "muscle memories" gone, I have a "broken swing", instead.
I struggle from the eighteenth hole; I think my brain is dead.

My "brain", that's it! Good Lord, it's what I have between my ears.
It's been right there from the beginning, all of these long years.
Equipment doesn't really make a difference in my game.
Persimmon woods, a mashie; graphite, steel, about the same!

It's what I have between my ears, my brain, and nothing more.
I play the game for fun; enjoy the process; damn the score.

COLORADO WEATHER REPORT—
LET'S GO GOLFING!!

The sun is shining brightly as it does most every day.
With golf bag on my shoulder, to my home course where I play!
There's not a cloud up in the sky; it's cool but it's not cold.
The mountains in the distance, so much beauty to behold!

The weather changes quickly, it is sunny; then it rains.
Right here beside the mountains or out on eastern plains!
I carry an umbrella and the rain gear I may need.
And watch the western sky for sudden changes I must heed.
Then on the course I concentrate on every shot I make.
My partners do the same for there's a couple bucks at stake.

We finish the front nine and make the turn out to the back.
Good company, good golfing, there is nothing that we lack.
The way we play's important but there's more to golf than score,
for golf's a metaphor of life, and sometimes even more.

We barely notice as the breeze increases to a gale.
For we are focused as we play, what each shot will entail.
Then on the putting green a gust of wind catches a ball.
And rolls it off the green; it's like the damn thing's in free fall.
Our hats go sailing from our heads; our golf clubs hit the ground.
The wind is whistling in our ears; debris flies all around.
The thunderheads are sailing from the west across the sky.
That's it! We stop our match. It makes a feller want to cry.

Wind from the west, a hurricane, one hundred miles strong.
It whistles through the mountains, every sound an eerie song.
The cottonwoods uproot; debris is blowing everywhere.
It's like God turned his back on us and doesn't seem to care.

There isn't any end in sight as gusts of wind explode.
Torrents of water everywhere as loose landfills erode.
A twister, a tornado forms out on the eastern plains.
Roofs blowing off of houses; flying glass from windowpanes!
The day has turned to night; the darkness shrouds the earth below.
The sun has disappeared and in its place, the Devil's show.

The thunderheads above announce the dangers to unfold.
No shelter for the faint of heart, or even for the bold.
The bolts of lightning bounce from earth to light the sky above.
The hailstones plummet to the ground like God gave them a shove.

So in the Clubhouse Patio, four "would be" golfers sit.
Describing for each other all the great shots they'd have hit.
A beer and then another as their golfing stories grow.
A Colorado afternoon, enjoying God's show!

DON'T MESS WITH THE "GOLF GODS"

A good day, you play bogey golf; a bad day, it's much worse.
Some days the golf gods smile on you; some days you feel their curse.
A lady, child or man, the "golf gods" never seem to care.
No matter how you plead or pray, the "golf gods just ain't fair".
Today you've got that feeling, practice tempo "smooth as silk".
You'll play this round like Mickelson, and others of his ilk.
Your body's so relaxed; you strut along like Vijay Singh.
Can't wait to start your golfing match; see what the day will bring.

With golf bag on your shoulder you walk out to the first tee.
You don't know who is in your group; a moment and you'll see.
A lady and her teenage sons are waiting there for you.
They look like rank beginners; you'll show them a thing or two.
The starter calls your names and you decide who'll tee up first.
You defer to the lady; you suspect she'll be the worst.
The boys will tee up next and you'll be last, a gracious move.
It doesn't matter anyway; your swing is "in the groove".
The lady's playing from the "whites", perhaps she's not aware,
the "reds" are for the ladies, to make competition fair.
It doesn't really matter; she'll take three shots, maybe more,
to even reach the green on this first hole; a short par four.
You chuckle as she sets up to her ball, adjusts her grip.
She swings; god, what a follow through; she gave that ball a rip.
Straight down the fairway and it's long; she'll have a wedge approach.
Her teenage sons then mention she's the high school golfing coach.
And they're her students on the high school team, ranked one and two.
They hit their drives, three hundred yards; both drives are straight and true.

The time has come; it's now your turn; you've gotten kind of stiff.
You set up; "pull the trigger", oh, my god, the swing's a whiff.
Moments ago your practice-swing, relaxed, felt smooth; felt right.

With body shaking, you now grip the club with all your might.
You'll execute a stroke like Tiger Woods in "Master's" play.
You swing and feel the contact; now your ball is on its way.
Yep, there it is, some twenty yards; it's on the lady's tee.
"How could the "golf gods" be so mean and do this thing to me?"

It didn't get much better as you played the round that day.
You'd earned the "golf god's" curse and there was nothing more to say.
The "golf gods" are impervious to gender, age or race.
They simply "exercise control" on challenges you face.

When winning you feel great; yes, it is winning you would choose.
Reflecting, you're aware that you "learn lots more" when you lose.

FROM WINTER TO SPRING—THE SEASON BEGINS

The winter's been a long one with the snow some four feet high.
I didn't practice once since fall, I didn't even try.
The temperature in single digits, freezing cold with wind!
Without my weekly "golf fix" my mind thought my body sinned.
And sinned it has, for with the warmth of this new day of spring,
I strain to swing each club, dear God; what will this season bring?

Last year a body, supple with a stroke that felt so smooth.
Not caring how I scored, for every stroke felt "in the groove".
That "old bat" in the mirror wasn't there out on the tee.
He'd been replaced by Arnie. Yes, that's how I "pictured" me.

Today's the first day of the season; tournaments each week!
My muscles feel like jelly; I can hear my joints creak.
I wobble when I try to swing; my head goes up and down.
Add red nose and some floppy shoes; there, now you've got a clown.
How come I'm suddenly so stiff? It hasn't been a year.
In fact it's only been three months; now something's kind of queer.
I've heard it many times; this question is not news to me.
"If you don't know how old you are, then how old would you be?"

I've exercised all winter, at home in my basement gym.
I've lost some weight, I'm slender; you might even say I'm slim.
I feel that I am in great shape, aerobics and strong core.
Yet all my clubs are strangers; barely know what they are for.

I can't remember, do I interlock or overlap?
I know the grip's important; can't remember, what a sap!
It doesn't feel natural either way, what could be wrong.
Now do I use a neutral left hand, or should it be strong?
My God, it's not my body. It's my mind that's gone astray.
It's not my missing hair but it's my brain that's turned to gray.

With grit, determination, with resolve to reach my goal,
I hit the links; I'm ready; let that ball drop in the hole.

447

TIPS FROM *GOLF MAGAZINE*

I pay for this damn thing; you'd think that I'd have better sense.
It hits my mailbox once each month, a buck and a few cents.
The stories are exciting, for they tell me what to do,
to shave strokes off my handicap, and more than just a few.

With hope I dig through pages written by the game's top pros.
Amazed, I study every word, how much each "teacher" knows.
I'll gain some twenty yards if I just close my stance a bit.
The ball will meet the club's sweet spot, with every shot I hit.
A little draw with lots of roll eliminates the rough.
How dumb of me to fight this thing, to think this game is tough.

I turn the page and there I find a tip that's really great.
I'll square my stance, relax, and then just let my wrists pronate.
The club head speed will be so fast, the ball will disappear.
The "swish" my swing creates will be the only sound I hear.
My ball will fly so far that I won't even see it land.
A wedge into the long par fours; my God, will that be grand!

I leaf through pages then I find the "tip" to hit it far.
Just follow what the pro advises and I'm shooting par.
I'll open up my stance and line up left of where I'll shoot.
It may look just a little weird, but who will give a hoot?
The ball will sail skyward; fade a little as it drops.
With carry that's so far that I won't care where my ball stops.

I've got these tips inside my head, the Wednesday tournament.
Excitement fills my body, like religious sacrament.
Today the golf course will be mine; I'll own all eighteen holes.
Already I feel sorry for my partners, three poor souls.
They haven't got a clue how far I'll hit the ball today.
They'd better have some "bucks" for I am going to make them pay.

You know the way it ends; how much these "golf tips" helped my game.
I couldn't break 100 and I've just myself to blame.
For I don't have the body of a touring pro, and more,
I know that I should "play my game" and then accept my score.

I QUIT THIS &%#@ GAME

I'm on the range and hitting balls to warm up for my game.
My golfing buddies join me there, all doing much the same.
We pitch a few; then try our middle irons and then each wood.
Each stroke feels smooth as silk; the balls arc high, the way they should.
There's laughter, banter, jokes as we are called to the first tee.
We're ready; yes, today's the day; four golfers all agree,
our scores will be so low they'll be the envy of the Pro.
We've buried all our "seeds of doubt"; they're dead; they cannot grow.

With confidence each tees his ball; now let the game begin.
A perfect setup; practice swing, we're here today to win.
Three balls sail long and straight; they hit the fairway, center cut.
Three golfers visualize a birdie, short iron then one putt.
I setup to my ball and take a practice swing, then two.
Now, something doesn't feel just right; I'm not sure what to do.
I check my setup, practice swing; I'm rushing it a bit.
Relax and focus, keep your balance; don't let your swing quit.
My mind is full of "swing thoughts", everything I've heard and read.
"The golf swing is too fast to think." I know I've heard that said.
No matter how I try the "do's and don'ts" run through my mind.
I've got to drive this ball; our group is already behind.

My body tremors as I swing! The ball and driver meet.
It takes a path straight to the sky and settles by my feet.
I want to "pack it in"; I'm not a quitter; I'll prevail.
My fairway wood; a mighty swing; my God how it will sail!

I'll make this story short; today was simply not my day.
I saw some places on the course that golfers never play.
Yet struggle as I did with shots that scoot along the ground.
I got through sixteen holes; two holes to go, an ugly round.

And just like that it came together, par on seventeen.
On the last hole a five iron put my ball upon the green.
A twenty footer; breaking right into the setting sun!
A single putt, a birdie, God, this game is so much fun.

IT'S LADIES' DAY

On Mondays they all congregate; each foursome gets ready
to play nine holes of golf. Today the ladies have the tee.
Yes, Monday morning is the time the ladies play nine holes.
Most "play for fun", yet some will focus solely on their goals.

On Thursdays ladies play them all, the front and the back nine.
You bet there's competition; it's okay; some pressure's fine.
A few can show the men the way the game of golf is played.
They hit the ball so straight and far you'd think they're being paid.

It doesn't matter; young or "old", the challenge is the same.
Each lady, all alone against the course; for that's the game!
Just you, your faith, your clubs, the little ball upon the tee!
The fairway out in front of you as far as you can see.
You "setup" to the ball to hit a fade, perhaps a draw.
And focus everything you've got, to swing without a flaw.
Relax and let the body and the club behave as one.
Then follow through and watch it fly; you've hit the ball "a ton".
How sweet the feeling as your clubface strikes the ball so clean.
Two hundred fifty yards out on the fairway; grass so green!
The rough, the trees, the bunkers; you just can't see them today.
They decorate the course to add some pleasure to your play.

A little conversation, then your concentration goes.
Too late you realize it's the beginning of your "woes".
Your shot "dribbles" in front of you. It's not gone very far.
There's no way you can reach the green and putt in for your par.
A bogey, double, maybe worse, you've just yourself to blame.
At times like this remember, this is golf, it's just a game.

As you'd expect, the ladies play for prizes, maybe more.
For when the round's completed and they tally up each score,
though low scores may be winners; others earn a "bragging right".
For "birdies" and those "sandy pars" are everyone's delight!

TAKE IT TO THE COURSE

Out on the practice range he hits a draw and then a fade.
If there's a score for practice shots, he'd make a perfect grade.
A pitching wedge a hundred yards; it softly hits the ground.
The sweet spot on a fairway wood; he simply loves that sound.
He takes the driver from his bag; it imbues him with strength.
He can't believe each time he hits this club; it's awesome length.
Then to the putting green to sharpen up his putting skill!
Each time he holes a twenty-footer it's a real thrill.
Soft hands, his head is quiet, as he strokes each practice putt.
The ball rolls true, into the hole as though it's in a rut.
He chips a few onto the green; they land and quickly stop.
Assembled near the hole; a single putt and each will drop.

He's got the touch; he's got the feel; his tempo's perfect, too.
His game is ready for the course; there's nothing he can't do.
Relaxed and filled with confidence, he walks to the first tee.
Today he'll shoot his lowest score; he'll show 'em, just you see.
His ball is on the tee; he checks his setup one more time.
He visualizes his first drive; it's straight and long; sublime.
A practice swing; a waggle and he's ready, let'er go!
Today he'll be the "centerpiece", the star of his own show!

A little doubt comes into mind; so much that can go wrong.
He hesitates a moment, got to hit it straight and long!
His focus changes to a "gaze"; his muscles seem to freeze.
What happened to the stroke that he was going to make with ease?
A bead of sweat upon his brow; his grip is way too tight.
Some demon took his body and won't let him do this right.
His legs have turned to posts; his arms as stiff as a broomstick.
He's got to get this done right now; he's got to hit it quick.
He swings with all his might, his body creaks; almost a fall.

Two hundred fifty yards away, he looks to see his ball!
He whiffed the thing; it's sitting on the tee; it hasn't moved.
Good God, what happened to that perfect swing that he had grooved?

As he moved from the practice range, a metamorphosis!
His supple body changed; his mind filled with analysis.
The golf course changed that youthful person on the practice tee;
transmogrified into the weak old man that you now see.

OLD GEEZERS

On Wednesday we "Old Geezers" play; we're most as "old as dirt"
We joke and laugh about our age; it doesn't help the hurt
we feel each time we swing the club, well, half a swing at best.
Yet, there's no quit in we "Old Geezers" as we seek our quest.

Yes, we've got goals; they may be slightly different than the kids.
They're "climbing up their ladders" while we "Geezers hit the skids".
Some "Geezers" in their fifties may have goals to shoot near par.
At sixty bogies are okay; our drives don't go "that far".
At seventy "Old Geezers" hope that they complete their round!
At eighty we just pray that we're not six feet under ground.

A few "Old Geezers" set a goal to yet improve their game.
While other Geezers pray that they can play about the same.
We "Older Geezers" hope that our decline is not too steep.
So when we tally up our score, it doesn't make us weep.

Don't get me wrong, we may be worn and play a little slow.
We may not hear the Marshal when he says, "Come on; let's go!"
But shuffle, limp or ride a cart, we play the best we can.
Each one of us remembers when he was a "better man".
That solid drive feels just as good today as "way back when"!
And we are just as mad as you when we record a "ten".
That chip that hits the stick and then drops down into the cup,
gives us exhilaration as we reach and pick it up.
We cuss when we miss a three footer, or when one lips out.
But we "Old Geezers" understand what golf is all about.

Don't pity us, no sympathy; remember as you play.
That if you're really lucky you'll be just like us, some day.
Each round of golf that you complete will be a real blast.
Cause at our age we just don't know which round will be our last.

THE "GORILLA"

It's Wednesday and we seniors have our tournament today.
As long as we can take a breath, we come out here to play.
Our swing's a little brittle but we do the best we can.
It's like the game of golf is the true measure of a man.

The game is played in "foursomes" but today we have just three.
We meet the designated "fourth" as we reach the first tee.
It's always great to make new friends; that's what this game's about.
We know our game; we've played for years; we've overcome all doubt.
So when our "designated fourth" stands tall to say "hello",
The three of us look up to him from way, way down below.
He's not just tall, he's big; there's meat and muscle everywhere.
I somehow cannot help myself; I just stand there and stare.

We're called to play and take the tee, the honor to our "guest".
A practice swing, a mighty coil, and you can guess the rest.
No matter how I hit my ball, it's always in my sight.
A chip, a pitch, an iron or when I drive with all my might.
But this "gorilla" has a ball flight like a "shooting star".
I've never seen a "senior" who can hit a ball that far.

We can't let this "gorilla" show us up; we play okay.
Just play our game; we know we'll be with him most of the day.
Don't let his drive mess up our heads; this game involves much more.
We'll play each shot like always, do our best and "damn the score".

We're on the green and he's away, his putt is twenty feet.
He takes a practice stroke like an experienced athlete.
And like his drive the ball departs his putter head with speed.
He's forty feet away, behind a tree, beneath a weed.
And then he chips his ball across the green into the rough.

Another chip, across the green, this game sure can be tough.
He takes his putter, hits it, hallelujah, on the green.
He's big and strong but he has the worst "touch" I've ever seen.
With three more putts and just like that, his ball drops in the cup.
The rest of us make par and find ourselves some five shots up.

You guessed it, the whole round of golf continues in this way.
He drives the ball a mile; on every fairway, we're away.
But up around the green that big "gorilla" cannot score.
He "drives for show"; finesse around the green means so much more.

MID-SEASON FORM

The first golf round of summer! Old man winter's" far behind!
Our home course is the place we come to see if we can find
the golf swing we remember from last fall, at season's end.
If we can find it quickly, it will be a real godsend.
A little play this spring, we didn't expect all that much.
Three months of deadly winter with no play, that's been our crutch.
We search the practice range. We look around the putting green.
We ask our golf companions, all, if anyone has seen
the setup, swing, the tempo we remember from last fall.
The "space between our ears" seems empty, nothing there at all.

It's a new season. Maybe we should check the clubs we use.
We don't want our equipment to become a lame excuse
for shots that go astray and putts that don't go in the hole.
This year we'll shoot a round at par. Now that's a worthy goal.

Let's see, our putter's kind of old. It's worn a little bit.
Perhaps a brand new mallet, with three "balls" adorning it!
Yes, a new putter's what we need to lower our golf score.
We'll one or two putt every green, goodbye to three and four.
And Hybrids are the thing this year; replace an iron or two.
A Rescue club for the deep rough, yes, that's what we will do.
And maybe a new driver, too, a Taylor Made R-7!
We'll hit that ball so far our friends will think it's gone to heaven.
Let's see, this sand wedge has some scuffs; it's not the latest thing.
A new flanged wedge with steel shaft; the sand saves it will bring.
A thousand bucks already, that's enough, we'll keep the rest.
We'll simply "groove our swing" and hit them out there with the best.

Ah yes, it's finally summer and it's time to do our thing.
The Senior Tournament; old Geezers with their "creaky" swing!
Some scores are high; some scores are low, but they do not display,
the fellowship, camaraderie, as round the course we play.

A "YOUTHFUL" MIND VERSUS AN "OLD MAN'S" BODY

It's Tuesday evening, dinner's past, there's nothing I must do.
My body needs some rest, although my mind is just like new.
I've finished all my chores and now I've got to get to bed.
Most mornings I sleep in till eight; golf days it's five, instead.
On Wednesday mornings we "old geezers" play a tournament.
Most times it's fun, yet other times it seems like punishment.
It takes about three hours, for my, "morning golf" routine.
I exercise and hit some balls; have breakfast in between.
I'm warmed up as I leave the house; I'm ready to begin.
With confidence I'm on the tee; today I'm going to win.

My mind is thirty years of age; has energy galore.
It visualizes every shot; and par is my worst score.
A practice swing or two; my ball is resting on the tee.
The center of the fairway; that is all my mind can see.
I setup to the golf ball, body flexed; I'll hit a fade.
Just swing with follow thru that's high; no need to be afraid.
The fairway's wide, a single tree, the lake is out of play.
Relaxed, two hundred fifty yards; begins a perfect day.

The body starts to take control as I address the ball.
My mind has disappeared; it's like it's not been here at all.
Or it has simply given up; it knows the real truth.
At almost eighty years of age, my body's lost its youth.
And every move, yes every swing, each drive and pitch and chip,
will endure pain from elbows, wrists; especially from each hip.
What can a mind that's youthful do when body parts are worn?
When concentration wanes because rotator cuffs are torn!
And eyes won't focus on the ball, a fuzzy mass of white.
My "old man's body's" in control; my mind has lost the fight.

I've studied mind control techniques; I've practiced yoga, too.
With fifty years of "muscle memory", I know what to do.
The golf swing is so fast you cannot "think about technique".
Just "grip that club and rip it"; let the bones and muscles creak.

GOLF PARTNERS

It's Wednesday morning early; we are ready to begin
the "senior tournament"; we'll hit it smooth; today we'll win.
The tournament's a "scramble"; "twosome" teams, old "geezers" all.
A partner who depends on me; oh, how we'll strike that ball!
We're playing "net"; our handicap is right where it should be.
We get a stroke on every hole; we'll win, just wait and see.
Two guys, two balls, a single score; all birdies, every one!
No, first tee nerves don't bother us; we're here to have some fun.

My partner looks at me; he smirks; he takes a warm-up stroke.
"Let's really play our best today; play smart, don't go for broke.
We'll stroke our balls with confidence; I'm sure you know your role.
Just fairways, greens and in the cup, net "birdie" every hole.
At eighteen under we will be the 'champions' for sure.
That's how the two of us will play; a 'fifty-two' net score".

My God, what does my partner want? I'm not a touring pro.
We're out here playing golf for fun; that's something he should know.
My confidence was at a peak until I understood,
my partner really expects me to play this round 'that good'!

And just like that my breath is short; my swing seems way too fast.
The confidence I had is gone; I'm trembling; can this last?
I'm here to 'play my game' and have some fun; but he wants more.
What if I disappoint my partner; really wreck our score?
The visions of my drives so long and straight, in the fairway,
are now all hooks and slices in a rough as thick as hay.
The chips and putts I know that I can make have left my mind.
I see 'thin hits' with 'lipped out putts', bad shots of every kind.

Then anger fills my mind; I feel relaxed as I can be.
Intimidation will not work; he can't do this to me.
I'll 'play my game'; it's just as good as his has ever been.
I'll laugh; have fun; for good or bad; somehow we may just win.

COURSE UNDER REPAIR—WHO CARES?

It's springtime in the Rockies and there's "weather" everywhere.
With wind, white clouds and thunderheads, sunsets beyond compare.
The temperature is fickle, freezing cold, then cozy warm.
Expect the unexpected; here that is the "weather norm".
We've made it through the winter; it's been dry, a little snow.
And now we brace ourselves against the blustery winds that blow.

The lake is dry; there's pipe and workers scattered everywhere.
Improvements to the course about which everyone's aware!
They're widening the first fairway; the lake's a trouble spot.
Your first drive in the water, that'll make you kind of "hot".
We'll have a few more yards with water almost out of play.
So any drive that's not a slice is right to start your day.

It's Wednesday; "senior" golfers at the golf course—many come.
We play our weekly tournament—old friends here for the fun.
At nine o'clock, a shotgun start, we only have nine holes.
Each "geezer" optimistic he will reach his golfing goals.
The driving range is closed, no warming up for us today.
We'll swing a club a time or two and we're ready to play.
Around the front nine—then again—we play the same holes twice.
It works for me; for all of us; in fact it's kind of nice,
the second time around comparing scores against our first.
It's okay; I'm quite happy when a bogey is my worst.

Out on the course we "lift and place", a club length anywhere.
Except when in a hazard; take a stroke or play it there.
With trenches down the fairways and black pipe in little piles,
We all envision how the course will be, with welcome smiles.
The work does not affect our game; it helps us concentrate.
With improved focus some of us may hit the golf ball straight.

About four hours, we complete the eighteen holes we play.
Then in the clubhouse, lots of talk, we have so much to say.
A little bragging—some complain—a glass or two of beer.
Excited sharing of the day is all that we can hear.
No matter how we scored today, next week we'll play once more.
And each of us is certain we will shoot a better score.

OUR "NEW" HOME COURSE

Some guys have golfed here thirty years; for me it's been just six.
From the beginning I could see some things they need to fix.
The greens are small but they're well kept, as smooth as they can be.
With subtle undulations that are difficult to see.
They're manicured about as well as greens are anywhere.
And though I miss my share of putts, I know the greens are fair.
In years gone by the fairways were quite dry, a little bare.
And bunkers unpredictable; sometimes no sand was there.
The rough was like a cow pasture, with clumps of grass and dirt.
An exit with a wedge would sometimes cause the ball to "squirt".
At times your ball stopped in a hole, a puddle or hard ground.
Yes, "through the green" was challenging as any course around.
The golfers bitched; they blamed the staff; they thought they should do more.
For every time they "played it down", it killed the way they'd score.

An irrigation system was installed; it took a year.
A lot of golfers moved to other courses that are near.
At "home" here we could play just nine, and play that nine again.
The only water for the grounds was from the summer rain.
It takes a while to fix a problem that's been there so long.
For every "fix" it seems like something else always goes wrong.
And even "old man winter" didn't help, with tons of snow.
You couldn't even find the course, no way for grass to grow.

Then comes the spring, with tender care; and lots of water, too!
With conscientious work by all, the greens keeper and crew!
The office staff, the pros and their assistants helped out, much.
They handled each complaint with grace and each their special "touch".
Our "home" course now has fairways that are "sculpted", well defined.
The "rough" is rough, but it is fair, though it's not always kind.
The bunker sand is "worked" each day; it's playable and fair.

I'll choose the bunker over rough; I'd rather play from there.
The greens are still like carpets and the break is hard to see.
Though we should one or two putt, there is still sometimes a "three".
Yes, it's a show place and the staff deserves our heartfelt thanks.
They've "stayed the course" and golfers have returned to fill the ranks.
The staff had lots of grit to see it through without complaint.
They're pretty special people, each, (though none may be a "saint").